Lawrence Sail has published eight books of poems, most recently *The World Returning* (Bloodaxe Books, 2002) and *Building into Air* (Bloodaxe Books, 1995). He has been chairman of the Arvon Foundation, a judge for the Whitbread Book of the Year and the Eric Gregory Awards, the UK representative on the jury of the European Literature Prize and director of the Cheltenham Festival of Literature. In 2004 he received a Cholmondeley Award. He is a Fellow of the Royal Society of Literature.

Lawrence Sail

# Cross-currents

Essays

ENITHARMON PRESS

First published in 2005
by the Enitharmon Press
26B Caversham Road
London NW5 2DU

www.enitharmon.co.uk

Distributed in the UK by
Central Books
99 Wallis Road
London E9 5LN

Distributed in the USA and Canada
by Dufour Editions Inc.
PO Box 7, Chester Springs
PA 19425, USA

ISBN 1 904634 19 2

British Library Cataloguing-in-Publication Data.
A catalogue record for this book is available
from the British Library.

Typeset in Palatino by Servis Filmsetting Ltd
and printed in England by
Antony Rowe Ltd

# A Response to Rothko

*A picture lives by companionship,*
*expanding and quickening in the eyes*
*of the sensitive observer. It dies*
*by the same token.*

Transgressions of the frame: the subject leaning
its elbow out of the canvas. The cloak's
crimson lining that spills,
molten, onto wood.

And *vice versa*, the nightmare world
sucked in, banged up in a box, glazed:
here, the worst of horror
is drained of blood.

By the same token, the citizens of art's
republic of loneliness struggle towards
hope, a horizon beyond
the surrounding truths.

# Author's note

The forty-two essays collected here are from a run of fifty written at the invitation of Michael Schmidt, editor of *Poetry Nation Review*, and published in the magazine as an unbroken series from 1995 to 2003. Publication in book form has given me the chance to edit, but in general the text remains very close to the original essays.

I am very grateful to Michael Schmidt for his invitation, and to Stephen Stuart-Smith at Enitharmon for the present book.

# Contents

1995

# The Cheshire Cat's Grin

I have always thought that one of the best things about *Alice in Wonderland* is the Cheshire Cat. Its claim that it is mad, along with everyone else, is the only unconvincing thing about it – probably part of its cover, and anyway if madness is universal it must have become the current normality. In all other respects it's a very cool cat, especially as it appears in Tenniel's four drawings in the text (though in the third one it is already in the process of disappearing) with its, well, yes, demented grin, and the way it hovers like a *felix ex machina* above the Queen's croquet ground, out of reach of the raging royals and the executioner's axe below. But most magical of all is its ability to become invisible, grin last.

A year or so ago Ted Hughes was speculating, in the course of a conversation, on the subject of invisibility. What if, in this age of relentless publicity and promotion, no one had really discovered the foremost writer of the time? Maybe he or she was working away entirely without recognition, perhaps even not having published anything as yet, and to be discovered only subsequently by some perspicacious literary archaeologist. This thesis may do less than justice to human vanity and the desire actually to communicate fully, and may also beg the question of what is meant by 'foremost'; but it remains intriguing nonetheless. As well as pointing to the provisional nature of critical judgements, the notion of the invisible poet seems peculiarly apt in the era of hype. As an image, it has a suggestive strength greater than that of an updated version of the garret-bound ghost of Romanticism. Besides, it is somehow rather appealing to think of a writer being represented, so to speak, entirely by *livres d'absence*.

Of course, when it comes to poetry, invisibility can be understood in a variety of ways. It may be voluntary, the stance of a writer either waiting to be discovered, or who already feels that

11

his or her talent has not received its due: a function of pride or wounded pride. It may be a matter of preference – not all writers want the limelight – or of forceful circumstances. Others (though few poets – perhaps the example of Ossian was enough) choose to wrap themselves in the cloak of a *nom de plume*. It may, though, be involuntary, a result of political or social pressures allowing at best for partial visibility, or of obliqueness of approach, poems of camouflage as much as revelation. On one level this might be a brutally straightforward matter of oppression and censorship, on another the socially predetermined invisibility of Gray's blushing flowers, the inaudibility of his mute Miltons. Or, internationally, it may be linguistic in origin, visibility depending on the choice of author made by a particular translator and the degree of his or her skill in rendering the work in another language. In this respect, it is interesting to recall Miroslav Holub's candid admission (in *The Poetry of Survival*, edited by Daniel Weissbort, Anvil Press, 1991) that at times his choice of subject and idiom for a poem might have been influenced, if not actually dictated, by its translatability: that is, by the prospect of an escape from invisibility by publication abroad, at a time when it would have been impossible to publish the poem in his own country. Then there is the invisibility of neglect, which is often the random work of time and chance ensuring that the race is not always to the swift, nor the battle inevitably to the strong. There is even the invisibility which can derive from over-intensive critical study, as T. J. Reed suggests has sometimes been the case with Goethe, 'half-hidden behind a scaffolding of scholarship, a long row of leatherbound volumes in the bourgeois bookcase' (*Goethe*, OUP, 1984). In English, Dickens and even Shakespeare might be seen as occasional victims of this invisibility of congealed reputation which can threaten to make them set books in more than one sense, revered as much as read, or with the actual texts blocked out by billowing clouds of commentary and the changeable weathers of critical fashion.

But in addition to all this, there is the invisibility which can be produced by the sheer welter of information, promotion and prizes which is, probably for better and for worse, a feature of the contemporary world of books and publishing. For the better, because there are good aspects of the welter, such as enabling books to make at least some impact alongside all the other products of a consumer society which might otherwise crowd them out altogether, not least videos and audio cassettes: or such as helping to enhance accessibility (though accessibility, like democracy, can only be a means to an end. It declares a good principle, while necessarily leaving open the matter of its substantive application). Patronage and encouragement of writers, publishers, magazines and books, whether from such bodies as the Arts Council of England, the British Council or even in the form of prizes, can also be a valuable counterweight to the raw judgements of the market, which are in any case rarely a matter of simple public preference. For the worse, because of the tyranny of fashion – and those areas of darkness intensified by the dazzle of oncoming lights from the endless procession of the new, as it flashes past on its traverse from printing to pulping, novelty to nothing. In this, hype – that coinage of the last quarter century – has become the agent of a debased idea of fame and significance, purveyed in language made flaccid by hysterical over-use: *major, acclaimed, brilliant, bestselling.* For the individual at whom hype is aimed, here is yet another shrill claim upon limited time and attention, along with junk mail, free offers and telephone calls from double glazing firms. Beyond a certain point, what vies for attention may become a blur of distraction. Hype, designed to influence choice, may in the end persuade us simply not to choose at all, to walk away from the clamour of competing market stalls. But one of its more worthwhile applications, as we approach the stock-taking which a millennium seems ineluctably to encourage, might be to reweigh the contents of at least some bushels hidden by lights.

Fame, that proof of lasting visibility, has often been seen as an antidote to the temporarily successful. Shelley seems to look upon it as the poet's natural right – 'Poets' food is love and fame' ('An Exhortation'), while for Bacon it is to be seen, in his essay 'Of Death', in the consoling perspective of eternity: for the man who has lived a good life, 'death hath this also, that it openeth the gate to good fame, and extinguisheth envy'. Yet fame, too, has its contingencies and vicissitudes: think of Bach championed by Mendelssohn, or Larkin's advocacy of Barbara Pym, or the renewed popularity of, say, Hopper and Macke. Against this, think of the relative decline in reputation of, for instance, the music of Meyerbeer, the novels of Arnold Bennett, the paintings

13

of Alma-Tadema. Today, even given our common knowledge of the planet's limited lifespan, and the existence of nuclear weapons (let alone peaceful nuclear uses such as Chernobyl), the finitude of fame is probably no more or no less oppressive an idea than was once the prospect of the Last Judgement. In every age and land poets have known how to measure the long odds of eternity and make them their own. Here, for example, is Ovid's *Metamorphoses*, xv, 871: 'Iamque opus exegi, quod nec Iovis ira, nec ignis, / Nec poterit ferrum, nec edax abolere vetustas' ('And now I have finished the work, which neither the wrath of Jove, nor fire, nor the sword, nor devouring age shall be able to destroy'). Among many versions of long-term optimism, there is Goethe's bracing exhortation 'Stirb und werde!' ('Die and become!') in the poem 'Selige Sehnsucht', with its image of the butterfly fatally attracted to the flame, yet also conveying a sense of metempsycholic continuance; or, in quite a different vein, Pasternak's memorable 1956 poem, here in a translation by George Bird, which begins 'There's nothing fine in being famous' and ends with these three verses:

> You let obscurity absorb you,
> and there conceal your every step,
> like country hiding in a mist
> so dense that nothing can be seen.
>
> Others in your living footsteps
> will follow inch by inch your path,
> but you do not have to distinguish
> a victory from a defeat.
>
> And must not by one jot or tittle
> cease to be the man you are,
> but be alive, alive, just that,
> alive, alive, right to the end.

While this may still suggest a somewhat Romantic view of posterity, it is a vigorous reminder that what demands attention is the job in hand, nothing else. Eliot makes much the same point (with a distinct echo of Goethe's *Faust*) in 'East Coker' – 'For us, there is only the trying. The rest is not our business'. But this lacks

Pasternak's dynamic zest which, even when considered apart from the difficulties of the author's own life, admirably puts the factitious energy of hype and the arbitrary fluctuations of fame in their place. Perhaps it is this sense of what really counts that the Cheshire Cat also knows, and which allows it to retain that broadest of grins even as it begins to fade away.

# Glimpsed in Passing

They are to be seen as you are heading north on the M5, shortly after leaving Bridgwater to your left. What you see is not, as you might think at first, Hamlet's cloud 'almost in shape of a camel' nor, quite, the Miltonic creature that 'wreathed his lithe proboscis' in Book IV of *Paradise Lost* – but, beyond doubt, an almost life-size camel and elephant which appear to be made from papier mâché. You come first to the camel: it stands close up against a hedge that runs at right angles to the motorway, and it faces towards you. An uncertainty about the hump arrangement might suggest a dromedary rather than a camel, but there is no mistaking the cameline set of the mouth, with its combination of smugness and obstinacy. From time to time the camel is repainted, in shades that vary from light beige to mid-brown. It displays a sensitivity to the seasons vaguely reminiscent of changing altar frontals: sometimes in summer it sports a pith helmet, and at Christmas time a woolly hat with, about its neck, a garland of tinsel. Since you are on the motorway, half drugged with speed and tedium and hardly expecting to see such a diverting and absurd thing, you have only just recovered from the shock of pleasure when, a mile or so on, you are racing past the elephant, four-square, properly grey and as if heading south.

That's all. No reasons, no notices, no advertisements – just these two gratuitous beasts, anonymous as cathedrals. The imagination soon gets to work. Are they by the same hand, or the work of keen rivals? Could they be the vanguard of a whole forthcoming menagerie produced in fierce competition? And what about the elaborately painted Egyptian death-mask which used to lie in the same field as the camel, but which seems to have vanished at some point in the last year? Perhaps they are emblematic: the camel with its endurance in the face of the desert-crossing ahead, the elephant with its legendary storage of the past. But even such

16

extrapolation may be too much. The memorable, the delightful thing, is that they are there to amuse and intrigue the speeding traveller, improbable dwellers in the green pastures of the Somerset Levels, with no design but their own to make on the passer-by. It's impossible to know, but not to imagine, how many journeys must have been lightened and how many spirits lifted by a disbelieving double-take done not once, but twice.

I was not, however, thinking of either of these splendours of the verge as I tuned in, earlier this year, to a Radio 3 discussion on literary theory, recorded at the ICA. In honour of the 15th birthday of the *London Review of Books,* a panel under the chairmanship of Christopher Hitchens and made up of Marilyn Butler, Terry Eagleton, Frank Kermode, Edward Said and Marina Warner had been brought together to consider the question, 'Literary theory: what has it done for us?'

The discussion was deftly conducted and certainly interesting, while remaining attractively within reach of the general listener. The liturgies of Saussure, Barthes, Foucault, Derrida, Lacan were rehearsed peacefully and fitted unproblematically into the discourse. Frequently there was an awareness of both the virtues and the limitations of what has now come to be called simply 'theory'. On the one hand, it was seen to have led to a greater sophistication and awareness in both reader and writer, to have brought about the democratisation of literature and a 'rapprochement', or even 'approchement', of the academy and the 'real world' (*sic*). On the other hand, there was seen to be a danger that abstract theory could absorb literature entirely, hindering close reading and finally doing itself to death in the toils of its own narrow jargons and orthodoxies. A number of interesting points were made along the way, in response to Frank Kermode's suggestion at the outset that there was the need to restore 'a kind of quasi-autonomous status to literature'. Marilyn Butler pointed out that, over the last thirty years, the identity of students of the English language (and so the potential readership for its literature) had changed radically, with the largest constituency probably now in Asia. For these students and others like them there was unlikely to be a real interest in a reading of literature set apart from politics and social science. The post-colonial approach which was one aspect of literary theory had opened literature up to these possibilities, enabling readers to ask questions about the

values of a text and the extent to which those values were con-
tested. Such an expansion and democratisation of literature
demanded flexibility and breadth of approach. Terry Eagleton
described literary theory as what had 'kept the revolution warm
in a bleak and chilly political climate' and suggested, later in the
discussion, that we all in a sense read theoretically anyway, even
those conservatives who lament the loss of literature. For him,
humanists were those whose theory had become naturalised,
accepted as intuitive, while for theorists (amongst whom he
counted himself) the 'technologizing techniques' of advanced
capitalist societies were there to be commandeered but also used
against the 'humanistic pieties' of such societies. Marina Warner
felt that we were in danger of sinking what had been, since the
late sixties, a vital revolution: for her, theory had certainly
brought the academy and the world outside closer together.
Indeed, all the real richness of literary criticism had been in its
connections with politics, as for instance with feminism: perhaps
now it was at the mercy of narrow abstractions. Edward Said
agreed that theory had changed the way in which we look at
texts, and for the better. The current situation, perhaps an
amalgam of past approaches, might be no bad thing, challenging
the critic to produce something more: but there had been a tremendous confusion between methodology and theory, with the
separation between the academy and the society in which we live
now almost total. Marina Warner disagreed: giving Angela
Carter and Toni Morrison as examples, she added that theory has
also profoundly altered creative writing.

And then, from the audience (evidently composed in part of
well-known critics and academics) came a question. Might it not
be that, in seeking to create for literature the quasi-autonomy
sought by Professor Kermode, there could be a place for such
concepts as value and pleasure? Yet contemporary theory, the
questioner ventured, is either embarrassed by such concepts or
simply denies them.

There was a swift response from Terry Eagleton, who agreed
but said that value was too often seen as the end of the argument
rather than, as it should be, a starting-point. For him, value was
a part of social living, and something also dealt with by theory.
There was a further contribution from a member of the audience
who took issue with Edward Said's talk of a total gap between

the academy and society: feminism had profoundly altered the academy as well as the world outside it. Said countered that there was now a great diminishment of the historical sense: all too often the past and its significance were forgotten. Then it was back to Frank Kermode, who made the point that theorists can also be wonderfully acute readers (Derrida was a good example), but it was the theoretical rather than the applied aspects of literary criticism which had been really followed through and which had become ends in themselves. And so to the chairman's thanks.

Of course a broadcast is not a written paper, and it is impossible for each strand of argument to be followed through. But it was interesting to sense the adjustments and modifications – the qualifications – that were being made to what once seemed so clarion clear and unstoppable. In particular, it was intriguing to hear that brief reference to pleasure come and go. At that moment I seemed to hear a faint but distinct echo coming from a more distant verge: 'The Poet writes under one restriction only, namely, that of the necessity of giving pleasure to a human Being possessed of that information which may be expected from him, not as a lawyer, a physician, a mariner, an astronomer or a natural philosopher, but as a Man'. One man's meat will always be another man's poison, of course, but there may still be something pertinent about Wordsworth's view that value has to do with a non-specialist human recognition and perception. And how long ago was it that the great French de-bagger of specialists and their languages wondered whether the really great rule, for a writer, wasn't to give pleasure? ('Je voudrais bien savoir si la grande règle de toutes les règles n'est pas de plaire'. Molière, *Critique de l'Ecole des Femmes*).

This is not to denigrate the interest or influence of theory (as Professor Kermode pointed out, criticism, which has been going on since Plato, is 'the fluid in which literature survives'). But perhaps, for a variety of reasons, there could be emerging a renewed alertness to what might, in quite a general sense, bridge the gulf between the theoretical and the applied: a process in which, as a literary criterion, the giving of pleasure might now assume a greater centrality than the preoccupations of recent years have made possible. It was that thought which, just then, recalled vividly to mind the camel and the elephant, standing their pleasure-giving ground beside the fast gray tracks of the motorway where speed reduces the surface to endless flicking hyphens of white, and the immediate landscape to a barely noticed blur.

# Veni, Video, Vici

Travellers and tourists vary considerably in their attitudes to what Tennyson in 'The Last Tournament' called 'the dirty nurse, Experience'. In their efforts to record what they see, they often go to considerable lengths – sometimes too far, as in the case of the visitor to southern England last year who, clamped to the viewfinder of his camcorder and intent on capturing the sweep of the landscape at a clifftop, decided that a step or two back would give him a better picture . . . Less drastic, but thought-provoking in its way, was what I saw the same summer at one of Romania's beautiful painted monasteries, at Voroneţ. A fellow visitor crossed the threshold into the interior of the church with its richly decorated walls, walking a little clumsily, with one eye closed and the other enclosed in the rubber socket of his camcorder. He proceeded to film as thoroughly as he could, taking in as many angles and images as possible, diving briefly out of the machine every so often to check that all was well, before finally walking backwards to the door, the machine still going. A moment later and he was gone – taking with him what would, with luck, be a striking record of what he had seen; or rather what he had not seen, except through the eyepiece of the camcorder. It is easy to understand his wish to encapsulate his experience in a way which would enable him to share some idea of it with those at home, but it did seem extraordinary that he had left the camera to do all the looking round.

Even more striking, not to say baffling, was this summer's sequel, enacted at Ax-les-Thermes, a spa town on the French side of the Pyrenees. Here, close to a hot footbath (77 degrees Fahrenheit) installed in the thirteenth century by order of Louis IX for the benefit of lepers, and now of great benefit to footsore tourists, was to be seen a man with a camcorder zooming in on one postcard amongst many displayed on a stand in front of a shop. He seemed to be filming only the card, and was so intent on his task that it was simple to look over his camera-loaded shoulder to see what the picture was of. A flock of sheep, it turned out to be, shining against the light and snapped in front of the abbey of St Michel de Cuxa. What could this possibly mean? Was he engaged on research into the frequency and nature of ovine representation on 2-Franc postcards? Or was this a cover-up for a failure actually to visit the abbey, perhaps making the best of a package tour on which time had run out? Was he ingeniously constructing a fake record of places he had never been to? Or could he simply be devising a good background for the credits to preface the home video he was compiling? In any case, the incident seemed to represent an intriguing comment on the relation of experience to the attempt to master it – rather as if, to turn round the Eliot of 'The Dry Salvages', someone had had the meaning but missed the experience. As with the Voroneţ visitor, one was left with the sense of travel as collecting, a compilation of video trophies shot for later display. Better this than the trophies shot by earlier travellers, no doubt, but there is still the question of why we should feel so strongly the urge to procure evidence of our experience, and the extent to which this quest sometimes vitiates or undermines the quality of that experience. Been there, done that, with the video camera building it all into a personal anthology capable of linking perhaps disconnected objects and places by the simple continuity of the same hand pressing the button. Our celluloid trophies ought, of course, to stimulate reflection rather than to remind us of our status as colossi bestriding the narrow world – but to record can be to dismiss from the mind; to film can be to file away. How many holiday videos or photographs are looked at more than a few times, or the objects, artefacts and buildings which some of them show considered more than fleetingly? The urge to video something, to take away an image of it, may actually interfere with a thoughtful consideration of it. 'Nothing ever becomes real,' wrote Keats to George and Georgiana in 1819, 'till it is experienced'.

This year sees the bicentenary of the publication of Schiller's *On the Aesthetic Education of Man*, so providing a reminder that discussion of the interplay of experience, ideas, meaning and their cultural contexts is by no means new. Set out in a series of twenty-seven letters addressed to the Duke of Holstein-Augustenburg, Schiller's intellectual constructions (which, as he acknowledges, owe much to Kant) are deeply felt and driven by a clear moral imperative, but also have a sense of symmetry and elegance as much geometric as philosophical: the language and style of the letters impressively enact their author's beliefs. He weighs the world of experience against the human capacity for ideas and artistic form, in a series of juxtaposed terms which are not simple oppositions, but which often set up a series of tensions, interdependences and qualifications. In broad outline, against the world of the senses he sets the world of form; against inchoate life, the deliberately formed shape; against the circumstantial and limited, the operation of reason and the will, and the impulse towards the moral and the infinite. He accepts that in the physical and historical world ideas can never find their complete embodiment, but rightly sees that this does not necessarily rob them of their force as ideals and influences. Not that he argues for a facile reconciliation of opposing forces – rather, for the proper appreciation of what he sees as the only context which will enable man to accept such oppositions but also to move on from them. And this means, for him, the realm of the aesthetic. Here, in what he describes as 'this condition of real and active determinability', man can exercise his instinct for play, his 'Spieltrieb': and only by this means, through the playful appearances of art which can combine 'life' and 'form' to become 'living form', can man hope to transform the (physically) real into the (ethically) true.

But what, for the individual, is the starting point of this process, which must clearly be somewhere in the world we inhabit, that of the senses? The twenty-sixth letter makes it clear: seeing and hearing, those senses which allow us to consider an object at a distance, are the key. 'The object of touch is a force that we undergo; the object of the eye and ear is a form that we create'. As soon as man appreciates the independent worth of seeing, 'then he is also already aesthetically free, and the instinct for play has come into being'. Seeing and hearing – these are precisely the two capabilities of the camcorder. By delegating these human faculties to a machine, perhaps we are endangering even the first step towards defining value, which is quite simply to give ourselves time to attend properly to the world around us, and to the art it already contains. As Schiller puts it, 'Contemplation (reflection) is the first liberal relationship of man to the universe which surrounds him'.

Two hundred years on, we may find Schiller's concluding delineation of 'the aesthetic state' hard to agree with on the idealistic terms he proposes: but his starting-point is, quite clearly, the political and historical circumstances of the world as they were when he wrote – and the continent in which he lived must have seemed in as much turmoil then as it does today. Much of what he has to say retains real interest and relevance, not least when applied to literature itself, and to read any number of twentieth-century writers on the issues he raises is to hear explicitly Schillerian echoes, however much their angles of approach and their intended destinations may diverge from his own. For instance, and chosen quickly from my bookshelves, Eavan Boland, Malcolm Bradbury, Donald Davie, Denis Donoghue (notably in his 1982 Reith lectures , published as *The Arts Without Mystery*, BBC, 1983), Terry Eagleton, Eliot (*Four Quartets* as much as any of the critical writing), Miroslav Holub, Frank Kermode, Milan Kundera, André Malraux – this alphabet could be extended without difficulty. These writers, among others, highlight some of the dangers of our own time, not least the possibility that our ways of looking, and the diversity and proliferation of the systems associated with doing so, may come close to ways of not looking, of not really attending to what we see. In the same way, our sense of meaning may be increasingly inseparable from our sense of context, whether in the form of biography, the assurance of a signature on a painting, simple fashion, or a critical *parti pris* whose imperatives may be a specific agenda. While there is no shortage of possible meanings on offer, our relationship with experience and events may be more attenuated than we like to think. Events, which Bradbury nicely characterises in *The Social Context of Modern English Literature* (Blackwell, 1971) as 'those things which happen twice, once because they happen and once because they are reported, filmed and published'.

For readers, all this may mean a willingness to engage first and foremost with the word spoken and written, with literary texts rather than interpretations of them. Even this does not always seem easy, given the number of books available, and the lack of any comprehensive critical perspective which could simply indicate good points at which to start. Yet – who knows? There may already, or still, be many more such readers than is sometimes supposed, for whom in a true Schillerian sense (and always supposing that such forms are not simply obliterated by others able to make more vociferous claims for attention) literature offers more evidence of valuable human experience, and more encouragement, than any interposing agency ever could. Meanwhile, new technologies, rightly used, surely have their own part to play. Perhaps, after all, the postcard filmer of Ax-les-Thermes was working towards his own version of the 'Spieltrieb'.

1996

# Paying Attention

It may be just a matter of temperament or generation, but I remember being much more likely to pay attention, when a student, to casual recommendations of books than to imperative injunctions. 'You might enjoy' was much more alluring than 'You *must* read', or a dauntingly long list of required reading – a bit like being given a hot racing tip in a low aside. It also seemed in keeping with the languid manner of some university dons and lecturers. The best nuggets were to be conveyed in the kind of soft-voiced parenthesis which, though it could sound like 'take it or leave it', might even have been a cunning way of outflanking the undergraduate need for definition by defiance. Anyway, this was how I came to read Percy Lubbock's *The Craft of Fiction* (Jonathan Cape), and so to re-read it more than once. First published in 1921, the book had reached its fifteenth reprint by the time I caught up with it in 1962. What interested me were not so much Lubbock's comments on particular works as what he has to say about books and reading in general:

> As quickly as we read it [the book], it melts and shifts in the memory; even at the moment when the last page is turned, a great part of the book, its finer detail, is already vague and doubtful. A little later, after a few days or months, how much is really left of it?

'To glance at a book, though the phrase is so often in our mouths, is in fact an impossibility', he suggests, concluding that 'the book vanishes as we lay hands on it.' This simple proposition – a caveat rather than a counsel of despair – reads like a forerunner of later critical views, but might seem hardly to apply to poetry in the same way as to prose (for prose a rule-proving exception might be the characters in Ray Bradbury's *Fahrenheit 451* who keep

29

literature alive, under a tyranny, by memorising whole novels). Yet even given the background of the oral tradition and poetry's traditional aids to the reader's powers of attention and retention – rhythm, metre, rhyme and, in the case of written poetry, its divisions and appearance on the page, poets have also often seen attention to the text as a problematical subject. Not all of them take Lubbock's view of the book as almost a closed book, or that of Mallarmé, who saw himself in the guise of a murderous cook approaching the poultry, as he attacked the uncut pages of books wielding a paper-knife in order to take possession of it, a procedure which for him involved 'la destruction d'une frêle inviolabilité' ('Quant au livre'). Or, to take another French instance, there is Valéry in 'Les deux vertus d'un livre' with his distinction between 'le texte lu' and 'le texte vu', the former being 'this successive and linear mode demanding *a focused eye*', the latter pictorial: 'A page is an image. It gives an overall impression, presents a block or system of blocks and strata, blacks and whites, a mark of figuration and intensity of greater or lesser felicity'. This reads like an eerie foreshadowing of the now quite common claim that computers will sooner rather than later replace the book (a recent television programme asserted breezily that computer screens would soon be made more convenient for the user to handle, though it failed to make clear how the computer version of reading in bed would be even a virtual pleasure).

But the situation is, of course, much more complicated than this, as is vividly illustrated by the extraordinary diagram included by I. A. Richards in his famous *Principles of Literary Criticism*, which appeared just three years after Lubbock's more modest undertaking. At this point in the book, Richards has already acknowledged the subjective nature of reading:

> It is unquestionable that the actual experiences, which even good critics undergo when reading, as we say, *the same poem*, differ very widely. In spite of certain conventions, which endeavour to conceal these inevitable discrepancies for social purposes, there can be no doubt that the experience of readers in connection with particular poems are rarely similar.

His diagram is part of an elaborate attempt to get beyond such subjectivity. It shows a vertical arrangement of vein-like or root-like lines above what seems a coil of bedsprings with, beneath them, the kind of wavy horizontal line you get from a cardiogram or seismograph when things are relatively quiet. Here

> the eye is depicted as reading a succession of printed words. As a result there follows a stream of reaction in which six distinct kinds of events may be distinguished. I The visual sensations of the printed words. II Images very closely associated with these sensations. III Images relatively free. IV References to, or 'thinkings of', various things. V Emotions. VI Affective-volitional attitudes.

To this scientific analysis of the act of reading he adds an important qualification about differences in readings of texts: 'some differences are, however, much more important than others. Provided the ends, in which the value of the poem lies, are attained, differences in the means need not prevent critics from agreement or from mutual service.' Eliot fished in the same waters – 'A poem may appear to mean very different things to different readers, and all of these meanings may be different from what the author thought he meant' ('The Music of Poetry'), and so did Auden – 'One sign that a book has literary value is that it can be read in a number of different ways . . . though . . . this number is finite and can be arranged in a hierarchical order' ('Reading'). As with Richards, much of this involves a quest for values objective enough to sustain the whole notion of literary criticism at a time of increasing uncertainties on many levels.

Since then the contexts of our reading have acquired excited and sometimes baffling proportions, directing and demanding our attention in ways often seen as inimical to previous notions of value. In general terms, no one has been a more acute chronicler of these cultural changes than George Steiner, notably in *In Bluebeard's Castle* (Faber, 1974):

> More and more literary texts and works of art now offer themselves as collective and/or anonymous. The poetics of ecstasy and of group feeling regard the imprint of a single 'great name' on the process of creation as archaic vanity. The audience is no longer an informed echo to the artist's talent,

a respondent to and transmitter of his singular enterprise; it is joint creator in a conglomerate of free-wheeling, participatory impulse.

For Steiner, however, one amongst various doleful consequences of such changes has been an end to the kind of historical cultural awareness which he sees as an essential prerequisite of reading fully.

Based, as it firmly is, on a deep, many-branched anatomy of classical and scriptural reference, expressed in a syntax and vocabulary of heightened tenor, the unbroken arc of English poetry, of reciprocal discourse that relates Chaucer and Spenser to Tennyson and to Eliot, is fading rapidly from the reach of natural reading. A central pulse in awareness, in the language, is becoming archival.

He admits that we hardly know whether things might not always have been so, and certainly it does seem very difficult to make exact comparisons between the reading habits and statistics of today and those of previous, often less self-conscious ages. But Steiner is sure about one striking difference: 'Activities such as reading, writing, private communication, learning, previously framed with silence, now take place in a field of strident *vibrato*. This means that the essentially linguistic nature of these pursuits is adulterated; they are vestigial modes of the old "logic".'

Participation rather than isolation; a new dominance of ear over eye; populism in one corner, the academy in the opposite one; immersion rather than attention – these, for Steiner, are the hallmarks of our culture (though it could be argued that the potential of television and InfoTech for encouraging isolation as well as the dominance of image over sound is at least as great as the purely auditory manifestations of what he calls the 'musicalization' of our culture).

As if this were not, in sum, more than enough to distract the reader, here comes Miroslav Holub's *The Dimension of the Present Moment* (Faber, 1990) to investigate, every bit as minutely as Richards and more wittily, the nature of the attention that we say we pay to things. Recent psychological experiments have shown, he reports, that 'in our consciousness, the present moment lasts about three seconds': and 'stimuli lasting more than three seconds cannot be maintained by our consciousness as a whole.' He goes on to apply this alarming limitation specifically to poetry:

> In 73 per cent of all German poems, from Gryphius to Hugo von Hofmannsthal, lines read aloud last from two to three seconds. Lines lasting over four seconds are, or can be, divided into shorter segments, and the reader makes a slight but noticeable pause in the middle of the line . . . Greek and Latin epic hexameters are divided by a strong caesura into two three-second fragments and the same time unit has been found in different English, French, Japanese and Chinese metred poetry (F. Turner and E. Pöppel, *Poetry*, August 1983).

Even free verse is seen as subject to the same law, and Holub broadens the argument still further when he writes that 'I dare to think that present-time frames are implied even in the process of thinking and feeling, and everything that is contained in the consciousness takes place in those tiny facets, in switching on and off, fading in and out, emerging and submerging'.

Whatever the neurography of the matter, getting beyond the tyranny of the present is as much the business of the imaginative reader as of the writer: and that essential act of stretching inherent in the very word 'attention' is, as philosophers such as R. G. Collingwood and Mary Warnock remind us (see, for instance, Warnock's *Imagination & Time*, Blackwell, 1994), a precondition for turning perception into an idea which the imagination can then keep alive. From Coleridge and his invented term 'esemplastic power', to Richards's 'imaginal and incipient action', poets and critics have long been aware of the kind of unifying concentration that books require. 'As for poetry in particular, it demands of its readers a greater diligence of attention, and it calls upon more concentrated powers of inference, drawn from a wider range of reference, than ordinary expository prose; for that reason many general readers of, say, cheap fiction find it impenetrable, and unworthy of their effort.' Thus Anthony Hecht in *On the Laws of the Poetic Art* (Princeton University Press, 1995), a wide-ranging book which insists on the craft of the art, as well as putting forward a view of our contemporary culture that has much in common with Steiner. Comparing poetry and music, poetry and painting, public and private art, the themes of paradise and wilderness, and the inner contradictions of works of art, Hecht also includes, in a preface, an extract from one of his own poems, 'Peripeteia', set in a theatre. To take an extract from the extract:

> Whether we like it or not, we are a crowd,
> Foul-breathed, gum-chewing, fat with arrogance,
> Passion, opinion and appetite for blood.
> But in that instant, which the mind protracts,
> From dim to dark before the curtain rises,
> Each of us is miraculously alone
> In calm, invulnerable isolation,
> Neither a neighbor nor a fellow but
> As at the beginning and end, a single soul,
> With all the sweet and sour of loneliness.

That instant, here described in an idiom not just theatrical but Shakespearean, seems to me an excellent evocation of the reader's best frame of mind, at the moment of reaching out for the book. If you have more than three seconds to spare, you might well enjoy the Hecht. It certainly repays attention.

# The Hole in the Flag

There are times when history produces images to equal those of the imagination, in their vividness and their consequent ability to live on in the mind. Even the rapid succession and short life of events on film and television news, which have often made them public in the first place, cannot dislodge them. Two such images stay in my head from 1989. The first, from China, is of a diminutive figure carrying a bag in each hand, facing a huge and cumbersome tank, matching its forward lurches to left and right, as if it were another person encountered in a narrow passage or doorway: defeating it, almost, simply by being there. For, in the face of that clanking engine of oppression, what could have been in those bags (which seemed to balance one another at the end of the carrier's arms almost like the scales of justice) but in one, hope, in the other, a soul? In the same year, newspaper and television pictures from Romania showed jubilant crowds celebrating what appeared to be the end of a dictatorship – a moment heraldically enacted by a round hole cut in the middle of the national flag, where the emblem of the régime had been. At the centre of those hoisted banners, a view through to blue sky, to the infinity of renewed potential.

If such moments reverberate in the imagination, in the world of historical contingencies they can sometimes appear all too fleeting, momentary stays against new or re-emerging tyrannies. Yet perhaps this is deceptive. It may be that their ability to have arched from instance almost to icon gives them a real, if unquantifiable, potency: a potency which may remain latent, but one day return to the world of events. Meanwhile, their influence is of necessity underground, complex, diffused.

Something of this trajectory might apply to relationships between the actual and the imagined in general – a negotiation which many writers of the twentieth century have felt to be ineluctable, and which some have found a test or a definition not only of conscience but of culture. 'And in the activity of poetry too, there is a tendency to place a counter-reality in the scales – a reality which may be only imagined but which nevertheless has weight because it is imagined within the gravitational pull of the actual and can therefore hold its own and balance out against the historical situation.' Thus Seamus Heaney, in the opening lecture which gives its title to the book that reproduces ten of the fifteen he delivered as Professor of Poetry at Oxford, *The Redress of Poetry* (Faber, 1995). He goes on: 'This redressing effect of poetry comes from it being a glimpsed alternative, a revelation of potential that is denied or constantly threatened by circumstances.' He has already alluded to Wallace Stevens's description, in 'The Noble Rider and the Sound of Words', of 'the nobility of poetry' as 'the imagination pressing back against the pressure of reality'. 'Nobility' is an awkward word, with its inevitable associations of aristocracy and rhetoric, but it may have validity despite that. Certainly there is no doubting 'the pressure of reality' – of which Andrew Waterman gives ample and specific evidence in his instructive article in *PN Review 107* (engagingly titled 'Seamus Riding Gently on the Fame') about reactions to Heaney's Nobel Prize. Pointing out that English poets are spared the kind of historical pressure which confronts Irish writers, Waterman praises Heaney for his 'profound understanding of the nature of the transaction between art and reality'. It is this transaction which runs throughout *The Redress of Poetry*, involving a choice which Wallace Stevens articulated clearly in 'The Noble Rider and the Sound of Words'. The poet has to

> come to a decision regarding the imagination and reality; and he will find that it is not a choice of one over the other and not a decision that divides them, but something subtler, a recognition that here, too, as between these poles, the universal interdependence exists, and hence his choice and his decision must be that they are equal and inseparable.

Though he does not quote this passage, Seamus Heaney succeeds impressively in fulfilling its intentions. In doing so, he firmly resists any conclusion based on a simplistic marshalling of opposing ideas and language, though the temptation to do so is there in the very subject matter (reality vs. the imagination, the actual and historical vs. the potential and Platonic, the indicative vs. the optative, enjoyment vs. endurance, hope vs. experience). For Heaney, 'Redress' is a granting of alternatives, an imaginative holding of them in such a way as to be not just a balance, but a constant readiness to adjust and amend, or to restore, in the interests of justice:

> Poetry, let us say, whether it belongs to an old political dispensation or aspires to express a new one, has to be a working model of inclusive consciousness. It should not simplify. Its projections and inventions should be a match for the complex reality which surrounds it and out of which it is generated.

And it is the nature of the course which Heaney charts very carefully through that 'complex reality' which is one of the most striking features of his Oxford lectures. He proceeds with a warmth of spirit and with the same talent for beguilement with which he credits the poetry of Marlowe, and sees the contemporary starting-point clearly: 'In any movement towards liberation, it will be necessary to deny the normative authority of the dominant language or literary tradition.' He acknowledges the injustices and exclusions of history, the oppression of minorities and the exploitation of the colonised: these, too, demand redress, and several find their place among the poets he discusses in detail, notably Clare and Wilde. At the same time, he defends the freedoms of poetry, suggesting that 'its integrity is not to be impugned just because at any given moment it happens to be a refraction of some discredited cultural or political system.' In 'a world of accusing ideologies and impugned ideals', he continues to assert 'the central, epoch-making role that is always available in the world to poetry and the poet'. 'Always' because potential, Platonic: 'in the world' because, as he also insists, the operational base must be the here and now, not some rhetorical or oneiric imposition on reality.

Heaney enacts his case by reference to a variety of poets, with frequent reminders that language and the joyful exploitation of its complexities and possibilities are intrinsic to the poet's business: and that this remains true even in instances where the poet has some specific political alignment or context, such as Marlowe's 'Hero and Leander', MacDiarmid's Scottish nationalism, or Wilde in 'The Ballad of Reading Gaol'. He emphasises both the immediate technical concerns which engage the poet and the areas of transcendence to which this concentration of creative energy may lead. Thus he quotes Brodsky's remark that 'intonation in a poem . . . stands for the motion of the soul': John Clare is, in a given work, 'led towards the thing behind his voice and ear which Nadezhda Mandelstam called "the nugget of harmony"'; Elizabeth Bishop's 'Sandpiper' is seen to offer evidence that 'the poet does to words what she does to details: she makes them beckon us into hitherto unsuspected places'; and despite reservations about Dylan Thomas,

> I would still like to affirm his kind of afflatus as a constant possibility for poetry, something not superannuated by the irony and self-knowing tactics of the art in post-modern times.

Above all, Heaney seeks to combine a view of poetry as an end in itself, as 'self-delighting', with a view of it as a means, as 'redemptive'. This can apply even to the bleakness of a world-view like that of Beckett, whose 'excellence resides in his working out a routine in the playhouse of his art which is both true to the depressing goings-on in the house of actuality and – more important – a transformation of them.' Of 'A Drunk Man Looks at a Thistle' he writes:

> It was a magnificent intervention by creative power into an historical situation. Its force was the force of the glimpsed alternative and it still gives credence to MacDiarmid's wonderfully stirring affirmation in another context that poetry is human existence come to life.

Heaney calls in evidence the Yeats of 'Under Ben Bulben', with a plea for poetry as crucial to the achievement of 'the profane perfection of mankind', though the impulse as well as the idiom of much that he writes is essentially religious, from his early reference to Simone Weil's *Gravity and Grace* to such remarks as the one he makes about Bishop's 'Sandpiper', that it brings 'a renewed awareness of that mysterious otherness of the world.' Interestingly, Larkin is seen to fall short, for all his technical excellence, precisely because in a poem like 'Aubade', 'its argument does add weight to the negative side of the scale and tips the balance definitively in favour of chemical law and mortal decline.' But the principle of 'redress' prevents any judgement from seeming too final, and retains sufficient elasticity to allow both detailed textual comment and such generalities as Heaney's evocation, in the context of John Clare, of Mandelstam's 'nostalgia for world culture':

> It makes sense to think of Clare in relation to the arrival of poetry in that longed-for place or state . . . The dream of a world culture, after all, is a dream of a world where no language will be relegated.

Here, as elsewhere, the 'glimpsed alternative' is reined in by being related also to the hierarchies of history, a process which finds its fulfilment in the final lecture, 'Frontiers of Writing' where, with absolute logic, Heaney not only summons the spirit of MacNeice ('if Hewitt was the projector of a Northern Ireland that failed to develop, Louis MacNeice is the sponsor of one struggling to be born'), but challenges Ulster Unionists to develop a 'two-mindedness' of the generous and inclusive kind that he has himself entertained for poetry.

> In other words, whatever the possibilities of achieving political harmony at an institutional level, I wanted to affirm that within our individual selves we can reconcile two orders of knowledge which we might call the practical and the poetic; to affirm also that each form of knowledge redresses the other and that the frontier between them is there for the crossing.

Wallace Stevens complements this view of individual freedom from a different angle, in 'The Noble Rider and the Sound of Words': 'No politician can command the imagination, directing it to do this or that. Stalin might grind his teeth the whole of a Russian winter and yet all the poets in the Soviets might remain silent the following spring.' Or they might have to cross actual frontiers as well as those of writing and language, as did Joseph Brodsky (whose untimely death occurred in January), who 'once suggested that the highest goal human beings can set before themselves is the creation of civilization', to take the opening sentence of Heaney's third Oxford lecture. Born within a year of one another, both inheritors of a context in which, however different, nationhood and frontiers, division and inclusiveness are unsettled and unsettling issues, Heaney the 'inner émigré' and Brodsky the exile frequently inform one another, sometimes by echo, sometimes by contrast. Both writers see poetry as an alternative world; both subscribe to a Keatsian view of a poetry of fine excess, and work that goes beyond the given and the expected. Both quote Mandelstam's notion of a 'nostalgia for world culture', both assert the fundamental independence of poetry, though Brodsky places much more emphasis on the ways in which the poet is, as he sees it, 'invariably at odds with the social reality'. In his essays, *Less Than One* (Viking, 1986), his view of the poet is often of a figure historically isolated, as was Mandelstam, by the simple truth that 'lyricism is the ethics of language' or, as he writes in his obituary of Mandelstam's widow Nadezhda, by the fact that 'there is something in the consciousness of literati that cannot stand the notion of someone's moral authority'. That sense of isolation could extend even to America, where a writer might feel bound to defend himself against possible charges of élitism 'from, of all places, the local campuses': cries which, Brodsky writes, 'must be left unheeded, for culture is 'élitist' by definition, and the application of democratic principles in the sphere of knowledge leads to equating wisdom with idiocy.' He concludes, with a blunt defiance, that 'basically, talent doesn't need history'.

If this is much more overtly confrontational than anything in *The Redress of Poetry*, it is also part of the story of a man who can still describe Nadezhda Mandelstam's memoirs as 'a view of history in the light of conscience and culture' and who, like Heaney, repeats Auden's hope that, even amid 'negation and despair', the poet may 'show an affirming flame'. Like any exile, Brodsky is acutely aware of the writer's need for readers: 'Consciously or unconsciously, every poet in the course of his career engages in a search for an ideal reader, for that alter ego, since a poet seeks not recognition but understanding.' Alongside this, we might consider Robert Pinsky's remark, quoted by Heaney, that the artist 'needs not so much an audience, as to feel a need to answer, a promise to respond'.

Ultimately, Stevens's 'nobility', Heaney's 'inclusiveness' and Brodsky's 'search for an ideal reader' are about such human fullness as the writer may achieve, by art and imagination, experience and hope, within the mortal and historical constraints of his or her circumstances. In Heaney's words, it is the work of the creative spirit 'reminding the indicative mood of history that it has been written in by force and written in over the good optative mood of human potential'. This is not an evasion, but a challenge which places real responsibility on the poet's conscience and responsiveness, as well as on the alertness of readers. As a critical standard, it may be impossible to systematise, yet any critical approach that ignores it risks desiccation, just as the state that thinks to shut it out will sooner or later find a man in front of a tank, and the 'o' of Heaney's 'optative' become a hole in the centre of the flag.

# Staying Tuned

One of the most common rhymes for 'June' is, of course, 'tune', as Browning's bean-flowers and blackbird and Burns's red red rose remind us: but when P. J. Kavanagh, in *The Spectator* of 1st June this year, wrote about the importance of 'tune' in poems, it was more in the context of a threnody, for he had two baleful items of news to deliver. The magazine was to stop publishing poems; and his own *Life & Letters* column had, as he wrote, 'been put out to grass'. So, the demise of an airy, enjoyable and thoughtful monthly page of prose, and another outlet for poems gone up the spout, joining such *chers défunts* as *The Listener, Encounter* and Radio 3's *Poetry Now*. Not that *The Spectator* has always been open to poems. Kavanagh relates the genesis of its hospitality, his suggestion in 1984 to the then editor (Charles Moore) and literary editor (Ferdinand Mount) that the magazine might 'put a few reasonably comprehensible poems under the nose of *Spectator* readers who had given up poetry for lost years ago'. He sets out clearly what qualities he was looking for in submissions – up to 200 poems a month, from which he would choose perhaps four: 'Tune, liveliness of observation and vocabulary, economy, shape. Perhaps the most important of these is tune – cadence, rhythm, euphony, that almost indefinable sound and sense of the right words in the right order.' Most submissions were easily rejected 'because their writers seemed to imagine that "modern" poetry had abandoned tune – T. S. Eliot is among the most mellifluous of poets – and to have forgotten that one definition of poetry is "memorable speech", and it is tune that makes it memorable.'

Perhaps few aspects of poetry have been as widely discussed, or have proved finally as resistant to precise definitions, as musicality and its agents – most commonly understood as rhyme, rhythm, stress and metre. Long ago Ecclesiasticus yoked together among his praiseworthy famous men 'such as found out musical

42

tunes, and recited verses in writing': and indeed relations between the two involve not just sound and sense, but the vocal cords (with their musical homonym) as much as the ear, utterance as much as reading with the eye. And how many 'Songs for St Cecilia's Day' are there? Among them is one by the founder of *The Spectator*. More likely to feature in the discussion is Verlaine: sooner or later someone is almost sure to come out with 'De la musique avant toute chose', even if it is sometimes forgotten that none of his contemporaries, several of whom wrote assiduously about the relation of poetry to music, quite had available to them the personal proof evident in his own poems, with their delicate evocations and subtle harmonies. Poets' general statements always chime with their particular talents – though Auden thought French poets in general possibly 'more prone than English to fall into the heresy of thinking that poetry ought to be as much like music as possible' because 'in traditional French verse, sound effects have always played a much more important role than they have in English verse' ('Writing'). Certainly not all those who quote Verlaine approvingly would necessarily feel the same about the Wagnerian *Gesamtkunstwerk* which is logically one of its evolutionary successors.

Pound strikes a typically admonitory note in his *ABC of Reading*: 'Poetry begins to atrophy when it gets too far from music.' In 'A Retrospect' he defines rhythm as 'to compose in the sequence of the musical phrase, not in sequence of a metronome', and it's a definition that seems to have worn well, like his comments in the same essay about translation: 'That part of your poetry which strikes upon the imaginative *eye* of the reader will lose nothing by translation into a foreign tongue; that which appeals to the ear can reach only those who take it in the original.' But can the music of poetry ever really be translated? In *The Dyer's Hand* Auden, for whom 'poetry is the most provincial of the arts', reads as if he might have been taking up Pound's point directly:

> The sound of the words, their rhythmical relations, and all meanings and association of meanings which depend on sound, like rhymes and puns, are, of course, untranslatable, but poetry is not, like music, pure sound. Any elements in a poem which are not based on verbal experience are, to

some degree, translatable into another tongue, for example, images, similes and metaphors which are drawn from sensory experience.

In 'Notes on Music and Opera', Auden has points to make from another perspective about poems and music, in considering what separates poems and songs. 'A verbal art like poetry is reflective; it stops to think. Music is immediate, it goes on to become' (is the same true of television, relatively, as regards the word and the camera?), and for him there is a crucial distinction to be made between lyric and song. 'A lyric is a poem intended to be chanted. In a chant the music is subordinate to the words which limit the range and tempo of the notes. In song, the notes must be free to be whatever they choose and the words must be able to do what they are told.' While acknowledging that some composers have set worthwhile poems (he cites Campion, Hugo Wolf and of course Britten as examples), 'the question remains . . . whether the listener hears the sung words as words in a poem, or, as I am inclined to believe, only as sung syllables'.

Eliot, in his 1942 essay *The Music of Poetry*, covers most of the angles, seeing the musical elements of poetry waxing and waning in different periods, though always to be measured by reference to the 'music latent in the common speech of its time'. In our own time, what gives the issue its edge is the conviction on the part of some writers and critics that the lyric is dead and indeed should be, as an element of what Tom Paulin calls in his cogent essays in *Minotaur: Poetry and the Nation State* (Faber, 1992), 'the magical transcendence of art', – 'that archaic humanist cop-out'. He quotes Holub's assertion that 'I strongly resent lyricism as adhesive tape over the mouth', but also includes the following sentence in which Holub acknowledges that lyricism may still be a better alternative than despair or aposiopesis. For Paulin, though 'the lyric speaks for unchanging human nature, that timeless essence beyond fashion and economics', its music is essentially to be heard as a reactionary force, and its closures are not to be trusted. He traces its progress, and challenges to it, from Coleridge (he is interesting on the contest between aesthetic pleasures or lyrical softenings and historical consciousness in 'Frost at Midnight' and 'Kubla Khan') through to Larkin's 'journeys into the interior, into the unknown heart – the maybe missing centre – of Englishness', and through the genre which he wittily describes as the 'England from a train' poem. *Minotaur* ends with a brief but warm consideration of Peter Reading, seeing in his work a positive idealism, 'a poetry of extreme risk' which is 'appropriate to the crazed astringency and philistinism of the present social moment'. Here the determining criterion is political commitment, the need to respond to the world as it is. Thus, 'as England regressed more and more into a nasty and brutal form of populism, Reading observed the national sickness and chucked torn gobbets of verse at his readers'.

Time and history certainly amend our view of what tunes may be permissible, as they do our ability actually to hear some of them. Perhaps a good musical analogy for our century might be Janáček's two string quartets or, even more, his piano music; particularly the Piano Sonata 1.X.1905, written in homage to a Czech worker killed by Austrian troops during a demonstration on that date, and 'On An Overgrown Path', haunted by memories of his daughter Olga, who died at the age of twenty-one. To hear in the music the tussle between such knowledge of public violence and private grief, and the composer's natural melodic gift, is to witness in miniature a paradigm of our contemporary self-consciousness. To return to poetry, one expression of this might be the way in which poets commandeer traditional forms and rhythms – for instance, Peter Reading's ironic use of classical metres, James Fenton's invigorating and unsettling ballads (that tuneful form has often had a political dimension, of course), or Tony Harrison's sense of dramatic incantation, as well as his natural lyric gift which co-exists to good effect alongside his sharp awareness of social divisions and historical cruelties. Carol Ann Duffy similarly combines lyricism with an acute social sense: in quite a different idiom, Eavan Boland's work brings together a feeling for the sensuousness of the immediate world and a cool though passionate weighing of the forces of history and society. And some poets, wherever they choose to pitch their tent, continue to write directly about the musical movements of poetry. Thus, for instance, Les Murray, in the essay 'Poems and Poesies': 'Poetry, in the form of verse or in the rhythms of properly tuned literary prose, alters our breathing and submits it to the laws of the dance. Where this does not happen, where there is an absence of what Alan Gould calls "some rhythmic principle" or other, poetry tends not to be fully achieved.' Like Ted Hughes, Murray is interested in myths, and he sees them as closest to the dream-nature of poems and to the dance. Opposed to what he sees as the deleterious effects of education and the academy on the enjoyment and understanding of poetry, Murray sees musicality as an important ingredient in what he calls 'the riveting wholespeak of poetry': you could say that one of Murray's chief concerns, as an avowedly Christian poet, is with a kind of soul music.

More recently, Ted Hughes's volume of occasional prose, *Winter Pollen* (edited by William Scammell, Faber, 1994), includes an excellent essay, 'Myths, Metres, Rhythms', in which he traces two distinct musical traditions, as he sees them, in English verse. The first, which he characterises as 'orthodox metre', is 'musically accessible to every kind of reader, even those with the least culti-vated ear'. He gives as examples Addison's 'Letter from Italy, to the Rt Honourable Charles Lord Halifax, 1701', Graves's 'The Revenant', and part of a Holub poem, 'Suffering', translated by George Theiner. He makes a convincing case for the simple met-rical principle which they have in common, their reliance on 'natural quantities'. As he writes of the Holub poem, 'all the lines are for every reader easily sayable, when spoken in a natural, con-versational way'. 'Unorthodox metre', the second musical tradi-tion, he finds in the work particularly of Coleridge (the first part of 'Christabel', and 'The Knight's Tomb') and Hopkins. 'Rather like Sidney before him, Coleridge was constantly digging through to a sea of music that he could hear but not reach. Like somebody imprisoned in a tossing galleon – his only release was into that music. And the three visionary poems, 'Kubla Khan', 'The Ancient Mariner' and 'Christabel' are the story of how the music burst in on him and took him by surprise.' In the case of 'Kubla Khan', 'that is the subject of the poem: the demon of song emerges and claims the singer.' In coming to Coleridge and Hopkins, 'the voice has to make a shift, from the speaking mode to what – for want of the right word – one might call the 'per-forming' mode. That is, it is a demand for creative musical input, from the reader'. The complexity of this becomes even greater when 'the line does not move obediently from beginning to end, or even for some part of its length, under a single simple law of 'natural quantities' that coincide correctly with a fixed metrical pattern. Instead, it explores its way through a field of flexing, contrapuntal tensions, between two simultaneous but opposed laws – that is to say, between a law of 'natural quantities' set in opposition to the law of a fixed, basic metric pattern.'

The ensuing examination of 'The Windhover' in the light of this is a marvellous instance of one poet paying close attention to the work of another, and producing at times a music of his own. Hughes is particularly good on language as power, 'the vocal code of the social and political ascendancy', and on the way in which succeeding generations revalue prosody and hear with an ear changed by new developments and possibilities. The fears of poets such as Coleridge and Hopkins that their work would be, literally, misheard because opposed to the prevailing metrical tradition, illustrates the same point, though for Hughes the test case remains Wyatt, for so long one among numerous victims of what Hughes describes as 'the chronic war between the New Chaucerian and the Old English tradition'.

None of this invalidates the point which P. J. Kavanagh makes about the need to write memorably. That challenge remains – to find for the given poem the tonality and the rhythms best suited to its intentions, the harmonies or the dissonances, as well as what Eliot called 'the music of imagery': in fact, all the means by which it may lodge in the mind of the reader. For that reason alone, as well as because of the flux of language and history, the continuance of the debate seems assured. Meanwhile, if you want to stay tuned to Kavanagh's civilised discourse, you will be able to find it in the pages of the *TLS*, the new setting for his column.

# Actual Emblems

Of what occasion this year has it been written that it 'will advance the cause of worldwide culture – establishing a sense of mutual trust and helping us all to address our disagreements through constructive dialogue . . . rather than through confrontation'? That 'history, in its unpredictable way, has in this instance conducted a unique experiment'? And that 'it is capable of provoking feelings not unlike those experienced by the relatives of an inmate released from jail after many years of incarceration'? Would it help to know that 'guns were still firing when Soviet troops began to discover these bunkers'? Or that, in the words of one of the people involved, 'I was lucky enough to get inside Special Storage thirty years ago. This was a blatant violation of the régime's directives . . .'? These bold, not to say dramatic remarks come from the foreword, preface and introduction to the catalogue of *Hidden Treasures Revealed*, the exhibition at the Hermitage of seventy-four paintings, mainly Impressionist but including Corot, Courbet and Daumier, as well as works by Rouault, Picasso and Matisse. Visiting St Petersburg for the first time in March, thirty years to the month after the death of Anna Akhmatova, I was just in time to see them – and memorable they certainly were, beginning with five wonderful Fantin-Latour flower pictures, and continuing with such riches as Renoir's *In a Garden*, Van Gogh's *The White House at Night*, two wonderful Monet paintings of gardens, amongst others too numerous to list here. As the catalogue points out, the pictures retain a vivid freshness which they owe to the long time they have spent in closed storage. Fresh as they are, they are also inseparable from the story of the violent historical moment which brought them here, often by tortuous routes. In this way they are a perfect introduction to a city described by Dostoevsky as 'the most abstract and the most premeditated place in the world', a description cited by Joseph

Brodsky, for whom 'this city really rests on the bones of its build-
ers as much as on the wooden piles that they drove into the
ground.'

But the three pictures which have stayed most vividly in my
mind from Akhmatova's 'granite city of fame and misfortune' are
not those in the Hermitage, though the first of them was also
framed and hanging on a wall. Issued at the behest of the
Directorate of the North Eastern Corrections Group of the NKVD,
it was easy enough to read:

| | |
|---|---|
| Height: | medium |
| Physique: | normal |
| Hair colour: | grey |
| Eye colour: | dark brown |
| Nose: | hooked |
| Other: | chest and abdomen covered with hairs, bald head |
| General speciality: | writer |
| Narrow speciality: | poet |
| Languages, apart from your own: | Russian, French, German |
| Admitted to this camp: | 12 October 1938 |

There was also a printed statement that 'I am aware of my responsibility for the submission of misleading particulars' and, at the
foot of the form, a signature: Osip Mandelstam. The form now
hangs in the small flat on the Fontannyy Dom occupied for many
years by his friend Akhmatova.

Then there was the monument recently created by the sculptor
Mikhail Shemyakin, on the Robespierre embankment immediately opposite the Kresty prison. It consists of two large bronze
sphinxes, full-breasted but otherwise emaciated. They face each
other several yards apart, set on tall plinths of brownish-pink
stone. Between them and on the actual parapet of the embankment wall, four blocks of granite surround a space barred like a
gunner's reticle, representing a cell window. One half of each
sphinx's face is cut away vertically to the bone, a half-skull.
Round and below the sphinxes are a number of quotations,
including lines by Brodsky (Brodsky, who wrote that 'Lyricism
is the ethics of language'), as well as the final verses of

Akhmatova's 'Requiem'. Impossible, then, as you look across to the grim red-brown bulk of the prison, not to think of Akhmatova's preface to 'Requiem', *Instead of a Foreword* (here from *Selected Poems*, translated by Richard McKane, Bloodaxe, 1989) in which she describes how she queued there in the hope of seeing her imprisoned son:

> During the terrible years of the Yezhov Terror I spent seventeen months in the prison queues in Leningrad. One day someone 'identified' me. Then a woman with lips blue with cold who was standing behind me, and of course had never heard of my name, came out of the numbness which affected us all and whispered in my ear – (we all spoke in whispers there):
>
> 'Could you describe this?'
> I said, 'I can!'

If both these images owe their potency to their challenging juxtaposition of the poet and the contingent oppressions of history, the third offers no such redemptive alleviation. At 72, the Avenue of the Unconquered, in what was once the village of Piskaryovskoye, about half an hour's drive from the city centre, there is laid out the huge cemetery where over 500,000 people are buried, mostly civilian victims of the siege of Leningrad. When I went there, almost fresh snow, trodden here and there by fine birdprints, lay across the broad tops of the mass graves. Each grave (and I lost count of how many there were) was marked with a single slab of stone bearing the number of one of four years: 1941, 1942, 1943, 1944. To undertake the considerable walk down the central avenue, towards the only monument, a statue at the far end representing the mother-country, was to be enveloped in silence. True, there was classical music coming softly from the loudspeakers deployed at intervals throughout the cemetery, but this seemed more than anything a reminder of the limitations of words or any other articulation. In fact there are some words here, lines carved on the end-wall behind the monument, and written by Olga Bergholts, who remained in the city during the 900 days of the blockade. They end:

We cannot number all their noble names here,
So many lie beneath the eternal granite,
But know as you look upon these stones,
That no one has been forgotten and nothing has
　　been forgotten.

Nowhere in St Petersburg, already so freighted with its cargo of grandeur and misery, does the weight of history seem heavier, the notion of individuality more forlorn.

The impact of such images is emblematic as well as actual: and as Václav Havel points out in his essay 'The Power of the Powerless', emblems 'often are important because they stand out against our own smallness and the shortcomings of our own society'. From the perspective of his own country and its history in this century, Havel can see that 'a person who has been seduced by the consumer value system, whose identity is dissolved in an amalgam of the accoutrements of mass civilization, and who has no roots in the order of being, no sense of responsibility for anything higher than his or her own personal survival, is a *demoralized* person.' In such circumstances, the temptation to idealise individuals acting heroically in far grimmer circumstances than our own is a strong one. For Havel, western attitudes can seem naive, and in another essay, 'An anatomy of reticence', he contrasts such naivety with the black humour, sense of irony and reticence of Europeans who have had to live under totalitarian regimes – qualities evolved by necessity, to which he adds 'an intense fear of exaggerating our own dignity unintentionally to a comic degree, a fear of pathos and sentimentality, of overstatement and of what Kundera calls the lyric relation to the world.' Yet he also acknowledges that, even if western 'peace fighters' can seem 'a bit too earnest, perhaps even somewhat pathetic', this is also partly a matter of 'an opportunity for life in a humanly richer community, for self-realization outside the stereotypes of a consumer society and for expressing their resistance to those stereotypes'.

The human need for models of behaviour has been emphasised by many writers and thinkers, from Emerson (who wrote of history, 'There is properly no history; only biography'; and of the poet, 'We are symbols, and inhabit symbols') to Primo Levi, who wrote in 'Eclipse of the Prophet':

51

We've had Eden, Cathay, Eldorado: in Fascist times we chose as our model (here too not without reason) the great democracies; then, depending on the moment and our propensities, the Soviet Union, China, Cuba, Vietnam, Sweden. They were preferably distant countries, because a model by definition must be perfect; and since no real country is perfect, it is advisable to choose vaguely known models that can be safely idealised without fear of a conflict with reality.

For Levi, the ambiguity of this idealising of a nation is repeated on the individual level: and he knows how close models can be to monsters. Yet 'no prophet dares any longer to reveal our tomorrow to us, and this, the eclipse of prophets, is a bitter but necessary medicine. We must build our own tomorrow, blindingly, gropingly . . .'

The subject is taken up in a different but related context by Donald Davie, in 'From the Marches of Christendom: Mandelstam and Milosz' (*PN Review 109*), where he discusses the Christianity – and, as he sees it, the differing heresies – of Mandelstam and Milosz. He writes that Mandelstam 'was concerned throughout to make of himself and his life 'a visual-biographical "emblem". And that is what . . . readers far outside Russia still seem to expect of their poets, nourished of course by the commercially driven fashion for biographies.' Davie criticises 'the awe-struck commendations of him by those who know his work only in arbitrary selections and indifferent translations', and compares him unfavourably with Milosz, who 'will have little appeal for those excited by spectacularly "emblematic" lives like Sylvia Plath's or Robert Lowell's'. There is a great deal else in Davie's article, notably about the decline of any real sense of Christian orthodoxy, but I want to focus on his view of the emblematic. I wonder about this. Does anyone choose to lead an emblematic life? There may be a choice, and often a hard one, in favour of an important principle — and the principle itself may well have the kind of breadth which is a prerequisite of the emblematic: but that does not seem the same thing at all. And could the simple or complex desire to lead an emblematic life suffice to bring it about convincingly? Everyone knows the muddy complexities of a life lived, and that biographies are often, for one reason or another, only somewhat less distorted and edited than our conscious memories. That only some temperaments have the potential to house the emblematic is as clear as the fact that only some of these actually become 'emblems': isn't this at least in part because it is others, or the historical moment, that make them so? Impossible, in thinking of Nelson Mandela or Daw Aung San Suu Kyi, to deny the overlapping of the actual and the emblematic: emblems by definition call attention to something other than themselves – in these cases to remarkable human persistence and moral courage embodied in hardship and imprisonment. And for Christians, isn't the figure of Christ the supreme, indeed the only example of an exact fusion of the actual and the emblematic? In the case of writers, it is surely the work itself and its readers that must validate in artistic and human terms, as well as help to explain, any emblematic aura.

This is not to deny the validity of Davie's contention that there is 'a gulf set between the Russian and the English ideas of poetry', but to challenge his view that 'we are right, I think, to be prudently aghast at how the Russian intelligentsia, before and after the Revolution, accorded to their poets (and also their musicians, notably Scriabin) the privileges of the mystagogue, the sage, and the scapegoat.' For writers like Akhmatova and Mandelstam, their art was set at the brim of historical circumstance and necessity – and the same could be said for many others in different times and places, including a number of writers whose work has come through to us in translation over the last twenty years or so, whether in the prison poems of Irena Ratushinskaya, or in the poems of involuntary exiles such as Bei Dao.

In St Petersburg it is as if time, which often seems to dilute the individual events of history as it accrues, has concentrated their mass, compacting the actual and the emblematic. In so doing, it lends a more than purely emblematic or sentimental weight to such lines as these by Mandelstam (translated by Clarence Brown and W. S. Merwin, in *Selected Poems*, Penguin, 1997):

Mounds of human heads are wandering into the distance.
I dwindle among them. Nobody sees me. But in books
much loved, and in children's games I shall rise
from the dead to say the sun is shining.

53

1997

# No Shortage of Questions

There are various ways of imposing or achieving silence. One of the most effective I have encountered was the work of a guest at a rather pretentious drinks party who, declining the canapés and asked whether any other food might be preferable, declared with serious and voluble enthusiasm that a jam sandwich would be just the thing. Recently, while attending the meeting of a jury considering a number of European books (poetry and prose) for a prize, I encountered another method, which seemed almost as effective initially. 'What is meant,' someone asked, taking up a phrase from the description of the award, 'by "a work of European significance"?'

The ensuing silence was impressive enough to make the suggestions which followed it sound somewhat tentative. Somebody spoke of 'the European tradition starting with Shakespeare'. Somebody else felt that 'durability' had a part to play. 'Diversity' was offered as a third contribution. I found myself thinking, not very helpfully, of that extraordinary stage direction in *The Dynasts*: 'The nether sky opens, and Europe is disclosed as a prone and emaciated figure, the Alps shaping like a backbone, and the branching mountain-chains like ribs, the peninsular plateau of Spain forming a head.' While not necessarily accepting Hardy's geotectonic anatomy, we might well agree on a description of the continent as extending eastward from the eastern shores of the north Atlantic as far as the Urals, following down the Volga, then through the Bosphorus and westward along the Mediterranean to Gibraltar. Nor is it difficult to think of the names of poets, dramatists and prose writers who are regarded as having European stature: but how much closer does this bring us to a specific definition?

Though we read and hear the word 'Europe' virtually every day, more often than not it is in the context of politics and economics rather than culture: and too often what we truly have in mind is western Europe, the corner nearest to Britain, rather than the whole continent. We are more likely to think of Brussels than Bucharest; of Luxembourg rather than Lisbon. Most definitions are, of course, two-fold by nature: those we make of and for ourselves, which we might call internal, and those made for or by others. In the case of Europe, perhaps one of the greatest difficulties is the problem of defining features which can be isolated as 'European'. The point is well put by Timothy Garton Ash, in his book *In Europe's Name* (Vintage, 1994):

If we regard Europe as a community of values, or of liberal democracies committed to mutual support and defence, the question immediately arises: why not 'the West'? Aren't the values of the West actually easier to define than those of Europe? . . . Beyond this, there was of course the even larger question: why not the world?

In many respects he sees even the question of 'Which Europe?' as problematical: '. . . the fact is that Europe does not have a single clear eastern end. It merely fades away. (Fortunate are the continents defined by seas).'

The question of a European cultural community and what it might mean was addressed in the mid-eighties by Hugh Seton-Watson, writing in *Encounter* under the title 'What is Europe, where is Europe?' He sees it as derived from 'an earlier allegiance to Christendom', which he defines as 'an area, as distinct from a belief', and as 'a higher ideal transcending narrower territorial and feudal loyalties . . . maintained by the reality of conflict, on sea and land, with Islam'. For him, from the seventeenth century onwards, and with gathering momentum up until the first decade of the twentieth, 'the idea of Europe began to replace the idea of Christendom in the west.' But alongside this 'allegiance of educated persons all over this continent to an overarching idea of Europe' there moved a dark shadow: 'healthy natural devotion to individual national cultures, variant flowerings of an overall European culture, became perverted into nationalist fanaticism . . . And the nightmares are still with us.' Writing as he was before the collapse of the Soviet Union, Seton-Watson makes a strong case for the needs of people in Eastern Europe, and shows himself sharply aware of actual and potential pressures, whether emanating from America, or internally, for instance from the European Muslims of Turkey and Bosnia. While bemoaning the slump in modern languages teaching in Britain, he makes participation in European culture sound engagingly simple:

> In order fully to belong to European culture one must be aware of other Europeans, know some history, know another language or several, take some pleasure in literature or painting or old buildings. Those who have such awareness have always been minorities, everywhere.

Such a formulation has something of the elegant imprecision of an eighteenth-century aristocrat waving affectionately towards corners of the estate, and is unlikely to satisfy those who demand a broader view of the arts. Seton-Watson is on less contentious ground in pointing out that a sense of cultural community may be essential for the long-term survival of European economic and political unity, while historically the converse is not true: and he is surely right to emphasise 'the need for a positive common cause, for something more exciting than the price of butter . . . a need for a European *mystique*.' At best, this could imply much more than an uncertain terrain somewhere between a local habitation and airy nothing. An important part of his argument, however, is that what starts as 'mystique' declines, sooner or later, to 'politique'.

The historical perspectives drawn by Seton-Watson compare interestingly with those developed by Robert Bartlett in *The Making of Europe* (Penguin, 1994), with its sub-title 'Conquest, Colonisation and Cultural Change 950–1350'. He gives an astonishing picture of what he calls 'expansionary migration' in western Europe, with external definition provided by the Crusades. He is particularly good on the way in which 'Latin' came to be 'a term by which adherents of the western Church identified themselves . . . It came to have a quasi-ethnic nuance, as in the phrase *gens latina*, "the Latin people", and even to spawn abstract nouns parallel to the usage "Christendom" . . . The category "Latin" thus had a role in the self-description of the people of western Europe and obviously helped lend a kind of conceptual cohesion to groups of very varied national origin and language.' Taking as instances of growing cultural cohesion such features as saints, names, coins, charters and universities, he concludes that 'by the late medieval period Europe's names and cults were more uniform than they had ever been; Europe's rulers everywhere minted coins and depended upon chanceries; Europe's bureaucrats shared a common experience of higher education. This is the Europeanization of Europe.' Perhaps most compellingly of all, now that we are embarked upon the age of the Internet and its surfers, he characterises the spreading cultural and political forms of the time as 'marked, like the alphabet, by a lack of local association and resonance: the western town and the new religious orders were blueprints, and that means they were neither coloured nor constricted by powerful local ties.'

Languages have always been a primary factor in any consideration of European identity, and they are appropriately the subject of the opening section of *Aspects of European Cultural Diversity*, the second book of four designed as an Open University course under the overall heading *What is Europe?* (Routledge, 1993). The course is itself a European project, involving institutions in Denmark, France, Germany and the Netherlands as well as the Open University. Here, European ideals are seen to be those 'of freedom, tolerance and democracy, which, though political decisions obviously often fall short of these, form the often-invoked keystone of the whole process of social and political *rapprochement*.' Hence the preference of the European parliament for a multilingual Europe rather than one particular language, or even Esperanto. An interesting comparison is made between the possible fate of English – already a pan-European and world language – and the actual one of Latin, 'i.e. to become progressively splintered, ultimately serving as a springboard for the development of new languages. . . . Latin made way for Vulgar Latin, which in turn provided the foundation for the Romance languages. In the case of English, too, centrifugal forces are to be found alongside centripetal tendencies.' (In this context, it is interesting to remember how both poetry and prose have been enriched by non-standard English from a variety of sources.) As is made clear later in the book, the language question is a complex one. German is 'the largest language population in Europe'; both French and English have been enriched by extra-European influences arising from the colonial past; and another important strand is represented by 'the current multi-ethnic composition of the population in large cities'. Even the commercially driven world of advertising exhibits the need to adapt to individual countries, providing further evidence of the strength of national differences and individuality.

Like Seton-Watson, the authors of *Aspects of European Cultural Diversity* acknowledge the flaws in 'the much debated European culture', which have produced 'not only the constructive and fruitful cultivation of European intellectual life but also the most terrible wars based on prejudices and stereotypes. Even today these divergent forces continue to have their effects . . .' Such European homogeneity as exists is to be found, it is suggested, in 'lifestyle': 'Thus in all countries there exists . . . the so-called "Euro-dandy", the young, urban, pleasure-seeking middle-class European, whose habits and preferences show the same basic structure, whether British, German or Spanish.' Yet it is questionable how far this is a European feature rather than typical of the consumerism to be found in all developed countries, as implied by the admission in the final section of the book, 'Everyday culture', that 'the international hamburger culture has conquered practically every country and continent.' Once again the question of what is peculiar to Europe seems answerable only by a balancing of opposites: 'on the one hand contacts between cultures have become closer . . . On the other hand, this "natural" convergence and mixing of cultures also generates defensive attitudes . . .'

The relevance of Europe to contemporary Britain is discussed in several contributions to *What Needs to Change* (HarperCollins, 1996), a collection of essays edited by the Labour MP Giles Radice, sub-titled 'New Visions for Britain' and sporting an introduction by Tony Blair. In 'Community and the Left', David Marquand suggests that, despite Britain's twenty-year membership of 'a proto-federal European Community', 'no one has managed to invent a new British identity, centred upon her new European destiny.' Stephen Tindale ('A People's Europe') produces an echo of the emphasis suggested by Seton-Watson, positing 'a Social Democratic vision for Europe' which 'envisages the EU expanding at least to the Russian border, and possibly beyond', and recommending the adoption by a Labour government of Helmut Kohl's proposal to let the first of the eastern

European states join the EU by the year 2000. The most forceful as well as premonitory note, however, is sounded by Neal Ascherson, in 'National Identity':

> The river of Eurosceptic xenophobia is beginning to converge with the river of intolerant English nationalism. If they become one torrent, England may rapidly cease to be a country where men and women with ideals would care to live – and not only men and women whose skin is black or brown.

Defining the United Kingdom as 'two ancient kingdoms united by treaty, one conquered Celtic nation, the rump of another and a scatter of islands', he contends that the English alone have failed to find their identity, and believes that any such identity 'has to be inclusive and "civic", turning away from old-fashioned ethnic definitions to a wider identity in which the cultural traditions of England's Asian and Afro-Caribbean populations can find a home.' He ends optimistically by asserting that 'at the end, the Union of Europe can replace the unions, forcible or contractual, around which the United Kingdom was built.'

At this point 'politique' and 'mystique' seem to join hands again. When it comes to defining what is European, the worthwhile attempts all seem to include an element of the visionary alongside the practical. In this realm, though it may defy simple definitions, the imaginative richness and diversity of European literature has been of great significance, not least thanks to the efforts of those translators and publishers who have enabled the dissemination of new works and ideas. In literature, as in the arts generally, questions are there to be asked, even when the answers are complex or not available in the neat packaging which politics and consumer societies seem to require. And almost throughout discussions of what 'European' might mean, strongly implied where not actually explicitly stated, there is the other E-word, the practical ideal of a broad and liberal education. In that area, too, there is no shortage of questions to be asked.

# Bosnian Fall

If there were a prize for the world's most tactlessly titled airport facility it ought surely to go to the transit lounge at Frankfurt where passengers have the possibility of refreshing themselves at a bar called the Ikarus: perhaps good business is insured by undermining travellers' confidence while simultaneously providing a way of bolstering it.

I passed by the Ikarus while changing planes on my way to Bosnia last October, to read in Sarajevo, Tuzla and Banja Luka, at the inception of a literature programme initiated by the British Council's Director in Bosnia and Herzegovina, Susan Barnes. In my luggage I had Noel Malcolm's *Bosnia: A Short History* (Papermac, 1996), a number of copies of the latest issues of *Poetry Review, PN Review* and *Stand* most readily provided by Peter Forbes, Michael Schmidt and Jon Silkin and, thanks to Neil Astley, copies of the Bloodaxe anthology *Klaonica: Poems for Bosnia* (1993, published in association with the *Independent*). Amongst the contributions to the book I encountered Icarus again, in James Sutherland-Smith's poem 'Musée des Beaux Arts Revisited', with its close stalking of Auden's poem, a procedure made memorable by the awareness that nowadays 'All the colours run / In the suave stink of what our charity becomes for us' and for the thinking wishfulness of the poem's ending:

Impossible
And beside the point to tell Old Masters what to do.
Yet that first Brueghel, for instance, if only the ship were a fable
Of the delicate informed heart which had somewhere else to go
But instead put about and looked for Icarus.

In the poem immediately preceding this one, Michael Hulse cites Milton and Wordsworth in defence of the claim that 'grief will have words'. He believes passionately, as his own poem on the Gulf War testifies, in the legitimacy of poets engaging with themes such as the disastrous Bosnian war, and he calls his poem 'In Defence of Making Nothing Happen'. The editors of *Klaonica*, Ken Smith and Judi Benson, make clear that 'this book is not made in anyone's interest or bias, but in whatever measure of solidarity is possible with the victims of this most vicious of wars'. On the back cover we are told that the anthology was 'assembled in a matter of days as an immediate if inadequate response to the suffering in Bosnia', and the poems themselves are accurately described as 'baffled, helpless, heartfelt, heartbreaking, angry, tender, grieving. Useless too: except that readers should find some comfort, some hope, in this book. And the book is published to raise funds for Bosnian relief.' Bearing this out, many of the poems seek to outflank presumption by articulating the writer's awareness of voyeurism, condescension, impotence, the dangers of any literary equivalent of disaster tourism. Many also raise, implicitly when not explicitly, that issue of the disjunction between the everyday and the epic, the chilling co-existence of the mundane and the disastrous which Auden brings to his reading of Brueghel, in which 'everything turns away / Quite leisurely from the disaster' of Icarus falling.

If the information society makes it nowadays impossible for us not to know the ways of the world, the issue raised by Auden persistently in his work – the gap between knowing and any helpful or morally justifiable human form of action – remains, and perhaps accounts for the continuing interest of his 'Musée des Beaux Arts', as well as the frequency of allusion to his assertion, in his poem in memory of Yeats, that 'poetry makes nothing happen'. Nowadays, the writer's response is less likely to be an artful retreat of the kind so skilfully (but not wilfully) displayed in 'Musée des Beaux Arts', which pointedly involves the double distancing of poem and painting, than a direct and unblinking confronting of horror: the emphasis is on honesty to experience rather than any sort of artistic reclamation of it, or any aesthetic counterbalance.

Not that Auden, or the issues raised by 'Musée des Beaux Arts', went away from my Bosnian visit. 'Poetry, we are told, makes nothing happen', were the words with which I was introduced at Sarajevo: and in the discussion which followed the reading, a university teacher mentioned that he had had great difficulty in persuading his students to give their approval to a Brodsky poem about Bosnia. 'I keep on telling them that it's a good poem', he said, 'But they say they are fed up with people using Bosnia and its problems for promoting their own feelings or careers'. Later on, at Banja Luka, where an audience of about eighty-five included some German, American and British soldiers from the NATO Implementation Force (IFOR), someone asked how poetry could be relevant to them, 'since the business of soldiers is killing'. At one point, where I was not allowed to cross a frontier ('No, you cannot pass. No, we cannot 'phone. You cannot 'phone. Go back.'), it felt as if I had actually been spirited into one of those early Auden poems involving secret agents, bridges, binoculars and maps. At Mostar the relation of art to historical reality seemed to have found a particularly direct expression. In a studio close to the famous Old Bridge destroyed in November 1993 by, in Noel Malcolm's words, 'a senseless act of vandalism by Croat artillery', an elderly man was painting picture after picture of the bridge as it had been – oils, watercolours, views from upstream, downstream, from the west side and from the east, all of them focused on the gone elegance of the bridge's high arch and fine brow, on the organic clusters of buildings at either side, now reduced to haphazard slabs of stone. Ironies abounded, as in the beauty of the deciduous woods on the road between Sarajevo and Tuzla, just turning to the full splendour of autumn red and gold, vitiated like so much of the countryside by the threat of uncleared landmines. In Sarajevo itself, 'roses' are what they call the patterns tattooed on the tarmac by shrapnel – another echo of the '30s: apparently 'Madrid roses' are still pointed out to visitors to the Spanish capital.

Even in a short visit it was possible to encounter wary optimism alongside weary despair; to witness some of the practical busyness beginning to be generated by the development plan amounting to $5 billion presided over by the World Bank; to take note of children on their way to or from school on the verges of roads patrolled by IFOR convoys; to be impressed by initiatives like those taken by the British Council, while being awed at the kind of will and morale obviously demanded if the country's physical structures and infrastructures are to be renewed; to admire the energy and commitment of some (notably the professors and teachers I met), while deploring the stubborn prejudices of others.

But nothing outdid the impact of what I saw on my first full day in Bosnia. Landing at Split in the evening, I had been driven south-east in the softening light along a coast of great beauty, one little harbour after another, each with its cargo of gleaming wooden boats surrounded by waters of intense turquoise and aquamarine. After passing Makarska and Ploce, we turned north-wards to follow the road running alongside the river Neretva to Metković, just short of the Croatia-Bosnia border, where we spent the night. The following morning we continued alongside the Neretva, soon crossing into Bosnia at the frontier town of Dračevo. Then it began: mile after mile of individual houses utterly destroyed, some dynamited, slumped in on themselves, others torched, flared with soot round the empty window-frames, roofs gone apart from a few charred beams, and chimney stacks exposed to the sky. Here and there, a fridge or stove thrown out into what had been a garden; now and then, a car burned out, or plundered, with the jaw of its bonnet agape. Black remains of vines were stuck raggedly in the untended soil. Here, with a three-dimensional immediacy which television could never convey, was evidence of purest malice, a malice as remote from compromise as from any justifiable tactical or military explanation.

Though it added nothing, in a sense, to what I already knew, or to some of the incidents that I was to hear about later, the inhumanity so clearly expressed at first hand in this wanton destruction, so expressive of the cruelty which was its corollary, was deeply shocking. For Noel Malcolm, such behaviour is historically not, as others have alleged, the upshot of inherent animosities but of external forces: 'The history of Bosnia shows that, leaving aside the economic conflict between landowners and peasants, the "national" animosities within the country have reached the point of inter-ethnic violence only as a result of pressures coming from outside Bosnia's borders.' He concludes that 'the real causes of Bosnia's destruction have come from outside Bosnia itself, and have done so twice over: first in the form of the political strategy of the Serbian leadership, and then in the form of the miscomprehension and fatal interference of the leaders of the West.' I met people in Bosnia who found the cogency of his arguments and of his moral condemnation entirely convincing, while others felt that an anti-Serb bias had coloured his approach and led him to over-simplify. There was no argument, however, about the fact or nature of the atrocities that had taken place on all sides. For a writer, that leaves the challenge at the heart of 'Musée des Beaux Arts' still to face: not just what to make of worldly and artistic indifference to suffering, but to consider the actual source of such suffering. If the final decade of the century is a time of lowered expectations and greater realism in comparison with the one in which 'Musée des Beaux Arts' was written, the concluding chapter of Valentine Cunningham's *British Writers of the Thirties* (OUP, 1989), 'Too Innocent A Voyage', makes for some instructive comparisons. Writing from a socialist perspective, he acknowledges that much remains unchanged:

> Unemployment, hunger, injustice, dictators, repression of the powerless, the destructive element of actual wars, and the arms race, the social divisions nurtured in the West by the hegemony of bourgeois capitalism and, in Britain still, by socially divided practices in education, the arts, and traditional culture: all these are still with us.

Yet Cunningham also sees signs of hope – a new liveliness of debate in the universities, and a realisation on the part of the new critics that 'the ground of theory must be sternly besieged as part of the process of making the reading and writing of books (and of all their textual neighbours) of more interest and pertinence to all the people.' And he goes on: 'A difficult and intransigent struggle demands realistic politics. The troubled '30s experience will not have been in vain if it drains expectations of unwary – even as we've suggested, childish – utopianism. Progressive critics nowadays, of course, scarcely bother to consult Christian wisdoms. Perhaps they should.' While he has clearly stated reservations about 'the '30s Christians', whether that 'they equated the good too promptly with the *status quo* or with fascism', or that 'they were driven . . . by their perturbed vision of humankind's sinfulness into anti-human, often inhumanly idealist, Platonic excesses', or that many were simply eccentric, he argues that 'for all that, the question of evil remained and remains'. He ends by calling in evidence Eliot's essay on Baudelaire, with its references to T. E. Hulme's view of man's essential sinfulness.

The issue has little to do with dogma or orthodoxy. It calls to mind the argument of Randall Jarrell's poem 'The Old and the New Masters' (from *The Lost World*, 1965), another gloss on Auden which begins nicely with 'About suffering, about adoration, the old masters / Disagree', and traces the gradual pictorial demotion of Christ from a position of centrality, ending with a final shift in awareness to a secular and reductive sense of cosmic relativity:

> The new masters paint a subject as they please,
> And Veronese is prosecuted by the Inquisition
> For the dogs playing at the feet of Christ,
> The earth is a planet among galaxies.
> Later Christ disappears, the dogs disappear: in abstract
> Understanding, without adoration, the last master puts
> Colors on canvas, a picture of the universe
> In which a bright spot somewhere in the corner
> Is the small radioactive planet men called Earth.

On another level, Cunningham's conclusion relates directly to a number of poems in the Bloodaxe Bosnia anthology, not least Brodsky's 'Bosnia Tune', which absolves us of nothing, least of all complicity: 'People die as you elect / new apostles of neglect, / self-restraint, etc – whereby / people die.' This, like the dark blight of those destroyed homes on the road to Sarajevo, suggests finally that in Brueghel's picture it is the splash of his own falling into the sea, the echo of his own cry, from which the ploughman turns away.

# Thresholds

In strictly practical terms, our approaches to art can have their indignities. Sometimes they involve peering and bending, to read what is written sideways on the spine of a book, or at the side of a picture in a gallery. Or stretching, being reminded that you are not only lower than the angels but also a good way below the book on the top shelf which you are after. Or struggling not to show unartistic irritation to the person who, unbelievably, brushes past your nose as you are actually bending towards the book, or who comes to stand plumb between you and the picture you are appreciating. Even, between the idea of going to an exhibition and the execution of it, there may fall the shadow of a privatised rail journey.

Sometimes we need to get as close to pictures as we do to books, as I saw at the recent London exhibition of Howard Hodgkin's paintings. The Hayward Gallery was not particularly crowded on the first Monday of January, and it was impossible not to be aware of the way in which, commuting between Hodgkin's tidal brushstrokes of colour (shimmering sealights; the most amazing greens since Chagall; the most arresting oranges, reds and tender pinks since Matisse), nearly all of us viewers were taking a first look at each picture, then stepping forward to stoop and peer, before retiring to undertake a more prolonged scrutiny. We seemed to be behaving like apt objects of study for those who compile graphs of animal behaviour.

'Too close a view of the picture will not only yield a new round of voluptuous sensation (say, the streaks of salmon-pink now visible beneath what read, when feet away, as cobalt blue). It will also remind the viewer of what is written beside or below: its title.' Thus Susan Sontag, one of the contributors to a handsomely produced book, *Howard Hodgkin Paintings* (Thames & Hudson / The Modern Art Museum of Fort Worth, 1995). She goes on to discuss the significance of Hodgkin's titles, suggesting that some 'seem to be drawn from the history of a love life ', while others 'hint at a submerged story, which we can be sure we're not going to hear'. She points out that what is at work here is 'as much an impulse to play down as to reveal the charge of some of the pictures', concluding that 'the majority of the titles are casually nominative or slightly ironic, which makes them nicely at variance with the pictures' proud exuberance of feeling'. In another essay in the book, 'A Long View', Michael Auping writes that 'the recognizability of Hodgkin's subjects . . . is often more a function of titling than appearance'. He puts it rather more accurately, I think, a page or two further on: 'One's initial impression of Hodgkin's images is that there is something there waiting to be recognized.' Just so: and the titles often help the viewer enjoyably to cross from uncertainty to recognition, though still with plenty of room for the play of the imagination rather than anything dully literal by way of definition. Some titles, such as *Talking About Art, Gossip, It Can't Be True,* set up a dynamic of witty disagreement, exploiting precisely the gap between word and image. Others challenge with a question: *When Did We Go to Morocco?, Haven't We Met?* and its sequel, *Haven't We Met? Of Course We Have.* Some of the titles are reminiscent of Klee: compare, for instance, these Klee titles – *Small Room in Venice, Will it be a girl?, What can she be hearing!, An insignificant fellow but exceptional, Open Book* – with Hodgkin's *Small View in Venice, Gossip, A Small Thing But My Own, Like an Open Book.* Less strikingly, given the currency of the word, a 1927 Klee drawing shares the name of one of Hodgkin's best known paintings, *Rain.*

A more radical exploitation of the interplay between word and image is offered by Magritte in his use not only of titles but of words carried onto the surface of the painting, as in *The Use of Words I* ('Ceci n'est pas une pipe') or *The Key of Dreams* (1927), where what throws the viewer is not so much the disjunction of word and image in three of the picture's four compartments (a bag described as 'Le ciel', a leaf as 'La table', a penknife with half-open blade as 'L'oiseau') but the rational alignment of word and image in the fourth (a sponge titled 'L'éponge'). It is this apparent reassurance which may set us off on a quest for associations in the other three compartments. Doesn't a table have leaves, after all? Isn't there something appropriately beak-like about the blade of the half-open penknife?

The way in which Hodgkin challenges the viewer is less con-frontational, but perhaps subtler. If the words of the titles some-times imaginatively sharpen our visual perceptions, in other instances they remind us that, as Sontag suggests, there may be limits to what we can construe from the verbal information given. 'This is most obviously true of the portraits – that is, the pictures whose titles are someone's name; usually two names, a couple. (The names, those of friends and collectors, will be unfamiliar to viewers.)' Titles may provide clues to identity, but they are not definitions, and may even be elliptical commentaries or evasions.

In many of Hodgkin's pictures the title is only one of several thresholds. There may be visual as well as verbal puns. Frequently the most obvious sill, the frame, is also painted, masking the border the spectator crosses into, for example, a room, a landscape, a theatre of columns, curtaining verticals. But there is no doubting the part the titles play in disposing the viewer to recall the possibilities of recognition, bearing out the reminder in the exhibition guide that 'Hodgkin says that his titles are absolutely specific'. Given this, one of the more enigmatic titles in the Hodgkin exhibition is *Writing* (a gerund, or the actual lettering?) in which, almost like a distant windspout, an inverted hoisted cone of blue, solid as an inkblot, seems to be sucking up a welter of fragments of the same blue, bits as ragged and torn as scraps of leaf or paper: all this over a ground of half-glimpsed rich reds, greens and blacks which themselves spiral upwards in a swirl of energy. If there is a Horatian link here between paint-ing and writing, it is well hidden; but it did set me thinking about titles and poetry. What when Magritte's assertion, in *Les mots et les images*, that 'in painting the words are of the same substance as the images' can no longer apply, when the words of the title are followed by more words?

Books have their own progressions. Usually we first see the title, on a shelf or a list or in a review, in tandem with the name of the author and, where the writer is well known, this certainly has its effect, as publicists know: 'A's new book'; 'N's latest col-lection'; 'Z's eagerly awaited Selected Poems'. And as a writer's career develops, we learn how book titles go together, may be seen as characteristic, from *The Hawk in the Rain* to *Crow* to *Wolfwatching*, or from *The Survivors* to *Friend of Heraclitus*, from *Fighting Terms* to *The Man with Night Sweats*, from *The Onion,*

*Memory* to *History: the Home Movie.* Often, though, book titles may engage our interest just because they give so little away. To take some recent examples, what are we to make of *Paleface, Masculinity, Stones and Fires, The Wellspring, Gunpowder?* Their very refusal to be anything other than themselves constitutes a challenge, one form of an invitation to read on – as with the Hodgkin paintings, to pursue in search of recognition. Beyond the title, perhaps we shall find a title poem, and in that poem a key of some sort with which to unlock the writer's central preoccupations. Or not. The opacity of a title is a reminder of the ways in which words can conceal as well as reveal. But this is also true of transparent book titles, those which describe their contents with apparent ingenuousness, in the simplest terms. At a stage in their writing careers early enough for the general reader to have few clues, Auden, Spender and MacNeice all produced volumes called uncompromisingly *Poems.* More recently, Douglas Dunn collected the entirely particular poems in memory of his first wife under the simple but apt general title of *Elegies.* It is hard to imagine how any more specific title could have done as well. When it comes to really cryptic challenges, Tony Harrison's *v*, Peter Reading's *C* or R. S. Thomas's *H'm* would be hard to outdo. In contrast, vanity presses and the like tend to give themselves away precisely by the dewy descriptiveness of their anthology titles, in which mists, spring buds or autumnal leaves tend to waft alongside other pastel measures of time, roseate dawns or soft sunsets.

However disguised, every book title is bait, an invitation to bite and not swim off. Lacking the instant evidence afforded by pictures in a gallery, the potential reader has to be hooked sufficiently to open the book and turn the pages: and with poems, will then nearly always face a long list of further titles, those of individual poems. They too can be invitations to further exploration which, if they fail, will result in the book being replaced on the shelf. As with book titles, those of individual poems may be restricted to information about their form or intention: ode, elegy, haiku, epithalamion, sestina, ballad, villanelle. These offer us the recognition of their form, the anticipated reassurance of a familiar structure, while refusing to tell us more. Sometimes the reader is offered a buried title: in a riddle, at the end of the poem or the book, possibly upside down; in an acrostic, at the margin. A few years ago there was a fashion for titles which ran straight on into the poem, themselves the opening of its first sentence. A title can be elliptical, or the spring of irony or wit. It can be evasive, or choose to signal tone or intention clearly. It can be the sleeve on which the poem wears its art. As in the case of Apollinaire's *Calligrammes*, it can account for the visual shape and typography of the poem. It may be replaced by a simple march of numbers. The relation between title and poem may be flat or dynamic: the first is not always inappropriate or an error of judgement. The great majority of poem titles are essentially nominative, descriptive, a summation, prefigurative as well as precursory: but they also tend to be short, minimal, there not to be made too much of or to give too much of the poem away. They issue an invitation, while taking care not to stage the party on the doorstep.

Shakespeare's sonnets provide one of the best known instances of untitled poems, though they do have the transparent description of form, as well as numbers, the latter offering a rich opportunity for scholarly investigation into the correct order. At least one editor, M. R. Ridley, has seen a potential for titles where there are none, referring to 'groups of half a dozen or so sonnets which might be distinguished by arbitrary titles such as "Night thoughts", "Love in absence", and so on' (*The New Temple Shakespeare*, Dent, 1939). He makes the point not to recommend it, but simply in support of the view that 'most readers . . . have the feeling that the sonnets, or the bulk of them, were intended to form a sonnet sequence'. Whatever our reading of the sonnets and their addressees, they have an organic quality which makes any notion of individual titles seem absolutely inappropriate.

For something of the same reason, it is very hard to see how individual poem titles could have been other than damaging in another famous example of untitled work, the poems of Emily Dickinson, which Tom Paulin has described as 'poised between existing as a series of unique speech-moments and a gathering of familiar letters' (in 'Writing beyond Writing: Emily Dickinson'). Here, what draws the reader in and on is the sense of a developing world which, in all its simultaneous vehemence and mysteriousness, is intently vivid and yet elusive. The words and phrases which materialise between the dashes that both link and isolate them could somehow never lend themselves to the kind of closure or the descriptive indexing which a title can imply at the outset. Though the numbers of *The Complete Poems* amount to 1,775 rather than the 154 of Shakespeare's sonnets, with Dickinson too the reader confronts something that is in many respects seamless, and which builds to something like the illumination that one poem (No. 1687) characterises memorably in its four lines:

> The gleam of an heroic Act
> Such strange illumination
> The Possible's slow fuse is lit
> By the Imagination.

This seamlessness is partly a consequence of the poet's own strategy, her position as the dramatising and dramatised centre and touchstone. It may also have something to do with what Ted Hughes describes as the idea of something unnameable at the heart of her poetry. 'It is', he writes (in *Winter Pollen*, Faber, 1994), 'the subject of some of her greatest poems, and all her best poems touch on it. It is what throws the characteristic aura of immensity and chill over her ideas and images . . . it was the source of the paradox which is her poetic self, and which proliferates throughout her feelings, her ideas, her language, her imagery, her verse technique, in all kinds of ways.' As with the paintings of Hodgkin, this takes us over all the obvious thresholds into areas of shade and ambiguity, those slant truths given their full force by the light which can shine in from the attentive imagination of the viewer or reader.

# The Helfgott Hiatus

Few recent films have given rise to as much commentary as *Shine*, the story of the Australian pianist David Helfgott, a child prodigy who suffered mental breakdown and has triumphed over it sufficiently, with the help of his wife, to resume playing. Much of the continuing interest has had to do with the international concert tour which followed the release of the film. In the *Guardian* Ian Katz reported that in America Helfgott made his debut, at the start of a 10-city tour, 'to a rapturous reception from a sell-out crowd in Boston's Symphony Hall. The next morning he woke to the kind of reviews that have reduced more mentally stable performers to nervous wrecks.' The report went on to point out that the film itself, though 'lavished with critical and popular acclaim, attracting seven Oscar nominations', had also been attacked for apparent distortion of the facts of Helfgott's life, while 'critics have savaged Mr Helfgott's performance of Rachmaninoff's (*sic*) Third Piano Concerto on a recently released CD – currently No. 1 in the US classical charts.' Almost at once *The Times* weighed in with a leader headed 'SHINING EXAMPLE: A grateful, graceful pianist – unless you are a US critic'. The writer has no doubt about the rights and wrongs of the case, praising 'the triumph of the spirit over mental breakdown, the redeeming power of love and the exhilaration of music', and contrasting the 'sour tantrums' of the critics with the public's standing ovations, 'a tribute as much to Mr Helfgott's return from the brink of madness as to his music.' The rhetoric homes to outrage: 'Has American criticism become so devoid of human warmth, so isolated in its purist aesthetic that it is blind to the strivings and achievements that inspire people?' After a brief nod to what the critics might consider their proper business, the writer cites John Ogden, Van Cliburn and Horowitz as other pianists dogged by mental illness or depression and concludes that, in the case of

Helfgott, 'his reply to the critics is as devastating as it is serene: "Mustn't be so *serioso*. It's all a game. Must be grateful."'

Under two weeks later it was the turn of *Newsweek* to note not just the hot demand for seats ('tickets . . . sold out in a day in New York; in L.A. they went in three hours; in San Francisco, two'), but also 'the tacky merchandising – "Get a Helfgott Rise & Shine mug FREE with purchase while supplies last" – and the media group-grope awaiting his arrival.' The concert programmes have titles, we learn: one is called 'The Celebration of Life', the other 'The Miracle of Love'. The book written by Helfgott's wife Gillian about life with him is called *Love You to Bits and Pieces*: there are more than 100,000 copies in print. Meanwhile, 'the "Shine" soundtrack tops Billboard's Classical Crossover (read schlock) chart; Helfgott's recording of Rachmaninoff's Third Piano Concerto is the top Classical album.' *Newsweek* gives a candid portrayal of Gillian which points up the difference between Helfgott's 49 years and her 65. 'She looks pale and harried next to her tanned, fit husband with his blissed-out, squint-eyed smile.' Yet it also acknowledges that she has stuck with him. As for the pianist himself, he is 'a hugger' who pours out 'a stream of free-associative hyper-speed commentary and self-addressed pep talk', and 'from the moment he runs out onstage, you know Helfgott's desperately trying to please you.' The standard of his playing involves not 'problems of interpretation, or even of technique, but problems of coherence', and 'while his Rachmaninoff CD is more listenable than his live recitals, it's still muddy, noisy, raggedy – and boring.' For *Newsweek*, 'David Helfgott's arrival is either terrific news – a plucky little indie film tells his uplifting personal story, creates a new audience for serious music and gets seven Oscar nominations into the bargain – or a dreary new cultural low-water mark.'

A month on, the BBC's *Music Magazine* described Helfgott's renderings of Chopin in Boston as having 'no elasticity or expressivity', with critics 'generally appalled' and listeners ill at ease, 'fearing he may not make it through the chosen piece.' Though everyone except the critics may have 'left with the experience they were looking for', the writer thinks that Helfgott would be unwise to hope for too much from his resumed career: 'once had, will people want it again?'

The texts which accompany Helfgott's CD of Rachmaninov's

Third Piano Concerto (BMG Classics / RCA Victor Red Seal) do little to help his cause. A prominent unattributed citation declares that 'the Australian pianist David Helfgott is a musical genius and an inscrutable mystery. After ten years in diverse psychiatric wards he ended up as a bar pianist in Perth. Then he met his wife, Gillian Helfgott, and today he is a universally acclaimed performer.' This is not only the hyperbole of marketing expressed as a mini-saga, but illustrative of the human need for fairy tales with their happy endings. After the slaying of the monster, the hand of the princess and the key to the castle. It is not all. There is also an article by Elisabeth Saugmann (reproduced from the *Jutland Post*) which lavishly lives down to its title, 'A Cosmic Hug'. Two sentences are enough to convey the substance as well as the tone: 'For David Helfgott is an enigma, a mental unicorn, a freakish angel with antennae stretching far out into the universe to catch impulses that find explosive expression in bursts of gut reaction. Having spent more than ten years in psychiatric wards, where he was forcibly subjected to strong psychopharmacological drugs, Helfgott's intellect operates on a completely separate wavelength which picks up cosmic noises and vibrations.'

Much is made in this piece of Helfgott's debt to his wife Gillian, who has given up her astrology career to marry him. '"Somebody has to take care of these fragile artists. Great talent means great vulnerability. Bastards bring other people down, but sensitive people bring down only themselves", she whispers.'

When the reader fights through to the actual CD and becomes a listener, it is clear that the recording occasionally startles with fistfuls of right notes, but too much is a mush which indeed lacks expression, and there are more than a few errors.

With all this indignation, apologetics and special pleading, it is easy to forget the complexity and variety of judgements to be made. How successful is *Shine* as a film? How truthfully does it depict the facts? Is it fair to Helfgott's father? Does it glamorise his wife (played in the film by Lynn Redgrave)? Should we not at least admire without reservation the quality of the acting, particularly Geoffrey Rush as the adult Helfgott? And what about Rachmaninov and his work? Has the film made a much wider public aware of his Third Piano Concerto, or will it produce little more than the very simplified piano part now available as a result of the film, and the abbreviation of the title to 'Rach 3'? Most unnerving of all, many reactions to the film seem to invite a trade-off between our critical judgement and the compassion we might feel for the performer: some commentators come close to staking a claim for critical immunity in the name of adversity overcome. At worst, this patronises the player and indulgently makes the audience feel better: an audience no longer of truly attentive listeners, but of complicit players in a sympathy orchestra. It also demonises the critics, who are seen as callous élitists.

Objectivity against human feeling – it's an opposition that surfaces in various guises, for instance in the debate following the plea from the ex-BBC correspondent Martin Bell for news reporting that is 'attached' to humanity. It informs and sometimes can distort judgements made about literature produced despite great personal difficulties, or under political oppression. Just when the papers were chewing over *Shine*, a literary parallel appeared, in accounts of a book produced by the Frenchman Jean-Dominique Bauby, suffering from Locked-in Syndrome following a stroke. Paralysed, speechless, his left eyelid the only muscle he still had the use of, he nonetheless managed to 'dictate', twitching assent letter by letter, a book of 130 pages, *Le Scaphandre et le Papillon* ('The Diving Suit and the Butterfly'). Subsequently reporting his death shortly after the book's appearance, the *Guardian* praised the book 'both for the quality of the writing and the unique insight into a rare condition' and quoted the Goncourt prizewinner Eric Orsenna as saying: 'I salute the work more than the courage needed to write it. This was not a performance but literature which explores what is left when only the essential remains – life itself.' Here, too, there is the fear that a favourable critical evaluation will wrongly be attributed to a sympathetic view of the author's appalling circumstances.

Yet, with Helfgott and Bauby, how can we disregard the effort and suffering that have gone into their work? If it cannot be good for the hearer or reader to offer 'forgiveness' for any artistic shortcomings on the grounds of hardship, how can it be humanly possible not to take mitigating circumstances into account?

In the case of the performing artist, one of the wittiest and shrewdest examinations of the relations between performer and audience is to be found in Kafka's story about a singing mouse, *Josefine, die Sängerin*. Here the artist is seen as both vulnerable and manipulative, though audience awareness of the artist's frailty, the thought that perhaps performance will be impossible for so fragile and exposed a being, is soon replaced by the cosy solidarity characteristic of the crowd. Josefine's singing is far from faultless. It is even suggested that a lack of perfection may make it more effective: in any case, given the realities of the world, perfection would be intolerable. Her singing is also somehow emblematic of the hard lot of mice: 'Josefine's thin piping in the midst of hard verdicts is almost like the pitiful existence of our people amid the turbulence of the hostile world'. In some respects she is seen as laughable, yet she is saved from ridicule by the audience's awareness of the need to protect the vulnerable artist – and this despite Josefine's own conviction that it is she who is protecting the people. Wilful and tyrannical though Josefine can be, the audience wishes to placate and indulge her. In an existence made even harder by the constant pressure of swiftly arriving new generations, Josefine's singing recaptures something of the brief childhood of the mice, 'something of the lost and never to be recovered happiness, but also something of the active life of the present, . . . its diminutive, inconceivable, yet persistent and irrepressible liveliness'. Finally Josefine overplays her hand, miscalculating the need of the mouse community for her, and vanishes from sight.

Kafka's tale, with its typically acute ambiguities and qualifications, is a reminder of how difficult it can be to make clear artistic judgements much beyond those of technical competence, or to attribute value in terms which take account of contingent circumstances acceptably. While criticism may offer some objective criteria, there can be no precise measure for the impact on spectator or reader of disabling conditions of one kind or another, no scale of permissible latitude. To shift from prose to poetry, it is equally impossible not to be affected by, for instance, the circumstances of a writer like John Clare. Take 'Song', with one of his frequent images of shipwreck:

> Born to misfortunes – where no sheltering bay
> Keeps off the tempest – wrecked where e'er I flee
> I struggle with my fate . . .

Yet awareness of that fate can distort a proper appreciation of the work, and has led critics such as John Lucas rightly to insist on

the wit, radicalism and art of Clare as against the sentimental condescension offered by some of his biographers. Again, our
reading of Ivor Gurney cannot but be informed by the knowledge
that the last fifteen years of his life were spent in an asylum.
The difficulty is tackled by Donald Davie, in *Under Brigflatts*
(Carcanet, 1989). Noting a new plainness of style in Gurney's
poems written in asylums, Davie quotes the following lines
addressed 'to God':

> Why have you made life so intolerable
> And set me between four walls, where I am able
> Not to escape meals without prayer, for that is possible
> Only by annoying an attendant. And tonight a sensual
> Hell has been put on me, so that all has deserted me
> And I am merely crying and trembling in heart
> For death, and cannot get it. And gone out is part
> Of sanity. And there is dreadful hell within me.

Davie comments that 'although it is the cry of a soul in torment,
it is also poetry', and he goes farther than some critics would in
forthrightly dismissing what might be allowable under the
heading of fellow feeling, suggesting that 'by this stage we are no
longer reading for pleasure, in any ordinary sense. If there is gratification (as there is), it is of the unearthly and inhuman sort that
has to do with the indomitable spirit of Man, or suchlike unman-
ageable notions.' Davie will have none of it: 'There are those who
positively welcome such disorder, as if it authenticated a poet's
vocation. But great poetry is greatly sane, greatly lucid; and
insanity is as much a calamity for poets and for poetry as for other
human beings and other sorts of human business.' This is hard-
hitting, but not hard-hearted: and it is in keeping with Davie's
refusal, elsewhere in the book, to make more than passing
mention of the burdens of blindness and deafness suffered by
another poet, Jack Clemo.

There is a hiatus here which no attempt at resolution can
entirely bridge. If we can avoid the temptation to see objective
criticism and humanity as opposed to one another, and allow for
co-existence rather than competition, our judgements may be
more complete, admitting the possibility that 'X has achieved this
against appalling odds, and (and, not but) what has been

achieved is, in artistic terms, flawed.' Meanwhile, it is perhaps significant that humour and the flexibility that goes with it are features common to Helfgott and to Kafka's story of the singing mouse, just as they inform this funny and serious Austrian poem from a collection (*Fingerzeig*, Carl Hanser Verlag) which appeared last year:

> At his last concert
> seeing my colleague Fischkemper
> levitating above the piano
> I couldn't believe my eyes
> but there he was in fact hovering
> while the grand piano
> continued to play by itself
> the E flat major trill of the Sonata Opus 111
> extending it by minutes
> so that even the most hardened sceptic
> might have the chance to register
> that here a mystical experience
> perceptible to all
> was being enacted

The author is the pianist Alfred Brendel.

# Beating the Bounds

The last Sunday in May; and a walk of twelve miles or so on the eastern side of Dartmoor revealing a world every bit as beautiful as Hopkins found the bluebells in Hodder Wood at the same time of year, in 1873, or D. H. Lawrence the Cornish ones, forty-three Mays and a whole changed world later. In the banks and hedge-rows of the lanes skirting the open moor were drifts of pink purs-lane, along with stitchwort, red campion, herb robert: at the edges of the moor itself, stands of bluebells, their elusive colour heightened by the sunlit ginger of last year's bracken among which they were growing. Here and there, creamy clusters of flowers weighting the upper branches of the rowans. And as a complement to all this, near the end of the walk, there came a view from the higher moor back towards the village from which we had set out. There was no mistaking the focal point of the church, with its square tower harboured by tall trees. To one side lay the lush green of a field tamed to a cricket pitch, where fifteen diminutive figures stood, each in his allotted place. They went about their rituals like figures in a dream: even a cry of 'Howzat!', the eagerness of it softened by distance, emphasised rather than diminished the impression of a scene out of time, closed off from the outside world, to be glimpsed now and then by Wellsian explorers topping some far ridge.

It is more than their own perfection which makes such sights a little unreal, and perhaps more than just a matter of the temper-ament of the beholder. The beauty of nature calls to mind what we know of threats to the environment: an idyllic village view, with its privilege of leisurely sport, can summon images of poverty, starvation and oppression of every kind. Localised wholeness becomes a mirror that gives back distorted images of wider fragmentation. Not that there is anything new about such tensions, even if the European Union may challenge our idea of

the local, or space-walks encourage a redefinition of the universal. Everyday usage offers a whole series of markers along a scale
running from 'parish' (pump; priest; magazine; politics; paro-
chial) through 'local' (attraction, the effect of the iron in a ship on
her compasses; government; derby; anaesthetic; the local; loca-
tive) and 'grass-roots' to 'county' (cricket; court; town) and
'province' (pejorative or not in 'provincial', but retaining the echo
of an ecclesiastical association, though now without two of its
earlier specific meanings, 'of foxhunting outside the shires', and
'of the roses of Provence'). Towards the far end of the scale,
beyond 'national' (bank; debt; insurance; anthem; pride) but
short of 'infinite' (space; joy) lie 'universal' (suffrage; joint),
'world' (bank; class; domination; view; war; peace) and 'global'
(strategy; warming; deprivation; globalisation). Temporal equivalents would, I suppose, include Kipling's 'unforgiving minute'
and Vaughan's vision of eternity 'like a great ring of pure and
endless light'.

The particular and the universal have preoccupied many,
perhaps even most philosophers and poets, and not only those of
a Platonist disposition. Pope, Shelley and Blake all weighed
them, each in his own idiom and to differing ends. Voltaire could
hardly keep away from the subject of particular evils and the universal good, while hymn writers have long enjoyed comparing
the local and mortal with the infinite and the eternal, to which
many have gone on 'while others to the margin come, / waiting
their call to rest.' Proselytisers of every sort have aimed to strive
beyond the local, whether in the interests of faith ('I look upon the
world as my parish', John Wesley wrote in his journal on 11 June
1739), or those of the kind of imperialism well represented by
A. C. Benson's aggressively expanding land of hope and glory:
'Wider still and wider shall thy bounds be set'.

The issue has also enjoyed a long run in the realms of literary
criticism and aesthetics, and it was interesting to see it surfacing
once more in Marjorie Perloff's essay in *PN Review 115*, 'What we
don't talk about when we talk about poetry: some aporias of literary journalism.' Lamenting what she sees as the amateurish
and unsystematic nature of most contemporary poetry reviewing, she acknowledges that given the pressure on reviewing
space, 'the reviewer simply doesn't have space to define his or
her terms'. One possible solution would be 'for a journal to limit

severely the number of poets it reviews' – but 'however this parochialism might have been justified in the 1960s and 1970s . . . it has become, in the mid-'90s, a way of denying poetry its very life.' She disapproves of poets reviewing other poets, tracing the practice to the world of the poetry workshop, 'still dominated by a regressively Romantic concept of the poet as a man speaking to men (or woman speaking to women)'. This she compares unfavourably with the century's 'exciting body of poetics, a discourse on poetry impressive in its richness and excitement'. This 'international poetic impetus . . . is committed . . . to the basic theorem that poetry is the language art, the art in which the "what" cannot be separated from "how" . . .'. However, anxious not to lose sight of the local, Perloff goes on to say that 'poetic language is never simply unique, natural, and universal; it is the product, in large part, of particular social, historical and cultural formations. And these formations demand study.' Seeking to know 'which of the countless poets now plying their trade are worthy of attention' ('plying their trade' – in what other context is that expression familiar?), she veers back towards the universal, praising an international anthology which transcends local antagonisms and prejudice in favour of 'attention to the materiality of language . . . to syntactic disjunction and visual constellation', and which can speak not for the old lyrical 'I' but for 'the larger cultural and philosophical moment' and so for 'characteristics of poetries produced around the globe.' All this goes hand in hand, she suggests, with a number of recent American anthologies which, though barely reviewed, 'are already being assigned for classroom use and discussed at conferences'. Then there is also the internet and 'electronic discussion groups', which might disseminate the kind of information lacking in literary journalism. Such a brave new whirl would seem to bypass not just literary reviewers, but also actual readers of poetry outside the seminar and the classroom: Perloff concludes, however, 'that a middle-class poetry public no longer exists, that poetics is now at least as specialised as is architectural discourse'. This takes her back to her starting point, a comparison of architectural and literary reviewing, but hardly resolves the issues raised. It will surely take more than the internet to protect poetry from the particular forms of parochialism which can develop from specialisation and expertise, and which thrive not least by encoding criticism in language so arcane as to exclude all but its initiates.

Writing in the same issue of *PN Review* 'On Imagination and Lyric Voice', Christopher Middleton also takes the measure of the local and the universal, and sees imagination struggling to survive under threat 'from barrack-brains and other desolating mind-sets', in a world where value has been debased to price and where 'the sky darkens, the rain-forests burn, *animula vagula* scents corruption and savours it.' The arts are 'by postmodern agitation divested of every last clout of contrariety, doctored by yet another internationale of functionaries', and as for imagination itself, if it 'is realised as an armature of the pleasure principle, with aesthetics as its curious science, then its influence must be both rare and warped as long as suffering, monstrous and regulated suffering, afflicts people the world over.' Middleton is careful, though, not to align the imagination solely with a 'spiritual quest'. Its role is both universal and local: it 'integrates in a luminous presence infinitely various figurations of time past and prefigurations of time to come', yet it has also (and this is the contemporary challenge) to rediscover an individual voice and 'to pronounce it in truth, freed from the stranglehold of the nondescript, individuated against collectives which have smothered it, vividly diverse against abstractions which have desiccated it.'

Marjorie Perloff and Christopher Middleton between them sent me back to two books. The first is Terry Eagleton's *The Ideology of the Aesthetic* (Blackwell, 1990), and in particular its final chapters. Considering Adorno, Eagleton writes, with a nod to Blake: 'We may forget about totality, but totality, for good or ill, will not forget about us, even in our most microscopic meditations. If we can unpack the whole from the most humble particular, glimpse eternity in a grain of sand, this is because we inhabit a social order which tolerates particularity only as an obedient instantiation of the universal.' Adorno, 'like Freud, . . . knows that individual particulars will never rest content under the law's yoke, that the central tenet of traditional aesthetics is a lie; and this friction between part and whole is the source of both hope and despair, the rending without which nothing can be sole or whole, but which may well succeed in deferring such wholeness to judgement day.' In the last chapter of the book there is praise for Raymond Williams's social theory, which 'refuses at once a

"bad" universalism and what we like to term a "militant partic-
ularism", holding together a deeply pluralistic commitment, a
keen recognition of complexity, specificity and unevenness, with
what became as he developed a more and more resolute emphasis upon the centrality of social class.' Eagleton goes on to make
what is, from the viewpoint of his own political and moral commitment, a crucial connection: 'The aesthetic is preoccupied
among other things with the relation between particular and universal; and this is also a matter of great importance to the ethico-
political. A materialist ethics is "aesthetic" in that it begins with
concrete particularity, taking its starting-point from the actual
needs and desires of individual human beings.' But for Eagleton
it is the drive towards the universal of social justice and a humane
society which alone will permit redefinition of the individual on
a higher level. He concludes that 'in the pursuit of this political
goal, there are meanings and values embedded in the tradition of
the aesthetic which are of vital importance, and there are others
which are directed towards the defeating of that goal, and which
must therefore be challenged and overcome'. Not all readers will
be convinced by Eagleton's conclusions, but he displays an
impressive openness to complexity that belies the confines characteristic of any ideology.

A book with an equally explicit agenda, though of a very
different kind, is Colin Falck's *Myth, Truth and Literature*
(Cambridge, 1989). In contrast to the bounds beaten by Perloff
and Eagleton, it is the middle ground that Falck seeks to renew
and expand, in the interests of 'a long-overdue revitalization of
practical literary criticism.' He suggests that a reason for the con-
tinuation in literature of the naturalist manner 'might be that
such a manner can help to make literature more accessible to our
practically-engaged minds; even perhaps that it can help literature to "feed back" into the practical world and to modify those
minds as we make use of them in our ordinary lives': and he cites
approvingly P. F. Strawson's conviction that 'the creativity or
inventiveness of our imagination is inseparably involved in our
most ordinary perception of the objects around us'. Much of
Falck's argument is directed specifically against post-
Saussurean literary theory (as Middleton's is against the influence of Lacan) and the dangers of over-specialisation in the field
of literary criticism. His starting-point is the way in which we

perceive the world, given what he calls 'our nature as embodied and striving beings': and for him the critic's function, a traditional one, 'is to illuminate or to interpret; or else it is to find fault, and to suggest, perhaps as systematically as possible, some of the reasons for the faults that have been found'. Falck shares with Eagleton, though seeing it in very different terms, a strong moral awareness, what he calls 'the great middle ground of action and commitment within which we live our actual reflective lives.' He, too, relates the particular to the universal, defining reason as 'our imagination employed to make the best conceptual sense that we can of the whole of reality', while pointing out that 'there are also imaginative fictions which invest that reality with a local habitation and a name.' He insists on the world outside the text, as well as on the human who perceives it, and considers the dangers of *naïveté* or sentimentality which might ensue from his views to be risks worth running in the quest to 're-connect with the most central meanings of human life', and in any case lesser evils than mere cleverness and sophistication in poetry. In an appendix added to the second edition, 'Romanticism and Poetics', Falck unsurprisingly quotes with approval Blake's assertion that 'Ideas cannot be Given but in their minutely Appropriate words'; that the artist paints 'not Man in General, but most minutely in Particular'.

'. . . Possibly it is only the sheer numbers of poets on the ground that make the poets of rare distinction hard to pick out', speculates Middleton. 'Whose conception of poetry is to count as poetry?' asks Falck. 'What *is* poetry anyway? Does anyone have a clear idea?' demands Perloff. 'How can the mind not betray the object in the very act of possessing it, struggling to register its density and recalcitrance at just the point it impoverishes it to some pallid universal?' enquires Eagleton, at the start of his chapter on Adorno. And now it's not a moor with a view that I'm thinking of, but a room – Montaigne's library, inscribed with a variety of maxims, one for each of the room's 57 bays. One inscription is the proposition by Sextus Empiricus that to every argument it is possible to bring an opposing argument of equal force: another, the declaration by Lucretius that 'every thing, including the heavens, the earth and the sea, is nothing compared with the totality of the great whole.' To this we might add Montaigne's own famous dictum: 'Chaque homme porte la forme entière de l'humaine condition' ('Du Repentir', *Essais*, Book III). Four anxious centuries on, poets and critics alike continue to face the challenge of somehow integrating the particular and the universal by being true to themselves, truthful in language and at the same time, however elliptically, according to the light of their own temperament and understanding, alert to the stink and the beauty of the world.

# 1998

# Dens and Displays

The visit to Helpston, undertaken in the company of participants in a writing course, might have been a disaster. It was scheduled sufficiently close to a Bank Holiday to have attracted rain. John Clare's cottage, now in private ownership, had a commemorative stone by its door, and attractive hanging baskets of flowers, but it was not possible to look round inside. His grave (not, we were told, the kind that he wanted) gleamed wetly, one side incised with a caveat gloomily germane to students on writing courses: *A poet is born not made*. The village butter cross, for all its attractive heart-shaped base, lacked its cross, culminating in the bare rusting spike which once held it in place. Opposite, the John Clare memorial had newly had someone's initials added to it. Occasionally, large lorries hissed and bumped past. Once or twice an air force jet roared over somewhere above the downpour.

Yet all these factors of forlornness counted for nothing when compared with the total enthusiasm of Peter and Mary Moyse, respectively Treasurer and Secretary of the John Clare Society, who took us round. They told us how each year Clare's grave was embellished with 'midsummer cushions' of specially grown flowers; they showed us the brickwork on his cottage which traced some of the original outlines; they talked about neighbouring buildings, including the barn where Clare had been a thresher; they took us along a footpath which skirted round the back of the village, giving a glimpse of a landscape much more like that of the poems; they ushered us into the church and read a number of the poems to us; and would have done more, they said, if the weather had been better. At the end, they took us back to their house, where they had set out in the hall a display of cards, books and other items relating to Clare.

Such commitment and vitality reminded me of my first visit to the château of Blois, years ago, and the dazzling energy of a guide who not only related the assassination of the Duc de Guise there in December 1558, but acted it out blow by blow. Now he was one of a group of assassins armed with daggers; now, one of another group with swords, hiding in a corridor; now, Henri III sending for Guise; now, Guise himself, attacked, staggering back, mortally wounded, struggling valiantly but in vain, repeating 'Oh! Quelle trahison! Quelle trahison!' At Helpston, rather less dramatically, there was the sense of a poet being kept warm and alive in an entirely unbookish way. Literary sites, as much as historical ones, owe an enormous debt – sometimes their very survival – to the dedication of curators and guides, as well as the many individuals loyal in all kinds of ways to an author's memory.

Some writers' houses have been settings not only for the life, but for the work, like Hardy's birthplace at Higher Bockhampton, which became Tranter Dewy's house in *Under the Greenwood Tree*, or Yeats's Thoor Ballylee. Some reproduce as accurately as possible the furnishings and atmosphere of the place at the time the writer in question occupied it: little stages set by fame, with the props carefully laid out. Others are museums of one kind or another. There is no shortage of relics, whether Jane Austen's modest writing-table at Chawton, Byron's helmet at Newstead Abbey, Fanny Brawne's gold bracelet at Keats's Hampstead house or even, at Orchard Side, Olney, the feathers from William Cowper's starved goldfinch (itself the subject of a poem). And there may be more than one house associated with a writer: Max Gate as well as the Higher Bockhampton birthplace; Rydal Mount in addition to Dove Cottage; Chiswick House and Stanton Harcourt, not to mention a grotto in Twickenham.

What of our motives in visiting such places? Most often we go as pilgrims, out of admiration for a particular writer, as well as plain curiosity. Perhaps there is a superstitious element, too, the feeling that admission to a building is also a way into the secret of a writer's success or appeal. In some locations, such as Little Gidding, we may be in search of a particular aura or *genius loci*. Whether or not we find satisfaction in the visit may depend almost as much on the heightened expectations we bring with us as on the condition of the premises, or such circumstances as weather and the journey to and fro. In the case of somewhere like Helpston, for instance, it is easy to forget that it would hardly have looked remarkable in Clare's day. Our reactions are likely to be as personal as our reading, especially given that writers' shrines are by definition, and in contrast with churches or battle-fields, intensely individual.

One caution worth bearing in mind comes from P. D. James, who points out that 'not every writer has cared particularly about the place where he did his writing, and not every writer's house has had a significant influence on the work produced within its walls.' Another pertinent doubt is expressed by Claire Harman, when she suggests that 'more may be lost than gained when a writer's house is preserved artificially.' A direct challenge to the visitor comes in a piece by Virginia Woolf published in the *Guardian* in 1904, and quoted by Jeanette Winterson. Woolf writes: 'I do not know whether pilgrimages to the shrines of famous men ought not to be condemned as sentimental journeys. It is better to read Carlyle in your own study chair than to visit the sound-proof room and pore over the manuscripts in Chelsea . . . The curiosity is only legitimate when the house of a great writer or the country in which it is set adds something to our understanding of the books.'

All these comments come from *Writers and Their Houses* (Hamish Hamilton, 1993), a joint venture involving the Arts Council of Great Britain (as it then was) and the National Tourist Boards of England, Scotland, Wales and Ireland. Edited by Kate Marsh, it is a highly readable book, with each house the subject of an essay by a modern writer. For many of the poets included, no less than the prose writers, this has produced some ingenious pairings: Douglas Dunn on Robert Burns's birthplace at Alloway, Peter Porter on Newstead Abbey, C. H. Sisson on Milton's cottage at Chalfont St Giles, Gavin Ewart on the three places associated with Pope, U. A. Fanthorpe on Sissinghurst and Vita Sackville-West, Glyn Jones on Dylan Thomas and the Boat House at Laugharne, Seamus Heaney on Yeats's tower. Peter Porter points out the closeness between Newstead and the final parts of *Don Juan*: 'Cantos 15 and 16 amount to a guide to Newstead, so that almost two hundred years after they were written they conjure up the mansion in a form recognizable to the modern visitor.' U. A. Fanthorpe writes generously about Vita Sackville-West's poem *The Land* and correctly diagnoses the problem of numbers at Sissinghurst, where 'the major hazard, even in an English May, is not the cold, nor the past, but other people.' Both Dunn and

Heaney reach out to a dimension beyond the purely material. For Dunn, the 'auld clay biggin' in which Burns was born is 'tantalizingly poetic in itself. It is a metaphor. Those in the habit of associating one thing with another might find themselves unwilling to forget the significance of the material with which the house was built . . . it is constructed to a large extent of the substance with which Burns struggled for much of his relatively short life – clay, earth, dirt, ground.' And Heaney writes that, in the case of Yeats, who 'once boasted that he had no house but friendship', Coole Park and Thoor Ballylee 'are not so much domestic situations as emblems of vocation and commitment. They were symbols before they were amenities, and what they symbolized were the values and possibilities of culture, poetry, inheritance and love.'

Part of the appeal of the book, like that of many of the houses, has to do with curiosities that feed our curiosity, or with poignant details such as the pop-hole still to be seen in William Cowper's house in Olney, specially designed for his three tame hares, Puss, Tiny and Bess who were 'allowed out each evening into the parlour to play'. Gavin Ewart notes the survival of Pope's chair, specially made to help his back trouble, in the tower at Stanton Harcourt, where there is also 'a piece of red glass from a window' on which Pope has scratched:

> In the year 1718
> I Alexander Pope
> finished here
> the fifth volume of Homer.

Incongruities play their part, such as the relocation of the chaise-longue on which Dickens lay dying at Gad's Hill, which is now to be seen at his birthplace in Portsmouth; or the fact that financial pressures have led to Gilbert White's house at Selborne, The Wakes, being devoted jointly to White and the Antarctic explorer Captain Lawrence Oates. Then there is Shandy Hall where, as Malcolm Bradbury describes, the house not only 'began to acquire the spirit of Shandyism and become part of the imaginative topography of the novel', but also came to express Sterne's feelings for Eliza Draper. 'He imagined her living in Coxwold with him, and he fancifully reconstructed part of the house for her to live in . . . but she never came to Shandy Hall, though his memorial to the relationship remains in the building itself.' The house is also another striking instance of determined loyalty, and 'the fact that it survives at all today . . . is almost entirely due to the efforts of two latter-day Sterneans, Kenneth and Julia Monkman.'

A strong case for visits to writers' houses is made by Richard Hoggart, writing about D. H. Lawrence: 'to see Eastwood and the mining countryside is to understand a little better, visually and imaginatively, the culture from which Lawrence came and its contribution to his work'. Likewise Frances Spalding, in her essay on Charleston, argues convincingly that the house, 'which itself seemed to foster creativity', offers a real insight into the world of the Bloomsbury Group. John Wain, whose subject is Samuel Johnson, bemoans the display at the birthplace museum in Lichfield, where 'the late twentieth-century fashion for explicit visual and aural presentation' leaves the viewer's imagination 'disabled by all the paraphernalia'. However, when it comes to the Doctor's London house in Gough Street, 'Johnson's fame has protected No. 17 from the developers, and this is his last and best gift to the city he lived in. One fine building is better than none.'

Also included in the book is a place with a powerful atmosphere, T. E. Lawrence's tiny cottage at Clouds Hill, not far from Hardy's birthplace. Lawrence's own description of it was 'bleak, angular, small, unstable: very like its owner', but what struck me when I visited it was the cosy secretiveness both of the building and its setting. It seemed strongly expressive of an individual temperament. Above all it is a refuge, a den. Or three dens – the book-room downstairs, with its leather-covered divan and, when I saw it, a fire burning in the grate; the upstairs music room with its huge E.M.G. gramophone; and the room with a ship's bunk, and two glass domes under which Lawrence kept bread, butter and cheese. Though, as Malcolm Brown points out, 'the book-shelves now house photographs and drawings, and various pictures and mementos have been imported', much remains unchanged for today's visitors. Clouds Hill is very much 'not a museum, but a house which still has its own life.'

A month after the visit to Helpston, I went to see Coleridge's cottage at Nether Stowey, on the northern edge of the Quantocks, a building described by Anthony Quinton in *Writers and Their*

*Houses* as having 'no great intrinsic claim to attention'. Here, as at Helpston, was an enthusiast to enliven the experience, in the person of the warden, Derrick Woolf, himself a writer and magazine editor. The cottage, converted into a pub in the nineteenth century, still looks rather like one, with a portrait of Coleridge hanging just like an inn sign at a front corner. It stands opposite a present-day pub called, obviously, The Ancient Mariner. There is little to suggest the small thatched cottage to which the poet moved with his young family on the last day of 1796. Inside, two dim rooms were open to the public, though it was planned to open two upstairs rooms following a successful appeal. For the moment, items on display included an assortment of books, pictures and memorabilia, along with four cuttings of Coleridge's hair (the last 'cut off by Mrs Gilman after his death') and the sword worn by Coleridge when enlisted in the 15th Light Dragoons as Silas Tomkyn Comberbache. A copy of *The Rime of the Ancient Mariner* once belonging to Derwent Coleridge, with the famous illustrations by Gustave Doré, lay open on a table. What was entirely lacking was any emotional weight, any hint of atmosphere which might have linked the place with a particular personality (in this respect it is the antithesis of Clouds Hill), let alone Coleridge's literary achievements during his time there. As well as *The Rime of the Ancient Mariner*, these included 'Kubla Khan', 'Frost at Midnight' and the first part of 'Christabel'.

Yet there was a satisfaction in this, too: to have one's attention redirected outside, to the beauty of the Quantocks which, as Richard Holmes notes in the first volume of his biography (*Coleridge: Early Visions*, Hodder & Stoughton, 1989), Coleridge established as 'his poetic kingdom' ; and then, to go back to the poems themselves.

# Border Patrols

Among the most memorable lines of Yeats's 'Crazy Jane' poems are the two which conclude 'Crazy Jane talks with the Bishop', a characteristic statement of the necessarily dark starting-point for any notion of healing:

> For nothing can be sole or whole
> That has not been rent.

This, like the conclusion of 'The Circus Animals' Desertion', might be seen as one instance of the model, embodied in many myths and religions, of a journey through darkness as a condition of the light. It recurs in the juxtaposed association of blindness and insight, in the Romantic view of excess and madness, in Eliot's wounded surgeon plying the steel. And Crazy Jane herself resurfaces in a Richard Dadd drawing, 'Sketch of an Idea for Crazy Jane', inside the front cover of *Beyond Bedlam* (Anvil, 1997), an anthology edited by Ken Smith and Matthew Sweeney and subtitled 'Poems written out of mental distress'. The upshot of some 5,000 poems submitted to the Bethlem and Maudsley National Poetry Project, with royalties going to the Mental Health Foundation, Mind and Survivors' Poetry (a national organisation 'dedicated to promoting the poetry and self-empowerment of users and survivors'), the book signals clearly the worth and worthiness of its intentions: no one here is playing Hamlet, or taking cover as a Bedlam beggar like Edgar in *King Lear*. The back cover promises 'poetry that is testament to the transforming power of the imagination, poetry that catches the reader in the full glare of its light, challenging the isolation, stigma and myths of mental illness': and a universal context for such affliction is suggested by one of the quotations which prefaces the text, Ibsen's assertion that 'our whole

being is nothing but a fight against the dark forces within ourselves.'

The approach to the poems has three thresholds. The first is
a foreword by Dr Felix Post, formerly of the Bethlem and
Maudsley, and author of a study of mental illness in writers. His
investigation showed that 'serious disorders of personality were
more common in artists and creative writers, while emotional
breakdowns, mainly depressive illnesses, had afflicted creative
writers twice as often as visual artists, composers, thinkers,
national leaders and scientists', but he also found that 'writers
who had published only poetry had suffered less often from
depressions, alcoholism, social and sexual maladjustments than
those who had also or only produced prose fiction or plays.'
Poetry may be better than other forms of writing as therapy, he
suggests: but he also flags the need for hard work at the craft.

The second threshold, 'Bedlam and Beyond', explains the
project committee's interest in considering the possibilities of
poetry for 'alleviating symptoms of mental distress', as well as
possible evidence 'of a real exchange between creativity and
"madness"'. We are reminded that the subject is 'a decidedly rich
one, historically, philosophically, artistically and clinically; from
the Renaissance fool to Surrealism, from Byron to Berryman, and
from Freud to Foucault. "Madness" has been both held to reveal
inner truths and condemned to silence and exclusion as something unintelligible by reason, and therefore threatening to
society and to humanity.' And, as Miroslav Holub puts it in
'Maxwell's Dream or, On Creativity': 'Somehow, Plato's divine
rapture of creativity, Pascal's sentence "l'extrême esprit est voisin
de l'extrême folie", and Lombroso's almost clinical correlation of
genius and psychic deviation still linger in our minds' (*The
Dimensions of the Present Moment*, Faber, 1990).

Then there is the editors' introduction, locating the common
ground between poetry and mental illness in the unconscious,
from which can emerge 'the jumps and sudden lurches that forge
new connections with things not connected before, new ways of
seeing', but which is also where 'the voices of the irrational lurk'.
For them, 'the act of writing can help offset the advance of chaos,
shaping it into the order of words.'

There is always a danger in such circumstances that the reader
will sense, if not special pleading, then a temptation to sedate the

critical impulse, rather in the way that John Berger suggested (in *Ways of Seeing*, BBC/Penguin, 1972) that our response to Van Gogh's painting *Wheatfield with Crows* is inevitably altered once we know that it was believed to be the painter's last work before he shot himself. Given the anthology's clearly stated intentions, it is impressive to discover how many of the poems succeed as poems, bearing out the editors' claim to have come across at least some 'that transmuted the original experience into art'. In part this is due to two excellent editorial decisions: to include poets of the past as well as of the present; and to order the book as a narrative journey into, through and out of madness. The first poems are about the onset of mental illness and its effect on appearance, behaviour and personal identity. Successive themes include language itself, dreams and visions, institutions, day rooms, visitors, family, recovery and the haunting which often stays in spite of it. Here, amongst others, Berryman, Blake, John Clare (a pervasive presence: not only his famous poem 'I am', but he is the subject of three other poems, and mentioned in another two), Emily Dickinson, Ivor Gurney, Hölderlin, Lowell, Sylvia Plath, Pound, Rimbaud, Anne Sexton and Christopher Smart keep the company of contemporary writers such as David Constantine, Paul Durcan, David Gascoyne, Selima Hill, Elizabeth Jennings, Sean O'Brien, Peter Reading, Harry Smart, C. K. Williams and Kit Wright, as well as many publicly unknown poets, some of whom have produced really striking work.

A significant number of the poems grapple with a sense of fragmentation, the self divided against itself, what Denise Jones in her poem 'The Intruders' calls the struggle 'to feel whole for ever'. 'For One is perfect and good being at unity in himself', as Christopher Smart put it, while the author of an anonymous poem smuggled out of the Arsenal Prison mental hospital in Leningrad, as it then was, wonders 'how to find myself in me'. In 'Blacker than Before', Claire Bayard-White is possessed by a blackness which is 'keeping me away from me and myself'. Other poems convey vividly the darkness of confinement, a fear that can range from a sense of betrayal to a loathing of being watched and controlled (let alone being given ECT, the subject of two of the poems). An excellent Peter Reading poem, 'The Euphemisms', sharply points to the role of language in judgement and exclusion, as does Sean O'Brien in a very different but equally good poem, 'Poem for a Psychiatric Conference', in which 'There are vast misunderstandings / Lurking in the syntax by the stairs'. C. K. Williams deploys the obsessive form of the villanelle to good effect in writing of a suicide's mother, and in 'The Cave' he memorably explores difficult negotiations between the so-called mad and the so-called normal. Kit Wright's 'The Day Room' is another highlight, its twelve sections making up the longest poem in the book. Here, at one point (and with an echo of Verlaine's 'Le ciel est, par-dessus le toit, / Si bleu, si calme!') is 'Unspeakable blue / Observed / Through unbreakable glass': and the image recurs elsewhere in the book, notably in Lowell's 'Waking in the Blue', in which 'Azure day / makes my agonized blue window bleaker'. And David Constantine strikes exactly the right tone in 'Clare Leaves High Beach', in an unforgettable picture of the poet:

> A face came over him, it had a crown
> That bulged from a wreath of hair, a face
> As large and a dome as bald as the moon
> Beamed down at him. It was his own:
> Good-natured, cheerful, and quite crazed.

The poems of re-emergence towards the end of the book make clear that even survival can include an ineradicable shadow of the past, as in Dermot Healey's 'The New Town'. Yet this same poem has the kind of formal shaping which enacts recovery in the poise of artistic control. The same is true of a poem by Paul Clark, 'On a Portrait of William Blake by Francis Bacon'. Here the distancing of the title's two removes is followed by a poem too good to spoil by brief quotation: sufficient to say that its close and dynamic attention to language makes its subject new and entirely immediate.

Mental distress may often be the work of inner forces: but they are not the only ones. Tyrants have all too often found madness to be a more convenient diagnosis for their opponents than dissent, and it is only sixty years since the wretched *Entartete Kunst* exhibition in Berlin sought to compare the likes of Van Gogh, Kandinsky, Klee and Kokoschka with the clinically insane. Here the languages of politics and medicine darkly elide in the vocabulary of asylum, confinement, alienation and control. If

*Beyond Bedlam* explores largely the darkness within, another recent anthology, included with *Banned Poetry*, a special issue of *Index on Censorship* (Vol. 26, No. 5), bears witness to the continuing need to assert human independence in the teeth of external threats. Edited by Harriet Harvey Wood and Peter Porter, it includes the work of poets from more than twenty countries, as well as accompanying essays by Abdullah al-Udhari, Jack Mapanje, Miroslav Holub, Michael Schmidt, and Gordon Brotherston with Lúcia Sá. Explaining in an introduction their choice of *Shadow Worlds* as the anthology's title, the editors write that 'the so-called free nations are not properly free while the oppressing nations go on being truly oppressive. Many regions inhabit some sort of tenebrous middle condition.' They point out that censorship is infinitely more subtle a matter than simple tyranny. It may be brought about 'by market forces and the imposition of the lowest common denominator': or it may be self-imposed. As in the case of aboriginal Arabic traditions, it may even simply be a matter of what is lost by being forgotten. Moreover, 'when political tyranny wanes it often allows other social discriminations to emerge. Religious orthodoxy, sexual intolerance, whether of women or homosexuals, racial hatred – these continue to flourish.'

All the poems here 'bear witness to the refusal of the human will to be diverted from its goal, whether that goal is to tell the truth about life in the writer's country or, equally importantly, to follow some artistic impulse running counter to embattled theocratic or chauvinistic forces.' Like the poems in *Beyond Bedlam*, these arise from a very specific context: and each one is prefaced by an account of the author's sufferings. All the better, then, that the editors deal briskly and directly with the matter of critical response, emphasising that 'this is a collection of poetry, not a journalistic dossier on persecution and state malpractice. No poem has got in only because its author has suffered.' They are also alert to the problem of translation, and 'have insisted on getting the best translations and realisations available.'

If some of the poems grapple with despair, often under the yoke of imprisonment or the imprisonment outside which is exile, the most common note is one of defiance and an absolute refusal to be broken by circumstances. Vedat Türkali's poem 'Istanbul' is typical, with its assertion that 'we haven't endured all these agonies for nothing', and the injunction to 'wait for history's dynamite'. The need to endure, along with a belief in ultimate justice, gives many of the poems a hopeful buoyancy. As Aziz Nesin puts it in 'Ten Minutes' (the time allowed for a prison visit), 'Clearly, they want to drive us mad. / But fortunately we know the value of laughter.' 'Ignore / the fastidious romanticism of prison', enjoins the Kurdish poet Recep Marasli in 'You're not alone'. 'Don't despair / wait for the new day' writes Kemal Burkay. For Min Lu, from Burma, it is scorn and sarcasm which are the energetic agents of defiance.

There is also plenty here to remind us of the world as it is: a poem by Ken Saro-Wiwa, beginning horribly 'Corpses have grown / And covered the land'; another by the Palestinian poet Samih al-Qasim which ends: 'When my children are born / Their tiny coffins are waiting for them'. In others, the fear of emptiness, a world grown indifferent or meaningless, strikes a note closer to the poems of *Beyond Bedlam*, as in the work of the Syrian poet Adonis, in which 'my body fights my body', and 'From time to time I feel as if I was someone else.' Or as in 'Darknesses', by Yang Lian (China):

> locked in the isolation ward     who isn't crazy
> delusions     more like fragments than flesh

The two books have other specific points in common, such as images of blue sky and the obvious division of inside/outside presented by confinement. Only one writer, Ginsberg, is represented in both anthologies. Like *Beyond Bedlam*, *Banned Poetry* also includes work by writers of the past, notably Mandelstam, whose 'Ariosto' and 'Old Crimea' are powerful reminders of the challenges still issued by poetry itself, whatever the context. But most of the poems have little recourse to colour or intense imagery: the characteristic idiom is that of Brecht.

The essays in *Banned Poetry* are distinctive, and each of them adds something of interest. For Jack Mapanje, 'writing was only one form of therapy; most of us did not write to seek fame or readership; we wrote to survive spiritually and to keep our sanity.' He describes from experience the way in which censorship itself can seem so nebulous and shadowy that it leads to self-censorship, and goes on to tell the appalling story of his friend

Blaise Machila, who tried to find him after his arrest, only to be imprisoned himself for his pains. 'He was eventually released after two and a half years. In that time he had gone irretrievably mad.' (This is reminiscent of Brodsky's point, in his essay 'On Tyranny', that a tyranny 'structures your life for you. It does this as meticulously as possible, certainly far better than a democracy does . . . the dream is to make every man his own bureaucrat.') Miroslav Holub offers a strong critique not only of 'free market "experts" who give priority to any "comprehensible" idiocy, from occultism to medieval mysticism, because "people want it"', but also of 'the new paradigm of "real" literature which must be postmodern, relativistic, "deep" (i.e. obscure)' . He concludes that 'the alienation of a broader public from the mainstream of present poetry is not the result of commercialism, but of an abdication by the poets themselves.' In 'Homework: invisible censorship' Michael Schmidt sees an author's revision and editing of his work prior to publication as two acceptable forms of censorship, but considers subsequent alterations inadmissible: 'A book or a poem in its integrity is part of the acknowledged record, whether the writer in the end likes it or not.' He also writes tellingly about copyright censorship, pointing out that 'sometimes those who practise it are the very writers who most vigorously champion the freedoms they privately curtail.'

Integrity, in its sense of wholeness as well as honesty, is the fundamental connective between these two books. Here is poetry in acute contexts. It deserves to be judged for itself, but equally by the standard implicit in the last of Václav Havel's 'Six Asides about Culture' (in *Living in Truth*, Faber, 1987). Havel is persuaded that 'every meaningful cultural act – wherever it takes place – is unquestionably good in and of itself, simply because it exists and because it offers something to someone. Yet can this value "in itself" really be separated from "the common good"? Is one not an integral part of the other from the start? Does not the bare fact that a work of art has meant something to someone – even if only for a moment, perhaps to a single person – already somehow change, however minutely, the overall condition for the better?'

The answers to such questions suppose, as Havel sees, 'an awakening human community' as a medium which may feed on and be fed by culture: and I wonder whether the questions themselves are not particularly relevant now. Both these anthologies were published shortly after the death of Princess Diana. The public response to that event was perhaps the nearest possible approximation, in an evolved democracy, to the moments of historical drama of the kind we have seen so often in recent years – the hole torn in the Romanian flag, the downing of the Berlin wall, Mandela's release. But to some what it suggested was alarming: that as a society we might be not only self-centred but soft-centred in a purely sentimental way. If that is so, reminders of two of the real borders are timely indeed.

# Seasonal Myths

The Palolo worm of Samoa and Fiji is really extraordinary in its time-keeping. Having spent most of the year lurking dully in its shoreline rock crevice, it spawns: and each year this occurs at exactly the same moment, as Anthony Smith relates in his book *The Seasons* (Pelican, 1973). 'The precise moment of spawning is at dawn, both on the day before and on the very day when the moon enters its last quarter . . . this Pacific worm then subsides until the right time of the right phase of the right moon the following year.' Human awareness of the passage of time may not be quite as acute as this, though circadian and circannian rhythms are well established phenomena, for us as for other creatures. Recently we have learnt that to be sad may be the result of Seasonal Affective Disorder – and our awareness of seasonal change and variation has been heightened by what appear to be gross and alarming irregularities.

The cycle of the seasons, which in temperate climates provides an essentially reassuring framework for local anomalies, has long been a part of our consciousness, reflected as much in literature as in the way in which we take it for granted in life. From Chaucer to Keats, Shakespeare to Wordsworth, Hardy to Hughes, the seasons have been a primary component of experience, and their effects on the landscape an essential part of expression. They are almost ubiquitous, from George Herbert's 'sweet spring, full of sweet days and roses, / A box where sweets compacted lie', to Housman's 'idle hill of summer' and Tennyson's liking for the conjunction of 'summer' and 'sea', to Arnold's autumnal view of Rugby chapel, to the wintry rigour of R. S. Thomas's Welsh hills. From the depths of winter to the height of summer, their polarities mirror the feeling heart. Together they describe the parabola of human life, as Thomson frequently reminds us in his version of *The Seasons*:

Behold, fond man!
See here thy pictured life; pass some few years,
Thy flowering Spring, thy Summer's ardent strength,
Thy sober Autumn fading into age,
And pale concluding Winter comes at last,
And shuts the scene.

Is all this changing in 1998? The turn of the year was soon followed by the Selsey tornado, and in some places January produced such mildness that there were reports of record temperatures at airports, camellias blooming and songbirds in full throat, evidently as much at ease as Keats's nightingale. Small details, perhaps, but enough to feed a growing anxiety that the old natural order is increasingly under threat. Television presents whole series of programmes highlighting earthquakes, tidal waves, volcanic eruptions and other cataclysms: equally well publicised are the contemporary problems of environmental barbarism, pollution, El Niño, global warming and holes in the ozone layer. Some would say that our sense of seasonal rhythms has also been altered, and no less radically than the genetically modified tomato, by international air-freighting of produce and the unseasonable cornucopia of supermarket shelves. The holding of harvest festival services at large retail shrines seems then only too horribly appropriate, though logically such rites could take place at any time of the year. As for literature, in January a *Guardian* leader lightheartedly envisaged a generation with 'no idea of the difference between winter and spring, spring and summer', leading to 'the rapid impoverishment of English literature as texts either become incomprehensible or are rewritten to be uniseasonally correct.'

In part this anxiety may be nothing more than the 'curious human frailty' noted by Anthony Smith, which means that 'each one likes to think his particular day and age is of enormous consequence. Climatic variation in one locality over a few years is assumed to be entirely abnormal, and a portent of greater change.' The tendency may be aggravated by a millennial susceptibility to signs and omens, as well as by a genuine fear that soon the seasons really will have no more significance for most people than the changing colours of altar frontals during the course of a year. Yet the truth is that contrariness has always characterised our view of the seasons, bringing out in many writers a gleeful sarcasm, to put alongside Charles II's view of the British summer as three fine days followed by a thunderstorm. Thus Cowper, in a letter of 1783, wrote of 'our severest winter, commonly called the spring', while 'Don Juan' refers to 'the English winter – ending in July, / To recommence in August.' For Coleridge, 'summer has set in with its usual severity', and Robert Graves commented that when we lived in the country we had seasons, but now that we are city-dwellers there is only weather. The seasons themselves offer plenty of evidence of exceptions and contradictions, as suggested by the various names for unseasonably warm weather – not just an Indian summer, but St Martin's, and St Luke's little summer too. Gilbert White wrote a poem 'On the Dark, Still, Dry, Warm Weather Occasionally Happening in the Winter Months', and there is plenty in *The Natural History of Selborne* to support the view that seasonal upsets are no novelty. One example is indeed the summer of 1783, which was 'an amazing and portentous one, and full of horrible phænomena; for besides the alarming meteors and tremendous thunderstorms that affrighted and distressed the different counties of this kingdom, the peculiar haze, or smokey fog, that prevailed for many weeks in this island, and in every part of Europe, and even beyond its limits, was a most extraordinary appearance, unlike anything known within the memory of man.' Similarly alarming episodes are mentioned in Kilvert's diary, and in many of the texts in Geoffrey Grigson's compilation *The English Year* (OUP, 1967), though few seasons are as Protean as the New England spring mentioned by Mark Twain, in which he counted 'one hundred and thirty-six different kinds of weather inside of four-and-twenty hours.'

In Shakespearean terms, any proper consideration of the seasons has to take account both of Berowne's preference, in *Love's Labour's Lost*, for 'each thing that in season grows', but also of dislocation like that brought about in *A Midsummer Night's Dream* by Oberon's jealousy, due to which according to Titania 'we see / The seasons alter: hoary-headed frosts / Fall in the fresh lap of the crimson rose.' To go back to Thomson's *The Seasons*, for all the overarching pattern that the poet descries in singing 'the glories of the circling year', there is also a fascination with the teeming multiplicity of the world – 'Full Nature swarms with life'

– and with the energy made explicit in the dramatic storms of 'Winter'. Much of the poem relies on the energetic interplay between a lost Edenic age and its ideals, most prominent in 'Spring' ('Man superior walks / Amid the glad creation, musing praise, / And looking lively gratitude') and a contemporary world in which 'Nature disturb'd / Is deemed vindictive, to have changed her course.' Working such contrasts, Thomson can leap boldly from a description of gambolling lambs or sheep-shearing to a pæan of praise for British power and enterprise, from the arcadian and bucolic to vigorous polemics in favour of philosophy, commerce and industry, and against France, public corruption and hunting. It is the author's own enthusiasms, such as his delight in birds and animals, rivers and mountains, which give his seasons cohesion and continuing life, just as his proclaimed patriotism, and his intention to 'meditate the book / Of Nature ever open; aiming thence, / Warm from the heart, to learn the moral song', set him distinctly apart from us. Finally, it is this moralising tendency, as much as the regularity of the blank verse, or the elliptical circumlocutions and Augustan poise of the language, which both defines and limits the poem. Here the seasons are terms in an equation, brought together in a series of *paysages moralisés*. Yet the solution is also a magical breaking of bounds and a return to Eden, in the concluding lines of 'Winter':

> The storms of wintry Time will quickly pass
> And one unbounded Spring encircle all.

The paradox of that final line would be appreciated, perhaps, by the author of the following ones. They describe Phaethon approaching the palace of his father Phoebus, the sun. On the silver doors which are 'like sheet flame' he finds a representation by Vulcan of the creation. It includes the seas, with Triton, Proteus, Aegeon, Dorcas and her daughters all disporting themselves, and also the land:

> And there, on earth, were the cities, the people,
> The woods, the beasts, the rivers, the nymphs
> And the spirits of wild places.
> Surrounding the whole thing, the Zodiac –
> On the right door six signs, and six on the left.

Once inside, Phaethon is dazzled by the presence of the god and those round him:

> To right and left of him
> His annual retinue stood arrayed –
> The seasons, the generations, and the hours.
> Spring, crowned with a flower garland. Summer,
> Naked but for a coronet of ripe corn.
> Autumn, purple from treading the wine-press.
> And Winter, shivering in rags,
> His white hair and his beard
> Jagged with icicles.

This comes from the second of Ted Hughes's *Tales from Ovid* (Faber, 1997), in which the seasons take their place as part of a cosmology both more universal and more dynamic than anything in Thomson. In these twenty-four tales Hughes recreates the all-embracing context of classical mythology, where human love and folly are played out in an elemental drama in which the gods fully participate. Here is a framework which, by definition, can contain all seasons, all possibilities – every conceivable metamorphosis. And it is apt that, discussing Ovid, Hughes refers to 'the swiftness and filmic economy of his narrative': his own versions of the stories have all the maniac verve of cartoons, and issue the same challenges to disbelief. Though full appreciation requires reading in full, something of Hughes's technique, as well as his outstanding control of rhythm, may be gathered from this description of Proteus, in 'Erisychthon':

> Proteus, who haunts the shadowy seas
> That scarf this earth, is glimpsed as a young man
> Who becomes of a sudden a lion
> That becomes a wild boar ripping the ground,
>
> Yet flows forward, hidden, through grass, without sound
> As a serpent, that emerges
> As a towering bull under bent-down horns,
> Or hides, among stones, a simple stone.

Often gory, destructive or cruel, these stories are also magical and consoling: the gods are sometimes capable of mercy as well as power. What makes the poems utterly compelling is the exact imaginative match between the original narratives and the gifts which enable Hughes to remake them as his own – a fantastical wit, vividness, pace and driving energy. As the introduction notes, 'above all, Ovid was interested in passion. Or rather, in what a passion feels like to the one possessed by it. Not just ordinary passion either, but human passion *in extremis* – passion where it combusts, or levitates, or mutates into an experience of the supernatural.' And Hughes views this individual dynamism against the background of an increasingly unstable Empire which, 'for all its Augustan stability . . . was at sea in hysteria and despair, at one extreme wallowing in the bottomless appetites and sufferings of the gladiatorial arena, and at the other searching higher and higher for a spiritual transcendence – which did eventually take form, on the crucifix.' These tales, he concludes, 'establish a rough register of what it feels like to live in the psychological gulf that opens at the end of an era. Among everything else that we see in them, we certainly recognise this.' This opens onto teleological perspectives in a way not dissimilar to our response to the seasons. With a brilliance that is not only wonderfully entertaining but implicitly optimistic, Hughes offers a convincing proof that the pattern may lie not in continuity, but in exception, unpredictability and variety: in all that, even towards the close of the twentieth century, is still available to be remade in new energies of language and expression.

# What's the Griff?

There are some questions which, once asked, go on rumbling round the mind like a thunderstorm that won't disperse, the occasional drumroll continuing to echo from the coiling cloud. One of them, for me, was the result of reading remarks made by James Fenton on the occasion of the publication of Ted Hughes's *Birthday Letters*. 'There is great excitement about this work, which has been kept so carefully secret. The content is obviously very interesting,' Fenton is quoted as saying. And he goes on:

> One or two poets have had the ambition for a long time to write a poem a part of the interest of which would be content. People would read that poem to find out what the information in it was. Hughes has succeeded in doing this.
>
> Everybody is fascinated to see what he felt. Content in itself doesn't guarantee the success of the poem, but content like this doesn't do much harm. What is striking is the intensity with which he still comes to the subject.

If part of the interest of this is the final sentence, which seems to make at least some concession to Housman's contention, in his Leslie Stephen lecture of 1933, that 'Poetry is not the thing said but a way of saying it', it was that word 'information' which really stuck in my mind. How much information can or should a poem contain, and to what end? And does 'information' mean only objectively verifiable facts? What about the information supplied by the imagination, the sub- or unconscious, our identity and our memories: by context, subtext, metatext? As often, the readiest clarifications seem to be negatives. Whatever the purpose of a poem, you can see that an overload of information might be injurious to its readability, just as inaccurate information would endanger its credibility, or the display of information

111

for its own sake, its modesty. But we live in the age of Information Technology, and the striking success of many meticulously researched novels, as well as the popularity of biography, suggests that readers like the anchorage of information almost as much as voyages of the imagination. And perhaps the awareness of the gulf between differing specialist uses of language, as well as a linguistic interest in the neologisms they spawn, also plays a part in the desire of some poets, as well as prose writers, to take account of the technological and the scientific.

Of course it is possible to think of poems in which information of one kind or another is central. Though we might not go to Tennyson in the first place for a factual account of the daring of the *Revenge*, there are poems like *The Battle of Maldon* to remind us of the value of the poem as chronicle. Its record of a battle against the Danes in 991 is, as Michael Alexander points out in his introduction to *The Earliest English Poems* (Penguin, 1966), 'a more sober and reliable account than is to be found in later Latin historians, and it must have been accepted as the true story by anyone who heard it.' The poem also offers an informative example of the inadvisability of the cricketing spirit when applied to battle. Allowing the Danes to cross unhindered to the landward side of a causeway and regroup may have been jolly sporting, but proved disastrous.

On one level, I suppose that allegory might be thought of as poetry of information; come to that, so might the *Georgics*, for those interested in such matters as beekeeping. As Fenton suggests, there may be information about relationships to be learned from poems, whether Hughes or Hardy; or autobiographical information as in *The Prelude* or, indeed, the work of Sylvia Plath. Poetry may also inform by reviving or sustaining half-forgotten cultural or mythical sources, and here too Hughes is one striking contemporary instance, with his *Tales from Ovid*.

I thought to have thought sufficiently about information: but a few days later it was in my mind again, translated this time into a few vivid frames from one of those World War Two films in which Kenneth More strides about in a bomber jacket, his brow crinkled by an anxious patriotic frown and biting his lip. 'Give us the gen!' he cries, throwing down or picking up his leather flying helmet. 'Gen', explains Eric Partridge (*A Dictionary of Slang and Unconventional English*, Routledge, 1984), can be pukka, duff or phoney, and is an abbreviation from 'for the general information of all ranks'. I remember it being in quite common use in the 1950s – and not only in films: it was not unusual to hear someone saying that they must 'gen up' on something, or 'get genned up'. The last time I encountered the word in a book was in Fenton's poem 'Dead Soldiers', from his 1983 collection *The Memory of War and Children in Exile,* in which Pol Pot's cruel and boastful brother 'tells me how he will one day give me the gen.'

On the other hand, I have no memory of hearing 'griff', also meaning 'information', a naval slang word (thought to derive from Anglo-Indian 'griffin', meaning 'a newcomer to the East') which Partridge describes as being in general use in Britain by 1950, in such phrases as 'What's the griff?' and 'Give me the griff on . . .'. Anyway, according to Partridge 'griff' was on its way out by 1980, so if you didn't catch it then you are unlikely to do so now. In its implication of not merely information but inside information, it overlaps with those two expressive American terms, 'dope' and 'low-down', which must have owed their popularity at least partly to gangster movies. By the time I had discovered from Joseph Wright's English dialect dictionary that in Lincoln (James Fenton's birthplace, incidentally), Sussex, Somerset and Devon, 'information' was used for 'inflammation' at the turn of the century (imagine 'a nasty information of the left knee' or 'a horribly informed elbow'), I was beginning to fear that I might myself be suffering from some early form of 'Information Anxiety', a coinage by the American Richard Wurman for 'feelings of panic or despair brought on by a surfeit of unassimilable information pumped out by the media' (*Brewer's 20th Century Phrase and Fable*, Cassell, 1993). Or perhaps I was becoming somehow tainted by the sneaky associations that shadow the word: 'informer'; even 'informant', in its anonymity.

Somehow there was no shaking the subject off. I found myself thinking about the kind of information that clusters round a poem rather than in it. Emanating from the critic or the biographer, such gen can make all the difference to our reading and understanding. And poets themselves may explicate their work in a footnote, or by introductions given at a reading. These may enhance a reader's or listener's enjoyment, but also run the risk of leaking the poem's energy away. It is not unknown to hear, at a reading, an introduction which the subsequent poem fails to match. Some poets refuse to make any explicatory comment, insisting that the poems must speak for themselves. Admirable though this may be, the success of it does rather depend on the poems in question, and on the extent to which the audience is in the habit of listening to poetry. On the page, too, there is often the temptation to surround poems with signposts of one kind or another. It was the sort which offer circumstantial or anecdotal embellishment that provoked Eliot's scorn in 'The Music of Poetry', where he wades into an annotated English translation of Mallarmé: 'When I learn that a difficult sonnet was inspired by seeing a painting on the ceiling reflected on the polished top of a table, or by seeing the light reflected from the foam on a glass of beer, I can only say that this may be a correct embryology, but it is not the meaning. If we are not moved, then it is, as poetry, meaningless.' Enter Housman again, with his assertion that 'to transfuse emotion . . . is the peculiar function of poetry.'

Les Murray is equally clear about what he calls 'managerial prose', in 'Embodiment and Incarnation', an essay deliberating his plans for two anthologies. They would, he writes, 'carry as little managing prose as possible, so as to leave more room for poetry, but more importantly, so as to give it its freedom and let it have its effect, without all the guide rails of commentary to which many readers will cling if they are provided. I would not even trammel my books with biographical data on the poets; other books contain those, and can be looked up . . . All the historical orientation I thought relevant went instead into the Foreword . . .'. In the same essay he goes on to distinguish between what he calls 'Wholespeak', which he defines as 'properly integrated poetic discourse', and 'Narrowspeak', that is 'discourses based on the supposed primacy or indeed exclusive sovereignty of daylight reason.' For him, 'the former embraces all good poetry including that of religion, the latter embraces most of the administrative discourse by which the world is ruled from day to day, as well as most of criticism.' It's an open question whether there could be room, in these terms, for a poetry of information, or useful information about poetry. Yet not all explication is redundant: sometimes it may be essential, as David Jones argues in the Preface to *The Anathemata*. 'It is sometimes objected that annotation is pedantic; all things considered in the present instance, the reverse would, I think, be the more true. There have been culture-phases when the maker and the society in which he lived shared an enclosed and common background, where the terms of reference were common to all. It would be an affectation to pretend that such was our situation today.' For Jones, the problem of discovering and using valid signs which will be understood by the reader is a central one.

Much of this comes down to the perennial debate about content, style and meaning. Eliot and Housman have opinions about this, too: and both are careful to guard their positions. For Eliot, 'style alone cannot preserve; only good style in conjunction with permanently interesting content can preserve' (*Charles Whibley*, 1931). And Housman, though critical of seventeenth-century wit and eighteenth-century intelligence alike in his lecture, concedes that 'poems very seldom consist of poetry and nothing else; and pleasure can be derived also from their other ingredients.' In at least some poems there may also be the matter of a balance between concealment and revelation, or a writer's liking for ambiguities.

Finally, I went back to Fenton's own work to see what he might have to say about 'information', since poets often tend to incorporate their own interests into remarks about the work of others. Here, as the blurb on the back cover of his first collection, *Terminal Moraine* (Secker & Warburg, 1972), puts it, 'there is certainly plenty of information available: geological, psychological, mycological, horticultural, architectural, and much else besides.' This is borne out by the acknowledgements and in poems like 'The Pitt-Rivers Museum, Oxford' where information is inventory, 'the chaotic piles of souvenirs', and 'A Frog', with its text taken from 'What the frog's eye tells the frog's brain', an article by J. Y. Lettvin *et al.* appearing in a 1940 publication, *Proceedings of the Institute of Radio Engineers*. Even at this early stage Fenton is keenly aware of what may subvert or dictate our view of the world as it is. As he writes in the 'Envoi' to his sequence 'Our Western Furniture', which won the Newdigate Prize thirty years ago:

> Even Bashō's experience of the flower
> Was, though acute, subjective, and if our
> Poem had aimed at reproducing *History*
> It would be largely Biochemistry.

Instead we offer you an almost-fiction
Constructed on a grid of contradiction.

Fenton's work as a journalist and his closeness then to the night-mares of brutal events give his writing a particular edge, at a time when we are all securely and insecurely chained at the cross-roads of information and impotence. The slippery linguistic inventiveness of much of his work is a reminder both of the unstable multifariousness of the world, and of the tyranny liable to accompany any prescriptive attempt to impose order on it. As his splendid 'Manila Manifesto' puts it, 'This is no time for people who say: this, this and only this. We say: this, and *this*, and *that* too.' Fenton's work, not least the sounding of private as well as public depths in his most recent book *Out of Danger* (Penguin, 1993), is a reminder that for the poet gen alone will never quite do. He gives us the griff on the world, but also knows that good poems always offer the reader something more, even when they come close to despair: in one way or another, you might say, gen and tonic.

# Sincerely

Ever since the graffito that manifested itself on the plaster of the wall at Belshazzar's feast, hoisted words, banner words, have claimed our attention in one form or another. Incised on monuments and memorials, they acquire a weightiness that seeks to imply durable worth; as mottos scrolled on flags, they command loyalty; foot-high on advertising hoardings and billboards, they act the courtesan or the sergeant-major, out to charm or bully; in the tags and aphorisms of graffiti artists they decorate grey cities of means with colourful ends suggestive of a different order. More transiently, they appear and flick away again in soundbites and shoals on the screens of our cinemas and televisions.

A number of them settled on the walls of the Bonnard exhibition at the London Tate Gallery earlier this year, by the entrance. They included the artist's assertion that 'in the subtle equilibrium between lies and truth, everything is relative, everything is a matter of more or less.' From which he concluded that 'extreme sincerity runs the risk of appearing either ridiculous or untenable.'

Does the observation earn its highlighting, its place on the wall, especially loaded as it is by the qualifying adjective 'extreme'? It's certainly the case that the matter of sincerity has occupied writers as well as painters considerably over the years, from Bacon, as when writing 'Of Simulation and Dissimulation', to Hazlitt, for instance in his essay on 'Good-Nature'; from Wilde, whether in 'The Critic as Artist' ('A little sincerity is a dangerous thing, and a great deal of it is absolutely fatal') or *The Importance of Being Earnest*, to I. A. Richards in *Practical Criticism.* The concept of sincerity offers an assurance, you would think, with its connotations of truthfulness and good faith, yet is often treated with suspicion, as if it were one of Keats's 'palpable designs upon the reader'. Either it is seen as flattening, a dead

end and indeed artless, or it appears escorted on one side by
*naïveté*, on the other by an embarrassment sometimes seen as
peculiar to the reserved English. It seems a notion unable to
shake off its moral pretensions, more suited to the work of a
hymn-writer such as Bishop Ken ('Let all thy converse be sincere,
/ thy conscience as the noonday clear') than to poetry. Sometimes it is discussed in terms which make it hard to distinguish
from the idea of originality or integrity. Like modesty, sincerity
relies for its credibility on being perceived by the recipient or
witness rather than being declared by its practitioner: to claim it
is at once to undermine it and conjure its converse. Enter the
ghost of the late Hughie Green, of the television show *Opportunity Knocks*, with his oily catchphrase 'I mean that most sincerely': eyes and mouth struggling vainly to match the words.
True, many of our letters are signed 'sincerely', but usage has
worn this to a transparent neutrality.

One of the most enjoyable exposés of sincerity and its implications is enacted in Molière's *Le Misanthrope*. Alceste wastes no
time in declaring to his friend Philinte, in the opening scene of the
play, his adherence to the principle:

> Je veux qu'on soit sincère, et qu'en homme d'honneur,
> On ne lâche aucun mot qui ne parte du cœur.

Philinte understands perfectly just how prescriptive and inflexible this high-minded aspiration must be, a form of extremism to
which he opposes the calm assertion that 'la parfaite raison fuit
toute extrémité'. The play goes on to show just how unworkable
Alceste's sincerity is, not only for others but for himself. Invited
to comment on a mannered sonnet written by Oronte, he proves
milder than he has led us to expect, even confessing that 'J'ai le
défaut / D'être un peu plus sincère, en cela, qu'il ne faut.' And in
terms of his love for the flirtatious Célimène, Alceste often
appears appallingly unreasonable and possessive. Both socially
and personally, the demand for sincerity barely masks an awful
insecurity: is indeed the articulation of it. What he seeks is not
truth – perhaps not even love – so much as reassurance. Yet for
all this, it is possible to discern within the ballooning comic exag-
geration something more substantial than hot air: absurd as he is,
Alceste has a point. 'L'art de feindre', the art of dissembling, may

be a social necessity if not a virtue, but it also makes room for hypocrisy and charlatanism.

When it comes to sincerity in poetry, the question put by Audrey in the third act of *As You Like It* remains central: 'I do not know what "poetical" is: is it honest in deed and word? Is it a true thing?' And Touchstone's famous answer, that 'the truest poetry is the most feigning', is taken as a title by Auden in a poem dedicated to Edgar Wind, where he makes clear which side of the argument he is on:

> Be subtle, various, ornamental, clever,
> And do not listen to those critics ever
> Whose crude provincial gullets crave in books
> Plain cooking made still plainer by plain cooks . . .

Auden's sprightly couplets make the case for flexibility and 'ingenious fibs' in a poet's treatment of matters personal and political, and his poem concludes with a rhetorical question. For man, 'the only creature ever made who fakes',

> What but tall tales, the luck of verbal playing
> Can trick his lying nature into saying
> That love, or truth in any serious sense,
> Like orthodoxy, is a reticence?

This teasing view of the sinuous route to truth-telling is reflected equally in Auden's prose. In 'Writing', he quotes Stravinsky's comment that 'most artists are sincere and most art is bad, though some insincere (sincerely insincere) works can be quite good', glossing it with his own comments. 'Sincerity is like sleep. Normally, one should assume that, of course, one will be sincere, and not give the question a second thought. Most writers, however, suffer occasionally from bouts of insincerity as men do from bouts of insomnia. The remedy in both cases is often quite simple: in the case of the latter, to change one's diet, in the case of the former, to change one's company.' At this point the reader may feel that the discussion has run aground on the lee shore of the urge to be aphoristic, but Auden soon launches off on a new tack, suggesting that 'when a reviewer describes a book as "sincere", one knows immediately that it is a) insincere (insincerely insincere) and b) badly written. Sincerity in the proper sense of the word, meaning authenticity, is, however, or ought to be, a writer's chief preoccupation.' This would be hard to disagree with, though Auden gives 'sincerity' a particular meaning here, that of the poet being true to self and aware of the scope and limitations of his or her own gifts. In 'The Poet & The City', he strikes a note akin to the poem dedicated to Edgar Wind, in asserting the writer's existential freedom which he has in common with all men: 'The peasant may play cards in the evening while the poet writes verses, but there is one political principle to which they both subscribe, namely, that among the half dozen or so things for which a man of honor should be prepared, if necessary, to die, the right to play, the right to frivolity, is not the least.'

Sincerity on parade can, it is true, make for an awfully dim religious gloom: often it is associated with solemnity. As Geoffrey Grigson put it in *The Private Art*, 'How solemn most of my latter day poets are, as if each insisted to himself "I must write *poetry*." No *jeu d'esprit*, nothing that seems thrown off, no snatch, no inconsequential rhyme of the kind we remember for life.' And he thought that this doleful situation was at least in part due to a growing disregard for form and rhythm. 'Each poet has to justify the anti-poetics of his form by being or appearing to be very serious indeed or very novel or very unexpected, or he tries to correct an inability by conforming to momentary dictates and postures.' But is this really just a matter of forms or a good ear? 'Partly', writes Grigson, covering himself, though he does not fill the gap he defines. Orwell may have been nearer to the core of the matter in 'Inside the Whale', with the suggestion that it is the pressures of history and politics which condition any notion of 'sincerity'. Comparing Julian Green's *Minuit* unfavourably with Poe's *Tales*, as an example of 'an insincere attempt to work up a similar atmosphere', it seems to him ' that for a creative writer possession of the "truth" is less important than emotional sincerity . . . talent, apparently, is a matter of being able to *care*, of really believing in your beliefs, whether they are true or false. The difference between, for instance, Céline and Evelyn Waugh is a difference of emotional intensity. It is the difference between genuine despair and a despair that is at least partly a pretence.' At the same time, Orwell sees the complexity of the matter, conceding that 'there are occasions when an "untrue" belief is more likely to be sincerely held than a "true" one.' In the aftermath of the Great War, he can appreciate the case for frivolity, for Prufrock rather than *The First Hundred Thousand* or Horatio Bottomley's *Letters to the Boys in the Trenches* ('What a relief it would have been at such a time, to read about the hesitations of a middle-aged highbrow with a bald spot! So different from bayonet-drill! After the bombs and the food-queues and the recruiting-posters, a human voice! What a relief!'). Writing in the middle of a second world war, he goes on to say that, for the writer, passive resistance to an age in which 'the autonomous individual is going to be stamped out of existence' is the most honourable procedure left: and he praises Henry Miller for it – 'he is a completely negative, unconstructive, amoral writer, a mere Jonah, a passive acceptor of evil, a sort of Whitman among the corpses.' This would certainly avoid what Auden saw as the real threat to a writer's integrity of 'appeals to his social conscience, his political or religious convictions', but it also looks like a counsel of despair.

In the late nineties, detachment of any kind might seem problematical : and if the kind of reassurance once offered by sincerity is not readily on offer, the demand for it is still there. Richard Hoggart described it very well nearly thirty years ago, in *Speaking to Each Other* (Vol. 2, 'About Literature'), writing about the teaching of literature to adults encountering it for perhaps the first time as an object of study:

> They expect the direct expression of emotion, the cry from the heart – 'my heart leaps up' or 'And then my heart with pleasure fills'; they expect to find joy about the accepted joyous things and sorrow about the accepted unhappy things. Hence the frequent use in early exercises of the epithet 'sincere': 'I like this poem; the poet seems to me sincere' often means that the poet has not roused mistrust by being oblique, that is, witty, satiric, or ironic.

Like Grigson, Hoggart suggests that there is a link between earnestness and a suspicion of formal aspects of poetry. 'Elizabethan sonnets, because they obey firm conventions of form and manner, are likely to be thought insincere. Even more, the conventions of a whole age may be mistrusted. The quiet, public deployment of moral abstractions by an eighteenth-century poet seems hypocritical. Cowper's easy traffic in such phrases as "dear eyes", "filial grief", "the perishing pleasures of man", "a frail memorial, but sincere", "constant flow of love", sounds artificial. Any man who uses words of that sort so easily must be phoney – as he probably would today.'

No doubt attitudes to the direct expression of feeling vary from age to age, as they do from writer to writer. One quite dominant contemporary idiom would seem to combine street cred and political correctness with a sentimentally or indignantly expressed compassion. For Hoggart the crucial yardstick, whether for literature or for society at large, is what may be seen as 'fully human' and expressive of 'common humanity'. Perhaps these are more spacious terms to use than 'sincerity'. If they are no less vague, at least they may be more able to accommodate rich ambiguities, and to be articulated in all manner of poetry by all means, whether elliptical, lyrical, ironic, formally playful or not, even allusive or difficult (the writing on Belshazzar's wall required Daniel's gift of interpretation, after all). They may also remind us of the limits of sincerity, not just socially, as Alceste discovers, but psychologically: 'a capacity for self-disclosure implies an equal capacity for self-concealment', as Auden writes in 'Balaam and His Ass'. And it is humanity that has Auden declare (in 'Robert Frost') his preference for Frost's epitaph ('I would have written of me on my stone / I had a lover's quarrel with the world') over that of Hardy ('I never cared for life, life cared for me. / And hence I owe it some fidelity . . .') or Yeats (*'Cast a cold eye / On life, on death. / Horseman, pass by!'*) 'And,' Auden concludes, 'when it comes to wisdom, is not having a lover's quarrel with life more worthy of Prospero than not caring or looking coldly?' Another rhetorical question but still, in the age of the soundbite and of relentless over-articulation, a good one.

# Island Treasure

The most bizarre experience of a July visit to Orkney and Shetland took place on Unst, on the road that leads towards Hermaness and Muckle Flugga, the northernmost point of the British Isles. It manifested itself as a two-seater cane sofa with cushions and a cotton throw; beside it, a cane table with two mugs, a television set and a small food cabinet labelled 'Hot Snacks', its contents somewhat ill-defined. There was also a smaller table on which stood a potted plant, an empty whisky or sherry bottle and a box of tissues. On the wall, a clock with an octagonal wooden case: round three sides of the room, at the top of the wall, a lace hanging which figured repeated pairs of geese. Only it wasn't a room, but a bus shelter with a bare concrete floor. Who? Why? The furnished shelter was oddly reminiscent of the displays to be found in Shetland at the Lerwick museum, or on Orkney at the Visitors' Centre at Maeshowe, of a typical islander's living room of times past. But here no explanation was on hand for what was effectively an instance of public art: no personal belongings, no poster, no collecting-box, not even evidence of sponsorship. No one. The peaty moorland stretching away. A small loch that glimmered in the background.

The incongruity of this tableau was heightened by the context of a sparse landscape in which any object stood out naturally, without such extravagance: the shelter alone, bright orange-red with panels of glass, would have been conspicuous enough. And what about the island on which the shelter stood? Perhaps any land enisled is given definition beyond the purely geographical by the surrounding water, as Kevin Crossley-Holland suggests in *Pieces of Land* (Gollancz, 1972), an account of journeys to eight islands. Writing of Inishmore, he suggests that 'we all have a dream of an unattainable ideal place. . . . Perhaps it is true that most of us think at once, like George Meredith, of an island. . . .

Why an island? Because it is a place apart. Because it is traditionally a place of retreat. Because it is surrounded by water. It is as
simple as that.' At Lindisfarne he notes as very much part of the
*genius loci* 'the coming and going of bright water; the sense of a
place that really is both one with and no part of the mainland; the
space; the long views to the black Farne islands, to the bulk and
bastions of Bamburgh. . .'. Visiting Orkney, he finds 'a way of life
. . . intelligent, courteous, in harmony with the natural world,
above all with the element water.'

  If Crossley-Holland's Orcadian visit focuses on Hoy, it also has
much to say about George Mackay Brown, about whom he
writes with an admiration tempered by awareness of the
dangers of writing that sometimes risks nostalgia for a vanished
past. He quotes a passage from Mackay Brown's *An Orkney
Tapestry* (Gollancz, 1969) which sees contemporary art as itself an
island:

> Nowadays our western art is autonomous, private, a cold
> lonely kingdom. It presents us with the human condition but
> makes no claim to do anything about it; being cut off from
> labours and hungers; being the preserve of sophisticated
> people, a small priesthood who can appreciate and under-
> stand, they alone.

To visit the islands is to be reminded that much of the long past
is also cut off. As *An Orkney Tapestry* puts it:

> Hardly a thing is known about these first Orkneymen (if they
> were the first Orkneymen) apart from the monuments they
> left behind them, the huge stones of Maeshowe and Brodgar,
> and the pastoral village of Skara Brae in the west. History
> can tell nothing: not a word or a name comes out of the
> silence – there are a few ambiguous scratches on a wall at
> Skara Brae. We wander clueless through immense tracts of
> time. Imagination stirs about a scattered string of bone beads
> found at Skara Brae.

Mackay Brown can acknowledge the greater prosperity of recent
times, but his artistic imagination laments the loss of 'the ancient
magical ceremonial quality of art'. His poems constantly weigh

loss against retrieval, want against plenty. With their cast of Norsemen, fishermen, ploughmen, tinkers, shepherds, crofters, shopkeepers and those for whom Edwin Muir's phrase 'the hardened old' would be apt, they vitally celebrate the richness of the island inheritance and the cyclical passage of winter darkness, summer and harvest. The 'first grace of light', the northern stars and the sea's 'bright girdle' all animate his view of 'the clay book' as he calls the earth in one poem, as well as 'the salt book', which is the sea in another. Richness is a good haul, endurance and faith a retrieved cargo whose value is set by the harshness of history and a hard-won home economy. Such virtues are often embodied, in the poems, in simple words and direct, end-stopped lines.

Something of the same interplay of sparseness and wealth also underlies much of the work of Edwin Muir, an Orcadian poet himself, even if he left the islands early on. For all the European or classical contexts of his poems, the lost Eden to which he frequently refers, like his sense of the heraldic and emblematic, is surely rooted in that islander's sense of apartness which he and Mackay Brown have in common. The visitor to Orkney and Shetland discovers something of the same: here hardly enough can become plenty. And just as it is the surrounding silence which winds the anxious call of the oystercatcher to an extraordinary tension, so objects acquire an emblematic significance from the space which surrounds them. It is as if perception itself slows down, attends properly to what there is: a small clinker-built boat on the beach; a white bone on a moor; a stack of cut peats by the road; the tormentil's little yellow flowers. Small wonder that an installation like Sullom Voe, on the Shetland mainland, looks alien despite careful landscaping. The hoisted gas flares of Europe's largest oil terminal, licking skywards with a roar of pressure, have an almost ritualistic presence.

To find on the islands the challenging interplay of objects and their context was also to be reminded of a visit, earlier in the year, to Kettle's Yard in Cambridge. Once the house of Jim and Helen Ede, this astonishing place contains work by, amongst others, Ben Nicholson, David Jones, Alfred Wallis, Christopher Wood, Henri Gaudier-Brzeska, Naum Gabo and Brancusi. Yet it sets out to be something quite other than the usual kind of gallery, as Jim Ede's introduction to the illustrated guide makes clear:

I found myself . . . dreaming of the idea of somehow creating a *living place* where works of art could be enjoyed, inherent to the domestic setting, where young people could be at home unhampered by the greater austerity of the museum or public art gallery and where an informality might infuse an underlying formality. I wanted, in a modest way, to use the inspiration I had had from beautiful interiors, houses of leisured elegance, and to combine it with the joy I had felt in individual works seen in museums and with the all embracing delight I had experienced in nature, in stones, in flowers, in people.

The aim of creating a domestic setting is pleasingly demonstrated to the visitor at the outset. To get in, you have to pull a bell rope and wait for someone to answer the door and usher you over the threshold: no turnstiles or ticket machines here, and no admission charge. And once you are inside, it soon becomes clear how everything in the house is intended to fulfil its creators' vision: not only the pictures and sculptures, but every item of furniture, the exploitation of light, the vases of fresh flowers, and every ornament. Many of these are unworked, taken directly from nature, such as simple stones and pebbles: the artistry is in their careful selection and arrangement. But Jim Ede also emphasises that Kettle's Yard is not intended to be merely a reflection of his personal taste. 'It is, rather, a continuing way of life from these last fifty years, in which stray objects, stones, glass, pictures, sculpture, in light and in space, have been used to make manifest the underlying stability which more and more we need to recognise if we are not to be swamped by all that is so rapidly opening up before us.' This sense of precariousness, of the danger of values lost beyond retrieval, makes common cause with George Mackay Brown. But if in nature and, maybe, a simple society, value of this kind can come free, in a more complex social setting its retrieval and maintenance cost: since 1966 Kettle's Yard has been maintained by the University of Cambridge. Whether in Orkney or Cambridge, there is the same underlying issue of the community and the artist's relation to it – how to achieve space, spaciousness, the proper honouring of objects in creation, while avoiding élitism, isolation, sterility, or merely another capitalist currency made from rarity.

The challenge of democracy seems to demand an art which, however sufficiently individual and distinct from the world, is still somehow integrated with it: more a promontory than an island. The pressures of a world increasingly crowded and, for all the talk of globalisation, in many respects increasingly fragmented, sharpen the pertinence of the question. Any answer must augment the openness of nature and the light-filled clearings of such places as Kettle's Yard with the spaciousness of the imagination, and what may be cherished and developed there. In this perspective Jim Ede's reference in his introduction to young people and their enjoyment of art has an importance beyond the contingent presence of students in Cambridge. The encouragement of the imagination must finally mean the sustaining of a creative approach to education. And our education system, with its current emphasis on performance and targets, sometimes seems in danger of crowding the imagination rather than liberating it. There are some encouraging signs, including the government's commitment to enabling free admission to museums and galleries to be maintained or, in some cases, re-introduced. Increased spending on schools also has the potential to help, though it must be hoped that the stand taken by such as Sir Simon Rattle and given a corporate existence in Professor Ken Robinson's National Advisory Committee on Creative and Cultural Education, will be properly heeded. And much will depend on the success of the National Literacy Strategy.

Meanwhile on Unst, whose shape is said to have been the model for Stevenson's Treasure Island, the imaginative life goes playfully on. In a second bus shelter, there is a small table at one side, and at the other a wooden chair of the kind to be found in churches: a setting for Beckett rather than Rattigan. A few miles away, from a third shelter a bright orange papier mâché sheep with very thin legs peers out, as if impatient for the next bus to arrive. I am told that, despite periodic cleansing of the shelters by the Shetland Islands Council, it is never long before new objects appear.

# 1999

# Winning the Bays

The submission contained a great many poems written by people who obviously put out a lot but took in very little, who thought that good writing and good reading were not connected, whose aesthetic ideas had been shaped when they first read the Georgians and never challenged since, and who were not interested in finding out how their pastoral/lyric world might be adapted to include things that were urban/political/rough-edged. Many of these offerings, indeed, seemed to me hardly poems at all (no shape, no rhyme, no subject) – which left me feeling puzzled as to why they'd been cast as such in the first place. The lure of 'being a poet'? Or sheer incompetence?

Thus Andrew Motion, in his introduction to *The Ring of Words* (Sutton Publishing, 1998), an anthology of winning poems in the most recent Arvon International Poetry Competition, sponsored by the *Daily Telegraph* in association with Duncan Lawrie Limited. Motion reports interestingly on the subjects which he and his fellow judges (Fleur Adcock, Grey Gowrie and Charles Moore) found recurring amongst the entry of more than seven thousand poems – 'love of places, love of loved ones, death of loved ones, death of Princess Diana' – and amusingly on the tendency of judges to moan while actually wading through. As for influences, 'the strongest pull was exercised by a mish-mash of the mighty dead, rather than any one or two contemporaries.' And as the winner of the first ever Arvon competition in 1981 (with an entry of well over thirty thousand, and judged by the formidable tetrarchy of Charles Causley, Seamus Heaney, Ted Hughes and Philip Larkin), Motion writes with authority of viewing competitions in perspective: 'I told myself the only sensible thing to do was to consider myself lucky, admit my good fortune, and try to write better in the future. I knew that if my poem was to have a life, it would have to be elsewhere.' But the puzzle persists, reminiscent of the ambiguities neatly planted as adverb and verb at the very entrance to Marvell's garden – 'How vainly men themselves amaze / To win the palm, or oak, or bays': why do so many people enter poetry competitions, when they are clearly not readers of contemporary poetry and have very little chance of winning?

Bardic contests of one kind or another, many of them involving recitation, have a long pedigree. Often they would involve a set theme: one of the most pleasingly mannered was the subject set by Charles d'Orléans, 'Je meurs de soif auprès de la fontaine', to which Villon amongst others responded, with his famous ballade. Nowadays there are competitions galore, varying hugely in scope and stature and with a corresponding diversity of reward, from publication in an anthology to a whacking four-figure sum. Feelings inevitably run high, not just about the preferences of judges but about the advisability of holding such contests at all. Arguments in favour include the encouragement of hitherto unknown talent, putting money into the pockets of poets (and often this means the judges as well as the winners), raising money for worthwhile institutions or causes, and greater public awareness of poetry in general. Some people are virulently opposed to the whole idea, whether because it often involves the extraction from the untalented of quite high entry fees, or for the reason given by Geoffrey Grigson in *The Private Art* (Allison & Busby, 1982): 'It is extraordinary, an act of illiterates, to give prizes for literature' (though even Grigson is sufficiently pragmatic to admit that 'every poet looks down on prizes, until he is given a prize. Then he recovers from this affront to himself and continues to look down on prizes. Rightly.') Between these two poles stand the temperate shruggers – it's better odds than the Lottery and, after all, no one is forced to enter.

A different, though scarcely more sanguine, view is expressed by Derek Mahon in his excellent long poem *The Yellow Book* (Gallery Books, 1997), accurately described on the back cover as a 'long poem [which] meditates on the idea of cultural decadence in its historical and contemporary manifestations'. It does so with wonderful verve and artistry: best of all, with earned wisdom. Rueful as he often is, Mahon never loses sight of the high stars which, throughout his work, have helped in steering through the dark. 'Remembering the '90s', the eighth section of the poem, recalls 'the hearties and the aesthetes' of Yeats's generation 'who died of thirst *auprès de la fontaine* / or tumbled from high stools in the Rose & Crown', and looks back from the perspectives of the future to what has been achieved:

> The most of what we did and wrote was artifice,
> rhyme-sculpture against the entangling vines of nature –
> a futile project since, in the known future,
> new books will be rarities in techno-culture,
> a forest of intertextuality like this,
> each one a rare book and what few we have
> written for prize-money and not for love.

Yet the hope of financial gain or of a claim to fame does not seem wholly adequate as an explanation for the appeal of competitions. Andrew Motion touches upon another possibility: 'Poets can be as clever, difficult, socially engaged and politically wired as maybe, but it does poetry itself a disservice if we ignore its value as a primitive emotional release.' And, he might have added, as a consolation, of the kind described in 'Patience Strong', a poem from U. A. Fanthorpe's first collection *Side Effects* (Peterloo, 1978). The first of the poem's two verses appears merely to mock:

> Her theme
> Always the same: rain falls in every life,
> But rainbows, bluebirds, spring, babies or God
> Lift up our hearts. No doubt such rubbish sells.
> She must be feathering her inglenook.
> Genuine poets seldom coin the stuff,
> Nor do they flaunt such aptly bogus names.

But the bite is in the second verse, which tells of a hospital encounter with an epileptic in his mid-fifties:

> His dad was in the Ambulance Brigade;
> He hoped to join, but being epileptic,
> They wouldn't have him. *Naturally*, he said,

*With my disease, I'd be a handicap.*
*But I'd have liked to help.* He sucked his tea,
Then from some special inner pocket brought
A booklet muffled up in cellophane,
Unwrapped it gently, opened at a page –
Characteristic cottage garden, seen
Through chintzy casement windows. Underneath
Some cosy musing in the usual vein,
And *See*, he said, *this is what keeps me going.*

This does not excuse triteness, but truthfully makes a point about what is, for many people, one of the points of poetry: not primarily a matter of aesthetics, but something that might help as part of an effort to understand, to endure, to round experience or to square it with some notion of shape and so of justice. And we seem to have no difficulty with this, where a poem is underwritten by historical necessity, oppression or personal hardship, even when it involves the direct expression of feeling unmediated by metaphor or image. What remains essential, however, is a regard for language – not only the avoidance of cliché, but respect for exactness and an awareness of what is linguistically alive. This is not just a matter for poetry, but in poems lapses in diction, vocabulary or rhythm stand out with particular clarity.

Recently I judged a poetry competition with just short of 2,500 entries, the best of which were good enough to make the work of final selection a challenge. I kept a record of the subjects of the poems and found that, as with the Arvon competition, the most popular theme was the business of love – requited, unrequited, often viewed in its aftermath, and sometimes seen in the context of family or of elegy. Almost as plentiful were poems focusing on the seasons (autumn more than the other three), weather or landscape. The passage of time, with its corollary of human ageing, accounted for another distinct group, as did regional or dialect poems. In contrast, there were also poems of travel and place which between them went from Bosnia to Bukaru to Beijing. There were poems in praise of animals (a clear preference here for cats), as well as a deal of light and comic verse. And, though fewer in number than I had anticipated, there were poems of occasion – indeed the death of Princess Diana, the Millennium, Hale Bopp.

Formally, the entries offered a similar variety. Alongside free verse that ranged from anarchic to apoious, there were sonnets, villanelles, sestinas, blank verse, even an acrostic whose initial letters were a lament for the untimely death of the poet Frances Horovitz.

Beyond the good poems, and those which were at least crafted, lay a huge hinterland cluttered with jumbled poetic ruins, where 'myriads' leaned against 'strife', 'twas' against 'o'er', where Man and Nature, Love and War strutted their Upper Cases. Though there were also poems here which answered to Motion's description of some of the Arvon entries in having 'no shape, no rhyme, no subject', the most striking feature of many was the widespread use of full rhyme, often going along with a rhythmic beat of furious regularity. And too often these weapons were either seen as sufficient to make a poem out of stated opinion (whether outrage or affection); or deployed with a bludgeoning disregard for the mood or intention of the poem. In the worst, the rage for rhyme involved the sacrifice of natural word order and vocabulary.

What seems to open up here is a gap between the respect accorded to the idea of poetry, as *the* vehicle for conveying feeling and experience, and any readiness to learn about contemporary instances: the gap between Poetry and poems. In the National Year of Reading, perhaps there should be a determination to submit one or two fewer poems per competition (and some submissions run to ten, eleven or twelve poems), and to spend the money saved on books. Derek Mahon's *The Yellow Book*, for one: and, if you can get hold of it, his earlier *The Hunt by Night* (Oxford, 1982) with, amongst other things, 'Tractatus', his riposte to Wittgenstein's opening sentence:

> The world, though, is also so much more –
> Everything that is the case imaginatively.
> Tacitus believed mariners could *hear*
> The sun sinking into the western sea;
> And who would question that titanic roar,
> The steam rising wherever the edge may be?

To honour that evergreen imagination must always, for poets, involve a lively awareness of form and of the evolving language.

135

Or, as the epigraph from *The Unquiet Grave* which Mahon places at the beginning of *The Yellow Book* (The Gallery Press, 1977) has it, 'To live in a decadence need not make us despair; it is but one technical problem the more which a writer has to solve'.

Meanwhile, I have to report by way of postscript that the winner of the competition I judged, the complete anonymity of entries notwithstanding, turned out to be the daughter of the winner chosen last year in the same competition by Les Murray. Quite apart from the mathematical improbability of such a thing, the thought that even the muse could be accountable to the genes might deter would-be competitors from parting with their entrance fee.

# Dog-days and Definitions

In 1998 the dog-days arrived horribly punctually, with the deaths in July of Miroslav Holub and Zbigniew Herbert, and extended themselves by doleful alliteration to the end of October, when the news that Ted Hughes had died shocked a world largely in ignorance of his illness. The seeming suddenness of the event gave it an impact which was further heightened by the Laureate's last two books: *Tales from Ovid*, a runaway prize-winning success, and the book of poems about Sylvia Plath that trumped it, *Birthday Letters*. And, as became clear from the extent and warmth of tributes both public and personal, the loss was not only of a writer of tremendous range and depth, but of a man who worked tirelessly and in very many ways for the encouragement of literature and of writers. In doing so he demonstrated his own profound generosity and his commitment to the art. His absence defined sharply the scope of his achievements. It also highlighted the distinction with which he had occupied the Laureateship, not so much for the poems to which the office gave rise, but for the claims which it enabled him to make for poetry in a national context and internationally – he played on a broad stage. His Laureate poems proved once again that the best public poems are those which enable the writer to commandeer an occasion in order to write another of his own poems: the notable instance is 'A Rain Charm for the Duchy', written for the birth of Prince Harry but simply a characteristically vivid Hughes poem as well.

Inevitably, there was much speculation about who the next Laureate should be, as well as about the office itself. Perhaps there should be, for the first time, a woman poet appointed, or an Afro-Caribbean poet; perhaps the office should somehow be disestablished, or no longer a lifetime appointment; perhaps the holder should be a 'people's poet' – a phrase that seemed to have floated in from the still hovering hazy adulation of Princess

Diana rather than any genuine radicalism. And even if the Laureateship were still a credible office, was it any longer genuinely British, or merely English? The wavering fortunes of the royal family in recent years, along with the democratising spirit of the age and the pressures of nationalism, encouraged discussion of a challenge to the *status quo*.

Even as the odds on the contenders were being weighed with relish by bookies and broadsheets, the extended dog-days produced another blow. The decision by Oxford University Press to axe its contemporary poetry list appeared all the more shocking for being done behind the back of its poetry editor, and in the context of a list which was not even making a loss. Quite apart from the many and emphatic protests in newspapers and magazines, by far the most trenchant comments which I have read appeared in the *Oxford Magazine* (edited by Jim Reed, and consistently interesting). There Jon Stallworthy, under the title 'Vandalism', rehearsed the case made in the 1950s for establishing an OUP list of contemporary poetry. Three points were then accepted. Firstly, since OUP did so well from the sale of dead poets' work, 'there was a *moral* case for ploughing a little of it back into publishing the work of their successors.' Furthermore, since OUP was not a commercial publisher, financial pressure on the list would be less. Thirdly, the case of Gerard Manley Hopkins was instructive, showing that 'OUP could usefully – and, in time, profitably – publish new poetry. The first (1918) edition of his *Poems* took ten years to sell its first printing of 750 copies. By the 1950s, however, a third edition was selling many thousands and, in addition, earning a substantial permissions income. OUP had published his *Letters*, his *Notebooks and Papers*, and had commissioned a biography. A lucrative Hopkins Industry was under way.' Predictably, in the post-Thatcherite (or neo-Thatcherite?) nineties, the OUP justification of their decision (published in *The Times*, Stallworthy tells us) was a bandying of sales figures and the sorrowful conclusion that, though the list did not make a loss, 'the university expects us to operate on commercial grounds, especially in this day and age.' Stallworthy weighs in with figures of his own, and a pertinent question: '. . . even if one were to accept (as I do not) that OUP's new poetry list "just about breaks even", why should a *charity* – the OUP is not a commercial publisher – ask for more?' And he has awkward questions, too, about the way in which the Delegates of the Press arrived at the verdict, challenging them to restore their credibility by denying a report in the *Independent* 'that they were convened to rubber-stamp a decision not only taken but implemented'.

Stallworthy's attack was reinforced by David Constantine, the *Oxford Magazine*'s literary editor, in a searing piece ('And the Profit and Loss?') which pulled no punches:

In this age of Poetry on the Underground, National Poetry Day, Poets in Schools, in Libraries, in Marks & Spencer, at board meetings, in hospital waiting rooms, on railway stations, among the lawyers, among the advertisers, in the supermarket, and when everyone has a Favourite Poem and a Favourite to be the Laureate, when there are poetry societies, poetry workshops, poetry festivals, olympics, jamborees and courses and competitions throughout the land, poor OUP can't sell the stuff.

Indeed there seems to have been something in OUP's attitude to its list reminiscent of the Rhodesian premier Ian Smith's policy on African education: by failing to promote it, prove it impossible. 'In the real world,' Constantine concludes, 'the writings of those poets on that list are greatly praised. They are writers who have won many prizes, who are well known abroad, who tour and read and teach, who take the craft and responsibility of poetry seriously, who affect our lives. Whoever thought they should be dumped should think again.'

And all this took place at the time of year when, even in a usual year, poetry is at its public apogee – not only National Poetry Day, which remarkably seems to have been received into the calendar almost as naturally as Hallowe'en or the phases of the moon, but also the announcement of the Forward Prizes and the Whitbread Book of the Year shortlists. In the autumn of 1998, when both the death of Ted Hughes and the axing of the OUP list saw poetry transferred, in journalistic terms, from features to news, there were also other ways in which poetry was brought to public attention. In September the Arts Council of England produced a document with the resounding title of *The Policy for Poetry of the English Arts Funding System*. The conclusion of a process which began with the 1996 Arts Council Poetry Survey, it is prefaced

139

with a quotation (translated by Joanna Trzeciak) from the Polish Nobel Prize winner Wisława Szymborska :

> Poetry –
> but what sort of thing is poetry?
> More than one shaky answer
> has been given to this question.
> But I do not know and clutch on to it
> as to a saving banister.

The Introduction identifies three areas of support – support for the individual poet, delivery of poetry, and readership and audience development – and goes on to declare that 'poetry is at the root of every culture and yet eludes simple definition. It can be both the vocabulary of great religious expression . . . and the utterance of simple thoughts in commonplace expression. At its best it is the distillation of intellect and passion in the crucible of language.' Furthermore, 'people need poetry. In moments of national or private grief, as with the Hillsborough football disaster and the death of Diana, Princess of Wales, at times of joy and celebration, in crisis and in contemplation, poetry is most often what Wisława Szymborska calls the "saving banister" to which we clutch. Poetry is most often the natural vehicle of expression to which people turn. It can be a great unifying force for good.' When it comes to the details of the policy there is, in addition to continuing support for individual writers as well as independent presses and magazines, a strong commitment to promoting particular interests, from the representation of contemporary women poets on 'a National Curriculum which reflects, through poetry, the diversity of cultures living in this country', to translation, literature in public libraries, literacy initiatives and reading groups.

There is an idealism at work here which lies a welcome planet away from OUP (though at one point hindsight brings irony to the assertion that 'research conducted by Dr Usha Goswami and others on behalf of Oxford University Press makes the educational case for the inclusion of poetry books in early years teaching.'). At the same time, the document begs some important questions, notably in attempting to provide answers to Szymborska's question about what poetry is. Perhaps inevita-

bly, given the Arts Council's central position and its responsibility to so many different constituencies, breadth of definition wins out over depth.

The autumn of 1998 also saw the publication of two anthologies aimed at the closing century: *The Penguin Book of Poetry from
Britain and Ireland since 1945*, edited by Simon Armitage and
Robert Crawford, and *The Firebox: Poetry in Britain and Ireland after
1945* (Picador), edited by Sean O'Brien. (They will not be the only
ones: next year there will be *Scanning the Century: The Penguin
Book of the Twentieth Century in Poetry*, with Peter Forbes as editor,
and no doubt other collections too.) All anthologies compiled by
practising poets tend to a greater or lesser extent to be read as
manifestos, and these two are unlikely to be exceptions. With
their emphasis on democracy and diversity (there is a reference
inside the front cover of *The Firebox* to 'the wild polyphony of the
contemporary scene'), both anthologies seem broadly to adhere
to the principles outlined in the Arts Council Policy document.
Certainly both contribute to the discussion of what poetry is and
what might constitute poetic value – an issue considered explicitly by John Lucas, writing in *Critical Survey* (Vol. 10, No. 1, 1998),
on 'Value and Validity in Contemporary Poetry'. After a brisk
canter through some anthologies of the last forty or so years,
beginning with Robert Conquest's *New Lines* of 1956 and taking
in on the way *Mavericks* (Howard Sergeant and Dannie Abse,
1957), *The New Poetry* (Alvarez, 1962) and *The Penguin Book of
Contemporary British Poetry* (Blake Morrison and Andrew Motion,
1982), he homes in on the 1993 Bloodaxe anthology *The New
Poetry* edited by Michael Hulse, David Kennedy and David
Morley. What Lucas perceives is a gradual loss of certainty and
blurring of vision, culminating in 'the fix that the editors of *The
New Poetry* have got themselves into'. To Lucas the reasons for
this are clear:

They are keen to subscribe to prevailing theoretical orthodoxies (which means privileging that which denies the pro-
priety of privilege) while nevertheless claiming that the
poetry they champion is not merely a verbal construct but
has value beyond its literarity. This is why we can sense a
very real anxiety lurking beneath their apparent confidence:
if the new poetry is remarkable for its diversity, who is to say

what, if any of it, is any good? Can aesthetic, or moral or political or social value have any meaning in a world of poetry which is so emphatically democratic?

Harry Clifton, writing in *Poetry Review* (Autumn 1998) about the Armitage/Crawford anthology, expresses a similar view:

Multi-ethnic voices sing high and low on the social scale, all contributing to a vast Hiberno-Britannic polyphony where nothing excludes anything else. Everything is positive, everything is good. Omni-tolerance reigns, bar some dark asides about America. Which, of course, is ironic, since the basic model here is American, the horizontal spread of equality-with-difference rather than the vertical value-discriminatory code with its dangerous, or politically incorrect, notions of ethical, aesthetic or spiritual authenticity.

By the time this is printed, there will be a new Laureate (assuming the appointment is made less sluggishly than last time) and the new anthologies will have been more widely read and reviewed. No one could deny the interest of the present moment, not least the way in which national and social identities are brought into play in considering notions of art and its possible definitions. If the underlying questions, those which expose the tensions between aesthetics and democracy, are likely to remain unresolved, the gap between them may also produce lively sparks arcing across. There are supplementary questions worth asking. Is there a danger of confusing access with success, or the proliferating means by which a poet might gain attention with artistic achievement? And is there a point, artistically speaking, at which democracy becomes ochlocracy?

Sooner or later some historical contingency or shift of interest will bring into focus the next new definition of what appears important or fashionable. In the meantime, there are issues which run deeper than appearances: on the one hand, plentiful evidence of philistinism (as OUP has recently reminded us) and on the other, the attentiveness of the poet to the next poem, the ambition of the maker to match the description which Ted Hughes gives, in *Poetry in the Making*, of any successful new poem – 'the unique living reality of it in the midst of the general lifelessness'.

# Escaping the Millennium

Some of the items that lodge in the memory, and the reasons for their survival there, seem as random as the way in which some household objects outlive others. Sometimes they lie hidden until some incident or thought recalls them suddenly to consciousness: or they float to the surface for no obvious reason. Recently, for instance, I found myself thinking of an American preacher who, almost half a century ago, toured the boarding schools of England, and is still quite widely remembered. Rejoicing in the name of the Reverend Colonel Lewis O. Heck, he was armed with a confident drawl and two sermons, one about Daniel ('Daniel just laughed and laughed and laughed') and one about Samson, which began, ringingly: 'If I had a million dollars, why, I would build a monument a hundred miles long, a hundred miles wide and a hundred miles high, and I'd call it The Mighty Failure'.

The reason for the re-emergence of this memory was, of course, the Millennium Dome, which I had been reading about. The Reverend Colonel's monument might have been a prescient vision of it, or at any rate of a widely held view of it. So much has been written and said about the project that it has begun to dwarf the occasion of its building. And when it is not the Dome itself which preoccupies us, or whether the millennium occurs at the end of the year 1999 or 2000, it is the business of how to survive negotiating the threshold: a dread of malfunctioning computers, plummeting planes and rumoured food shortages, compounded by anxiety that we may fail to celebrate in the best way, or that it may all be a horrible anti-climax, as New Year's Eve already is for many. Quite apart from the paradox of celebrating time with material objects, which seems like erecting a tent of wool and iron to celebrate moths and rust, any religious significance the occasion might harbour has become as much a sideshow as the Spirit Zone is shaping to be in the Dome.

Escape may seem the only sensible course: but how and to where, given our mortal tether? Poets, as exploiters of the ability of the imagination to outgrow its housing, have mapped an assortment of routes. Often they adopt the guise of lovers, from the Shakespeare of the sonnets to, as a twentieth-century instance, the lovers in MacNeice's 'Meeting Point' of sixty years ago, the point at which, even on the brink of a world war, 'Time was away and somewhere else'. And, in the last but one verse, the poet celebrates directly the outflanking of time:

> God or whatever means the Good
> Be praised that time can stop like this,
> That what the heart has understood
> Can verify in the body's peace
> God or whatever means the Good.

But if it's an actual location you want to escape to, try Venice. Not that time has done anything to lessen the number of visitors crowding in: the Baedeker Guide for 1906 was already noting an 'enormous annual invasion of strangers', while the Lonely Planet Guide for 1996 reckons an annual total of more than 23 million tourists. Yet nowhere is the confrontation of time and beauty more exquisitely registered: and no time of year conveys this better than winter, when the city is least crowded, and when its fogs and its days of clarified light work together to brew a compelling mixture of the monumental and the phantasmagorical. Spread out on its narrow shelves, halfway up between the green waters of the lagoon and the blue of the sky, the city is almost too much to take in. Somewhere in the middle distance, the precise details of its frontages and façades blur to uncertainty, and it is hard to know whether it is the mind or the eye which has reached its limit. Even a short stay, such as mine last December, is likely to provoke a glut of unforgettable sights: rounding a corner to find, as strange and wondrous as if it had just landed, the perfect marble box of Santa Maria dei Miracoli; equally strange, the pale pyramidal monument, in the church of the Frari, that contains Canova's heart; the view across the Guidecca Canal to Palladio's church of the Redentore (closed for restoration), its outline barely to be guessed at in a morning mist diffuse with baffled sunlight; the city at night, modestly lit, almost Dickensian in the fog, with an acoustic that loads footsteps with portent; even the broad grubbiness of the Lido, with the huge hulk of the casino looming in the background, and in the foreground ugly broken concrete, remains of piers at the edge of the slackly washing Adriatic, and pigeons intent on the instant when your picnic is unwrapped.

One of the most powerful memories is of the last morning of our stay, when we went to the cemetery island of San Michele. On our way to take the ferry across, we passed the hospital of Saint John and Saint Paul. A coffin appeared just in front of us, borne awkwardly on the shoulders of two men who then handed it down into a small motor boat (in Byron's day it would have been a gondola, no doubt – itself 'Just like a coffin clapt in a canoe', as 'Beppo' has it). Reaching the walled island, we found it bright with red and yellow flowers even in mid-December, with crosses as close as in a war cemetery. The place was alive with figures stooping to tend the graves, to arrange flowers, even to polish the marble surfaces. Here and there a priest or monk offered consolation. It was a peopled threshold, Venice's answer to the Phlegraean Fields: hard, here, not to believe in the underworld, and in the continuity of life going on. The atmosphere was extraordinary: there was something in it not only of sorrow but also, aptly, of a powerful serenity and affection.

Back on the Fondamenta Nuove, we walked down a street whose small shops included one displaying beautifully produced bookplates in its window. A casual glance caught the name on one: Joseph Brodsky. Brodsky, who frequently wintered in Venice, and whose *Watermark* (Penguin, 1997) is one of the best evocations of the city at that time of the year, as well as an affectionate memoir of a past love. Fanciful, anecdotal, rapt, mildly philosophical, the book's short sections beautifully mirror the magical properties of the city, in which 'it is as though space, cognizant here more than anyplace else of its inferiority to time, answers it with the only property time doesn't possess: with beauty.' As for the winter light in Venice, 'it has the extraordinary property of enhancing your eye's power of resolution to the point of microscopic precision . . . and the consequence of this is that art becomes a way of coping with all that the eye sees but the brain cannot retain.' To Brodsky, for whom 'water is the image of time', beauty is 'a *fait accompli* by definition' and the winter light its perfect agent, whose 'particles' only ambition is to reach an object and make it, big or small, visible'. And, he concludes epigram-matically, 'an object, after all, is what makes infinity private.' Though he is well aware of the threats to the city from winter flooding, industrial pollution and agriculture, Brodsky distrusts initiatives that he sees as driven by money and vested interests, forces which he equates with 'the future'. For him, '... the idea of turning Venice into a museum is as absurd as the urge to revital-ize it with new blood. For one thing, what passes for new blood is always in the end plain old urine. And secondly, this city doesn't qualify to be a museum, being itself a work of art, the greatest masterpiece our species produced. You don't revive a painting, let alone a statue. You leave them alone, you guard against vandals – whose hordes may include yourself.' Perhaps Brodsky would have been pleased by the recent cancellation or at least postponement of the project to construct floodgates at the entrance to the lagoon, in favour of lesser, palliative methods of controlling the winter tides. Perhaps he would have joined with Ruskin and William Morris in their impassioned opposition to the incompetent restoration of St Mark's. In the end, *Watermark* reasserts the claims of beauty's presence over against the future: 'By rubbing water, this city improves time's looks, beautifies the future. That's what the role of this city in the universe is. Because the city is static while we are moving . . . Because we go and beauty stays. Because we are headed for the future, while beauty is the eternal present.' As Brodsky wrote in his poem 'Lagoon', 'Time rises from the goddess's frothy tide, / yet changes nothing but clock hand and bell'.

Yet the conflict persists: if beauty stands still against time, time still gnaws at beauty. Are they to be reconciled only in the pictur-esqueness of ruins and the partiality of memory? Often inscrip-tions on stone are eroded to illegibility in time, and finally become invisible altogether. But words can also prove more durable than stone, rather as Ruskin's exact and ecstatic descrip-tion of St Mark's (in *The Stones of Venice*) may, perhaps, outlast the architecture it records. So, for that matter, might Canaletto's pic-tures, even though Ruskin hated their arbitrary colouring and the painter's 'miserable, virtueless, heartless mechanism', which 'gives no single architectural ornament, however near, so much form as might enable us even to guess at its actual one'. Certainly the same criticism could not be levelled at Ruskin's account of the west front of St Mark's, which fully enacts Brodsky's 'micro-scopic precision' of the eye. Here is a fragment of a sentence, about three fifths of the whole:

> And round the walls of the porches there are set pillars of variegated stones, jasper and porphyry, and deep-green ser-pentine spotted with flakes of snow, and marbles, that half refuse and half yield to the sunshine, Cleopatra-like, 'their bluest veins to kiss' – the shadow, as it steals back from them, revealing line after line of azure undulation, as a receding tide leaves the waved sand; their capitals rich with inter-woven tracery, rooted knots of herbage, and drifting leaves of acanthus and vine, and mystical signs, all beginning and ending in the Cross; and above them, in the broad archivolts, a continuous chain of language and of life – angels, and the signs of heaven, and the labours of men, each in its appointed season upon the earth; and above these, another range of glittering pinnacles, mixed with white arches edged with scarlet flowers . . .

It's possible to share Ruskin's sense of giddy delight in the object of his attention while at the same time sensing that finally the very richness of the description strains at the limit of what words can do. For all that, the soaring tone, with its echo of Ezekiel as much as Revelation, conveys and recreates an exaltation that springs clear of its architectural foundation.

Something of the same springing clear is no doubt what the perpetrators of the Millennium Dome hope for. They might ponder that one of the lasting markers of the most recent turn of a century, if not of a millennium, has been a simple poem about 'an aged thrush, frail, gaunt, and small, / In blast-beruffled plume'. This bedraggled figure, in Hardy's 'The Darkling Thrush', defeats all that is piled against it – the desolation of 'the weakening eye of day', where 'tangled bine-stems scored the sky / Like strings of broken lyres', the land laid out like 'the Century's corpse', and the poet's sense that he and the world are 'fervourless'. Defiant, if not heroic, the thrush is the singer of a song that is of 'joy illimited', alerting the poet to the continuing possibility of hope. Yet while Hardy is able to identify the bird's singing as joyous, he feels excluded from it, given that the world offers 'so little cause for carolings'. But the poem, just by being there, announces a frail optimism which goes some way towards overcoming the poet's dubiety.

Perhaps one consequence of focusing on a given moment of time is an underestimate of the possibility that the best hope for hoping may lie in the base hum of time's continuum, rather than in a single high note. Poets' reaffirmations of the timeless present, and their embodiment of it in ever-changing and evolving idioms and language, may have a cumulative effect greater than the sum of the parts. Like polyps, we die upon a reef we help to make but whose final shape is, after all, still hidden by time.

# Bread and the Big Match

In translating quotations from other languages the editors of the third edition of *The Oxford Dictionary of Quotations* have, they write, striven for 'a livelier rendering than earlier versions', and their treatment of Juvenal's opinion of the citizen's concerns ['Duas tantum res anxius optat, / Panem et circenses'] seems apt for the idiom of our time: 'Only two things does he worry about or long for – bread and the big match'.

There is more to this than the snap of satire: and as our century draws to its close, escorted by prophecies and retrospects, the issue of 'entertainment' and its possible relation to any sense of value is well to the fore. In one sense the issue of entertainment confronts every poet who undertakes a reading, especially if he or she is the kind of poet whose work is suited more to the page than the stage. To choose those poems which their writer knows most likely to succeed in performance may be simply sensible: to choose only such poems may be to sell poetry short. And it is a part of the age's sense of its democratic self that poets who have come off their high horse should sometimes ride the pantomime one. We like to play it both ways: and the ability of humour to go hand in hand with pathos and despair, as well as being a truism, suits the bad conscience imposed on us by knowledge of the world's miseries. Perhaps we also categorise too glibly: thus Wendy Cope, in her introduction to *The Funny Side* (Faber, 1998), deplores the term 'light verse' which 'seems to imply that a poem can't be funny and serious (weighty) at the same time . . . In fact, much humorous writing arises from despair and misery. In this book you will find poems about being broken-hearted, about obsessive love, about dissatisfaction with a marriage or a life, and about feeling suicidal. Experience has taught me that genuinely funny poems on such subjects can be enormously helpful at some of the darkest moments of one's life.'

Traditionally, the notion of entertainment or humour in poems often involves the exploitation of full rhyme and pulsing rhythm (or plays upon expectations of rhyme and metre by thwarting them), as do three-quarters of those in *The Funny Side*: virtually all the unrhymed poems here are by contemporary poets. As Byron and Auden amongst others remind us, the tone set by form cues our expectations. And traditionally, what we expect of verse that entertains is distinct from work with loftier aims. We associate what is entertaining with agreeable amusement provided for the moment, while reserving the title of art for what we perceive as in some sense living beyond its moment. Yet what might once have been considered as adjacent rooms in the same house can now often appear as fortifications politically opposed to one another: 'entertainment' drained of the hospitality, the companionable transaction built into the word, 'art' accused of turning its back on the world.

Stephen Moss, writing about contemporary culture (in the *Guardian*, 26 February 1999), suggests that 'we value cleverness over integrity, entertainment over meaning, the means over the end, the hype over the substance. In fact, we are somewhat suspicious of substance – of, say, a fat novel that offers a non-ironic narrative.' Contrasting Sir William Haley's 1948 manifesto for the then new Third Programme ('Let it often become dull. Let it often make mistakes. Let it arouse controversy and not seek to muffle controversy. Let it set a standard . . .') with the modern 'fear of boring the audience, of encouraging it to switch to a rival', Moss argues that 'the best evidence of the dumbness of contemporary culture is the low quality of the debate about dumbing down and the rigid positions adopted by both sides.' Evoking a pre-Romantic vision of the artist integrated with society, he makes a traditional stand for the importance of art: what matters is that it should be 'true and vital, that it has something of enduring value to say.' At the same time, he admits that 'truth, at the end of our century, poses problems, however. What do we, as a society, believe?' What he goes on to describe is in fact a new assimilation of the artist, a culture in which 'earnestness, foreignness, the Haleyian "dullness" cannot be accommodated.' In this situation, 'artists become media personalities, their work cultural events; and often promotion is in the hands of agents and publicists who confuse – or encourage us to confuse – medium and message.'

The point was taken up in the same paper a few weeks later (3 April 1999) by Don Cupitt, though from a different perspective. Contrasting the relative decline of Easter with the flourishing of Christmas – a contrast of the serious business of the Resurrection with the retail trumpetings which have engulfed the Nativity – he concludes that 'post-modernity in the West is increasingly an entertainment culture. We are highly reflexive, and we like everything double-humour – parody, satire, jokes, black comedy and so on. But straight seriousness we do not like. We like feelgood religion, religion for children, but we do not want close-up contact with the grown-up stuff.'

All this suggests that considerable growths have sprouted from the ground traversed earlier in the century, for instance in MacNeice's argument with himself, in *Autumn Journal*, about the nature of culture. Though, in 1938, it seemed clear to him that 'We must do as the Romans do, cry out together / For bread and circuses; put on your togas now / For this is Roman weather', he appeared to believe that the fear of dumbing down was an unnecessary one, even if his need to state it gives it some kind of residual weight:

> It is so hard to imagine
> A world where the many would have their chance without
> A fall in the standard of intellectual living
> And nothing left that the highbrow cared about.
> Which fears must be suppressed. There is no reason for thinking
> That, if you give a chance to people to think or live,
> The arts of thought or life will suffer and become rougher
> And not return more than you could ever give.

Where MacNeice comes closest to the spirit of our own time is in spotting the aridity and the hypocrisy which can infect so-called culture:

> As it is, the so-called humane studies
> May lead to cushy jobs
> But leave the men who land them spiritually bankrupt
> Intellectual snobs,
> Not but what I am glad to have my comforts,

Better authentic mammon than a bogus god;
If it were not for Lit. Hum. I might be climbing
A ladder with a hod.

What he could not have foreseen is the way in which technology
and market forces would transform 'entertainment' into a relentless succession of claims on our attention. Recent anthologists
and critics, as well as poets themselves, have provided their own
accounts of its effects. For Peter Forbes, in his preface to *Scanning
the Century* (Viking, 1999), 'as the century ends, a trawl through
the papers and media suggests that our lives are dominated by
crime, sport, new technology, sex and a dumbed-down Hooray-
Hello! cult of celebrity-for-celebrity's sake. No doubt this is a distortion but to ignore these aspects would be to falsify the picture
. . . .' Sean O'Brien, in his afterword to a book of essays shot
through with the underlying question of what might constitute
value (*The Deregulated Muse*, Bloodaxe, 1998), asks: 'In seeking an
audience, does poetry itself risk not simply change but dilution?
The climate seems to favour poems which court popularity by
tailoring the work to the market, dealing in crowd-pleasing
effects at the expense of more serious artistry.' For him, entertainment 'is a term which can encompass – and acknowledge – only
a small fraction of the experience which poetry can offer; at the
same time, its tendency is to deny what lies outside its limits.
"Entertainment" has become the core of the culture. It is the
homogenising force which drives Radio 3 down-market and
makes television drama exclusively realist in style, while also
extruding Cilla Black and Bruce Forsyth. Its pressure can even be
felt in education, in the disguise of "relevance".' Peter Jay, in a
compelling afterword to *The Spaces of Hope* (Anvil, 1998), an
anthology celebrating thirty years of his Anvil Press, argues that
'much of the poetry that is written and published today is unfo-
cused. It is formless, despite seemingly shapely presentation,
tone-deaf in its insensitivity to rhythmic nuance, superficial in its
propensity towards disturbing subject-matter, as if unsettling the
reader were a worthwhile goal in itself. Sometimes it is driven by
self-importance and has all the moral vigour of a style advertise-
ment. But poetry is not alone in this.' And George Steiner, in his
lecture 'The Humanities – At Twilight?' (printed in *PN Review*
126), laments 'a vulgarization of culture on an unprecedented

and now ever-accelerating scale . . . the proportion of the community that, given a free, which is to say, a market-choice, between trash and quality, continues to choose the former.'

Disparate as these writers and their books are, the conclusions they reach are various but not dramatically opposed to one another. Forbes, an admirer of MacNeice who considers that his 'ability to find beauty in everyday life rather than in conventionally exalted subjects, is one of the glories of the century's poetry', judges that 'the late twentieth century got itself into a tangle about art and élitism, popular versus serious culture, tabloid values versus high art.' He suggests that 'the best popular art and the most accessible high art meet on the same ground. . . . The more arid reaches of contemporary art and the braying vulgarity of tabloid culture are distorted caricatures which feed off each other. . .'. Sean O'Brien, while conceding that 'it is not hard to see how the vast bulk of what is made available could become the exclusive sphere of what is readily and even immediately comprehensible, with the resulting identification of simplicity (and popularity) with value', homes to

a conviction which is probably not popular at present, given the confusion of homogeneity with democracy. It is the conviction that art has something to offer the audience – enlightenment, a sense of wonder, a clarification of feeling, an extension to the map of experience – of which the audience is not already in complete possession. The distinction between Art and entertainment is to be sought in this area. Our concern or lack of concern with that distinction will govern our cultural health, not only in the microcosm of poetry but far beyond it.

Peter Jay also insists on that distinction: 'If poetry is to be more than another entertainment, another branch of the performing arts competing for attention with the whole array of arts-related leisure activities which our culture deems to be necessary, it must assert itself positively and stand firm on its particular ground . . . The qualities that have always contributed to good poetry will continue to do so. Imagination is unprescribable and unquantifiable. The moral quality of honesty is still relevant and it is concomitant with the quality of accuracy or precision which informs good poetry: the right words in the right order. And poets should reject too easy alliances with anything.' Even George Steiner glimpses a glimmer of hope, though he locates it in a world not unlike that of the exiles in Ray Bradbury's *Fahrenheit 451*: 'Very possibly, and in some measure of analogy with the so-called Dark Ages, clusters of men and women, maddened by the erosion of privacy, by the systematic annihilations of silence and space for thought that, today, seek us out, may turn to the almost forgotten arts of serious reading, of commitment to personal memory, of collaborative critical enquiry, which are the essential means of *litterae humaniores*. Word of mouth, word of heart may resound in shared privacies of rediscovery.'

Both Forbes and Steiner write interestingly about science in relation to the arts: Forbes pointing out that 'for writers like Primo Levi and Miroslav Holub . . . science provides a value system because it is the one domain immune from human sentiment', Steiner arguing that 'only some "ingestion" (Ben Jonson's hungry word) of the sciences and of elements of mathematics into the fabric of the humanities will restore to these the self-respect, the celebration of difficulty now lacking.' I am not entirely convinced by either of these statements. Can poetry ever relate profoundly to a value system immune from human sentiment? And is *all* contemporary poetry lacking in the richness of difficulty? Still, it is good to be reminded of the possibilities of the sciences, at a time when children fortunate enough to have them are said to be bored by the company of their bedroom computers; and when my computer's spellcheck suggests that 'litterae humaniores' ought to be 'lottery homeowners'.

Amongst contemporary poets, it is perhaps Tony Harrison more than anyone who has explored the ground between entertainment and art, not only in its political and class dimensions, but in his quest for a language that is sufficiently direct to speak to a wide audience, notably in his film and theatre work. In a March edition of *The South Bank Show* centred on his first feature film, 'Prometheus' (out this year), he repeated his view that 'art has to measure up to the worst things that have happened in the century', and his hope that his acquired eloquence could be more publicly directed: towards people like his own parents. Standing at Delphi, he recalled the strength and integration of Greek culture, in which 'the poets were central to the whole ability of the culture to understand itself': a culture which he sees as one 'of art and literature and sport that's before the catastrophe of Christianity'. And the polygonal wall at Delphi becomes a metaphor for his search 'for words that lock themselves together in the face of the seismic events of the 20$^{th}$ century.' In the furtherance of his aims, Harrison mobilises accessible, deep-rooted poetic forms, rhymes and rhythms and sets out to commandeer the medium of film and television. Yet his tone is far from that of an entertainer: often elegiac, a tolling tone that often takes on the pressures of the worst, as he says poetry should. And the bases of his own work are complex and personal as well as political, however true it may be, as he says, that much of it 'has come out of a retrospective aggro against RP [Received Pronunciation]'. Above all, Harrison writes with a seriousness and a fierce passion that finally outrun irony. Under all its devices (which may include ironies of the most bitter kind), his work is predicated on the basic human ideals of community, of home, of language, ghostly positives that emerge from the negatives of power: optatives to challenge the often dire imperatives of history.

As Harrison's formal skills may help to remind us, entertainment and art have in common the need to get and keep the hearer's or reader's attention, to engage the imagination and to be memorable. Or, to go back to Peter Jay and his afterword to *The Spaces of Hope*, 'Poetry is not poetry until it is absorbed, it is not what you read but what you re-read . . . Poetry – one might say art in general – is nothing if it does not bring the reader to thoughtfulness.' And this in turn may point to a crucial deprivation, as we tumble into the next century: the lack, for too many people, of any chance to slow down, to savour the human voice and its complexities in stillness, as well as thrilling to the roar of the big match.

# Buzz Words

One of my favourite pictures in the National Gallery was painted some time around 1470 by an unknown artist in Swabia, in oil on silver fir. It shows a woman about whom we know only what the inscription at the top left of the picture tells us: that she was a 'geborne hoferin', born into the Hofer family. The calm expression of her pale, smooth features as she looks into the distance, and the beginnings of a slight smile, add to the tease of anonymity. So, even more, do the meticulous details which give the picture its individuality – the great billow of her ruched headdress with its fine pinning and needlework, and its train which falls to the right shoulder, then leads across the front of the sitter's dark dress to disappear over her left shoulder; the precise rendering of the clasps on her dress, and of the zig-zag thread or lace fastening the collar at her throat; her right hand, with two rings on the little finger, across her heart; her left holding a sprig of forget-me-not delicately between forefinger and thumb. And there, towards the top of the coif, invisible to the woman but clear in every detail to the viewer, poses a single fly, casting the slightest of shadows. It is tempting to consider the fly as a reminder of mortality, as the text on the wall by the picture suggests it could be, though there is also the possibility that it might just be the artist showing off, even a *trompe l'œil* designed to fool the spectator into thinking that the fly might have alighted on the surface of the picture. James Hall, in his *Dictionary of Subjects & Symbols in Art* (John Murray, 1979) suggests that flies or bluebottles to be found in paintings of the period 'seem to have been without symbolic meaning since the subject matter of paintings on which it appears is widely varied, though usually religious. The painted fly is serving as a protective talisman against the real insects which otherwise might settle and leave their dirt marks on the brushwork of a sacred theme.'

I was reminded of this picture on seeing in Krakow, earlier this year, the main square's market stalls with quantities of amber for sale, the more expensive pieces with insects caught in them as if bubbled in barley sugar. And I already had flies in my bonnet, as I was on my way back from a visit to Ukraine for the British Council which had included really interesting discussions with university students of several poems considering suffering and our reactions to it, among them Miroslav Holub's well known 'The Fly' (the others, also much appreciated, were Auden's 'Musée des Beaux Arts' and Douglas Dunn's 'I Am a Cameraman'). Holub's fly's-eye view of the battle of Crécy was hugely enjoyed for its witty playing off of the life cycle of the fly against historical details, and of anonymous violence against rank and title (can it possibly matter that it was 'during the four-teenth charge of the French cavalry' that the fly mated, or that its mate was 'a brown-eyed male fly from Vadincourt'? Or that the blue tongue on which the fly alighted belonged to the Duke of Clervaux?). The human slaughter is here reduced to rather tedious background activity ('the shouts, / the gasps, / the groans, / the trampling and the tumbling'), so that the perspec-tive established is not unlike those moments in Voltaire's stories when he takes a cosmological view of the earth, to consider whether the plight of men really impinges on the consciousness of God any more than would rats drowning in a king's ship on the mood of the king himself. But in Holub's poem the parallels of the fly's life cycle and, here, human violence, are not just incon-gruously juxtaposed: like Aesop's fly, which thought itself responsible for raising all the dust as it sat on a chariot axle, Holub's has its near-human illusions, sitting at one point 'on a disembowelled horse / meditating / on the immortality of flies', only to be rewarded with a come-uppance in the final verse:

> And thus it was
> that she was eaten by a swift
> fleeing
> from the fires of Estrées.

That use of 'thus' seems very Voltairean, though perhaps the association most likely to be made is with Lear – not just 'as flies to wanton boys, are we to the Gods', but Lear's linking of human and insect behaviour: 'The woman goes to it, and the small gilded fly / Does lecher in my sight. / Let copulation thrive . . .'.

Once the mind has settled on literary flies they soon begin to swarm, as befits a species whose lord, Beelzebub, features in writers as widely dispersed as Milton, Sartre and Golding. Sometimes it's just the distracting or interrupting noise of them, rather less appealing than Keats's sensuous evocation of 'the murmurous haunt of flies on summer eves.' As Donne explained in his sermon at the funeral of Sir William Collayne in 1626: 'I throw myself down in my Chamber, and I call in, and invite God, and his angels thither, and when they are there, I neglect God and his angels, for the noise of a fly, for the rattling of a coach, for the whining of a door'. For Emily Dickinson (in No. 465 of *The Complete Poems*, Faber 1970) it can even be a sound apprehended at the same moment as that of death. It breaches the room's stillness, which 'Was like the Stillness in the Air – / Between the Heaves of Storm', just when the poet has 'willed my Keepsakes', as if cued by this reminder of mortality and material things:

> – and then it was
> There interposed a Fly
>
> With Blue – uncertain stumbling Buzz –
> Between the light – and me –
> And then the Windows failed – and then
> I could not see to see –

Here the blur of sound ('uncertain, stumbling') is brilliantly carried over to the loss of sight and the memorable image of the windows themselves failing: the fly's interference leading to the failure of both the organs and objects of sight. Blocking the light, it has become almost the agent of death, its little instigator.

Eighteenth-century flies seem frequently to be sipping things, an activity which quickly leads to moralising comparisons of one kind or another. Thus Macheath in *The Beggar's Opera*, finding himself in chains in Newgate, and left by the warder Lockit to his 'private meditations', has no trouble in rhyming entomology and Eros:

The Fly that sips Treacle is lost in the Sweets,
So he that tastes Woman, Woman, Woman,
He that tastes Woman, Ruin meets.

And William Oldys, in his anacreontic 'On a Fly drinking out of his Cup', welcomes the beast as a companion, finding little difference, in the perspectives of eternity, between the fly's life cycle and his own ('Thine's a summer, mine's no more, / Though repeated to threescore'). In John Wolcot's poem of 1792, 'To a Fly, Taken out of a Bowl of Punch', the affinity is obvious, for 'Thus 'tis with mortals, as it is with flies, / For ever hankering after Pleasure's cup', a theme developed over the following forty-one lines with their light castigation of human imprudence, impulsiveness and greed. But the fly, retrieved by Wolcot, succeeds in sobering up and finally makes good its escape, leaving the poet to imagine it the wiser for its brush with death. Charmed by his own conceit, he exhorts the lucky insect to be content in future with buns and sugar, harmless in comparison to punch, 'the grinning merry imp of sin', which 'Invites th' unwary wand'rer to a kiss, / Smiles in his face, as though he meant him bliss, / Then, like an alligator, drags him in.'

Perhaps the most literary of sipping flies is the one which alighted on Walter de la Mare's manuscript one evening and 'At the wet ink sedately sipped, / Then seemed to put the matter by', though as the poem's title 'Unwitting' suggests, here the emphasis is on the difference between the watching writer and the unawareness of the fly. The fly finds itself locked into a small poem of ten lines, yet whose last two lines imply, even if less intensely than is the case in Emily Dickinson's poem, that the insect's appearance has somehow affected the atmosphere: 'Silence; and wavering candlelight; / Night; and a starless sky.' It is as if the fly has replaced the manuscript the poet was working on, its minute distraction summoning an alternative poem. And that silence might even trigger an echo of a Yeatsian sub-species, the minds of Caesar, Helen and Michael Angelo, that each 'Like a long-legged fly upon the stream / . . . moves upon silence.'

Finally, though, it is the conjunction of flies with decay and death which produces the most powerful images. These can make us shudder with revulsion, by bringing together the helpless flesh and the insects' crawling presence: often they seem to make mention of the human eye, as with the flies on the face of the idiot in Sartre's *Les Mouches*, 'Elles sont douze sur son œil comme sur une tartine', or as in the Holub poem, where the fly

> . . . began to lay her eggs
> on the single eye
> of Johann Uhr,
> the Royal Armourer.

Something of the same helpless disgust pervades another well-known poem about a battle and its aftermath, Keith Douglas's 'Vergissmeinnicht', in which the body of a German soldier lies alongside 'the dishonoured picture of his girl / who has put: *Steffi. Vergissmeinnicht* / in a copybook gothic script.' But here, though the soldier's enemies see him as defeated, even 'mocked at by his own equipment / that's hard and good when he's decayed', the tone and feeling are quite different from the Holub poem, the remorselessness mitigated by the poet's imagining of how differently the soldier's girl would view the scene:

> But she would weep to see today
> how on his skin the swart flies move;
> the dust upon the paper eye
> and the burst stomach like a cave.

Another forget-me-not: another German woman. And suddenly here it is again, that picture in the National Gallery of the 'geborne hoferin': the calm expression of her pale, smooth features as she looks into the distance, and towards the top of the coif, a single fly casting the slightest of shadows.

# Robinson Crucial

A participant in a writing course approached the tutor with an anxious query. Following work on a poem, it turned out that there was 'this bit of lyricism left over', and the question was whether the tutor might have any idea how use could be made of it. This rather enchanting concern, as of someone left with an end of roll remnant from a bolt of one of Yeats's heavenly cloths, suggests a real interest in the economies of creative production, as well as a real ignorance of its processes. It could have been tempting, though probably not much help, to remind the questioner of what Auden wrote about art in 'New Year Letter':

> . . . it presents
> Already lived experience
> Through a convention that creates
> Autonomous completed states.

One of Auden's own notes on these lines quotes the preface to *The Spoils of Poynton*, and seems to approve Henry James's view that what distinguishes the writer is, essentially, the ability to spot the 'germ', 'the precious particle' of a story which, encountered in real life and recognised by the imagination, is all that is needed for the artist to elevate and fashion it into something of value.

Definitions of art and its processes have recently become hot issues, particularly in the context of education, with the publication of *All Our Futures: Creativity, Culture and Education*, the report of the National Advisory Committee on Creative and Cultural Education chaired by Professor Ken Robinson. On the cover, an entranced girl contemplates a globe spinning at sufficient speed to blur any divisions or boundaries (or is it another planet, a brave new world?). One hand, turned down, rests easily on the base of the globe: the other, palm upward, suggests a readiness to receive. The world indeed seems all before her, where to choose. Behind and above her, like oncoming weather, float eight words of varying size, luminosity and prominence: *creativity, curiosity, motivation, self-esteem, culture, identity, imagination* and *adaptability*. Intending readers should not, however, be put off by the massing words, nor by the bulkiness of the report itself, which runs to over 170 pages. There is much here worth pondering.

Central to the report's philosophy is the conviction, stated at the outset in the Introduction and Summary, that 'creativity is possible in all areas of human activity, including the arts, sciences, at work at play [*sic*] and in all other areas of daily life. All people have creative abilities and we all have them differently.' But it is also made clear that 'creativity is not simply a matter of letting go. Serious creative achievement relies on knowledge, control of materials and command of ideas. Creative education involves a balance between teaching knowledge and skills, and encouraging innovation.' (Here and elsewhere you sense the need to reinvent the term in a way which distinguishes it from perceptions of the 1960s, as well as a genuine quest for a balanced view.) Many contributors to the inquiry 'believe that current priorities and pressures in education inhibit the creative abilities of young people and of those who teach them. There is a particular concern about the place and status of the arts and humanities.' The supply of teachers, their training and an overloaded curriculum are all seen as further areas of concern, while a strong pitch is made for working partnerships between schools and organisations outside the school system.

One of the report's real strengths and, you'd think, also one of its most potent political selling points, is the closeness of the link it perceives between creative education and cultural education. The authors' broad view of what is creative is signalled early on by quotations from Tony Blair ('A successful creative economy is one of the Government's priorities, and a key source of jobs of the future'), Chris Smith ('Creativity in its widest sense is at the heart of much of what we in this country are good at. It is the foundation of a new generation of high-tech, high-skills industries') and John Wybrew, Executive Director, Corporate Affairs, British Gas: 'The business world is in a turbulent process of change from the old world of steady-state mass production to one of constant innovation and the pursuit of creativity in all forms and on a global scale.'

The report goes on to dedicate an entire section to the meaning of creative education. 'The word "creativity",' it is suggested, 'is used in different ways, in different contexts. It has an "elusive definition".' (A note at the back relating to this tells that 'Calvin Taylor and associates have traced "some 50 or 60 definitions" of creativity'). A delicate path is then traced between three distinct definitions: Sectoral ('Many people associate creativity primarily with the arts . . . but creativity is not unique to the arts'); Elite ('The élite conception of creativity is important because it focuses attention on creative achievements which are of historic originality . . . These achievements constitute the highest levels of creativity'); and Democratic (a definition 'which recognises the potential for creative achievement in all fields of human activity; and the capacity for such achievements in the many and not the few'). The elusive quarry is apparently run to earth with a definition of creativity as 'imaginative activity fashioned so as to produce outcomes that are both original and of value.' But this involves further pursuit, of course, of what might be meant by 'value', defined then as 'of value in relation to the task at hand . . . There are many possible judgements according to the area of activity . . . The criteria of value vary according to the field of activity in question.' This may avoid criticising a top hat for not being a bowler, but hardly constitutes any real value system beyond that suggested by the great catch-all stop-all word of our time, 'appropriate'.

Another approach to the question of value comes in the section on 'Cultural Education'. Here the opposition of high art and popular culture is seen as false, while two values in particular are noted as underpinning many others to form the core of our national life: 'The first is a commitment to the unique value and central importance of the individual . . . A second touchstone of our national culture is the idea of contingency: the view that things might be different from how they seem or are currently believed to be.' The rest of this section goes on to discuss the processes of creativity, as well as the nature of intelligence, and does so convincingly, emphasising 'the mutual dependence of freedom and control at the heart of the creative process.'

But can creativity be taught? The Introduction claims just that, though the inverted commas placed there round the word 'taught' seem to express uneasiness. Given its terms of reference, the report inevitably focuses more on the needs of pupils than of teachers, though it does see that 'teachers cannot develop the creative abilities of their pupils if their own creative abilities are suppressed.' And the detailed recommendations include one that 'school plans for staff development should include specific provision to improve teachers' expertise in creative and cultural education', while another proposes 'a national programme of advanced in-service training for artists, scientists and other creative professionals to work in partnership with formal and informal education'. Yet can in-service training entirely meet the needs of the case? Whether as teachers or pupils, it is surely true that people's creativity can only really, fully be explored when the kinds of pressures so often built in to the education system – exams, league tables, accreditation – are not present. And the demands of the system create a busyness, a sheer lack of time which militate against any such relaxation or creative playfulness. Moreover, while it may be true that more artists are eager to contribute to the community than is sometimes thought, the desire in some quarters for accredited artists and quality assurance runs the risk of smothering the imaginative spark, indeed the risk-taking, which is fundamental to what artists have to offer. And from 'accredited artists' to politically approved artists seems a dangerously small distance. There is another important point here. Artists who go into schools know that the success of their visits depends at least in part on the confidence of the staff concerned: and this often has to do with the teachers' own experience and knowledge of the art in question (this is not, though, to deny the responsibility of the artist to be properly aware of the school environment). Yet the impossibility, for many teachers, of any opportunity to explore their own creativity under favourable circumstances is a real deprivation not only for them but, ultimately, for their pupils. To make provision for this (difficult, but not impossible) would also go some way towards showing teachers more of the respect that is all too often denied them, and so improve their morale.

How can it be done? Robinson has practical suggestions to make – not only greater flexibility in the revised National Curriculum and schools making their own decisions about creative education, but the possibility of redefining the school day and year – and these absolutely straightforward measures might turn out to be as important as the underlying philosophy. It remains to be seen how much notice will be taken of the report by the politicians, and to what extent resources will be made available to fund and develop its proposals. It would be shameful if the challenges Robinson and his committee have put forward were to be ground down in the fine mills of politics or by the education system itself: a report which sees the centrality of the imagination as crucial not only to any worthwhile education system but for society at large deserves better. Even so, to go back to 'New Year Letter', 'How hard to stretch imagination / To live according to our station' – lines for which Auden provides, by way of a note, an extract from a letter written by Chekhov to his brother Nicolay: 'You have only one defect. Your false position, your sorrow, your catarrh of the bowels are all due to it. That is your extraordinary lack of education.'

2000

# The Joyfulst Day

It may have been less common through the ages than the elegy, the epitaph, the eclogue or the epigram, but the epithalamion has certainly had and held its place among poetic occasions. The tendency of poets to see weddings as opportunities for praise, and to commission themselves accordingly, seems an entirely sympathetic one, even without allowing for the chance it offers to outflank yard-long wedding lists despatched by department stores. And given the new freedoms about where and how marriages may be celebrated, you might even expect a new flowering of poems to meet the circumstances. Nowadays a civil ceremony may be held almost anywhere. Licensed premises (*sic*) range from hotels and stately homes to moored boats and football grounds. As Kate Gordon's *A Practical Guide to Alternative Weddings* (Constable, 1998) makes clear, 'the only stipulation for obtaining a licence for premises is that they must be fixed (i.e. not mobile), open to the public, suitably solemn and indoors'. In Scotland, as no doubt befits our devolved state, the law is different: there it is the celebrant who must be approved, not the place. North of the border, presumably anywhere to which a consenting official can be lured is acceptable, whether a balloon in mid-flight or a waterfall in full uproar.

Yet, to return to England and Wales, it is not quite as simple as you might think. Given that the ceremony is wafer thin – a life-long commitment articulated in the briefest of events, so that even the word 'ceremony' seems somewhat overblown – it is not surprising that many people try to make something more of it. Often they think in terms of poems, as an enrichment. But not only must the premises be approved for a civil marriage, so must any poems read at the ceremony. And when it comes to deciding what may be read, the situation seems hardly clearer than the Church of England's muddled thinking over the remarriage of divorcees in church.

At first sight the rules appear simple to the point of ruthless-ness. The law does not permit the inclusion in the ceremony of any readings or music with religious connotations, even of the flimsiest kind. Inadmissible, therefore, is anything from the Bible, much of the obvious musical repertoire and any text, whether spoken or sung, which makes mention of God, salvation or any-thing at all which might be associated with religion. The think-ing, so I was told by one registrar, is that if you want God, you have a church wedding: if you choose a civil wedding, you do without. This must have been the case for some time, but the issue seems to have become more prominent with the present tendency towards tailor-made marriage ceremonies. Whatever the rationale, the situation hardly seems ideal. To quote from Kate Constable's book again, the insistence on God's absence 'seems extremely unfair and bureaucratic, since it can have no bearing on the actual legality of the ceremony'. It may be just one measure of the distance between marriage as a sacrament and the fancy dress of a themed wedding.

It gets worse. As an inevitable consequence of this ruling, texts to be read have to be perused and approved by the superintend-ing registrar. One registrar to whom I spoke even referred to 'pro-scribed texts', and a young couple planning a civil wedding told me that they had heard of an extract from *Howard's End* being vetoed, though they couldn't give chapter and paragraph: I'm still intrigued by this. A call to the office of the Registrar General in Stockport was hardly more illuminating. Ultimately, I was told, the decision is that of the local superintendent registrar, though the General Registry could arbitrate in case of disagree-ment. And some religious words could be uttered, if used in a non-religious sense. When I asked for an example, after some consternation 'heaven' was offered as an instance: presumably, it was acceptable to be in the seventh (provided, of course, that you don't make the association with 'seventy times seven'). And I was reminded that the same rule applied to any faith, not just Christianity. Everyone I spoke to was very helpful, but nothing erased the impression of muddle and, worse, a kind of censor-ship. I asked about unfortunate Church of England divorcees, potentially caught between an institution that refuses to remarry them in church and a legal system which won't allow God among the guests: but the only answer I got was that once the registrar had left the premises people could do, say or read anything they liked. This conjures an image of the registrar not at the centre of things but, rather, in the peripheral role of the notaries who tend to appear briefly in the final act of Molière plays. Or it absurdly suggests the possibility of disappearing behind the bike sheds for a quick outburst of religious language while the registrar isn't looking. There must also be occasions when the local registrar, caught between a couple's earnest wish for a reading from, say, *The Prophet* (a popular choice, but forbidden) and the ruling, finds him- or herself unhappily adding to the quotient of stress endemic to wedding arrangements.

Since it is a matter of a match, I thought it might be interesting to see how a team of eleven epithalamions would fare under the present rules. The most obvious first selection, the epithalamion Edmund Spenser wrote to celebrate 'the joyfulst day that ever sunne did see' of his second marriage, seems to have a built-in defence in the form of the poet's declared intention of singing 'unto myselfe alone'. At first all seems well: the garland-bearing nymphs would surely pass muster, likewise the descanting Mavis and warbling Ruddock, but the 'merry Larke' that 'hir mattins sings aloft' might be in jeopardy, as would be 'Joves sweet paradice of Day and Night'. The picture of the bride 'clad all in white' would need curtailing, since 'So well it her beseemes, that ye would weene / Some angell she had beene', while some of the details of 'all her body like a pallace fayre' might well offend the registrar's sense of solemnity. But even without the joyful description of the wedding night and the hope for a fruitful outcome and future blessings, a decisive dismissal would result from mention of 'the temple gates', 'the Almighties view' and angels singing their alleluias while the bride is in church. Perhaps George Chapman's short 'Bridal Song' would be more acceptable, especially since the poem is couched in terms of a secular, almost proto-Baudelairean, conflict in which 'Love calls to war: Sighs his alarms, / Lips his swords are, / The field his arms' : but it would be done down by 'sheaves of sacred fire' and references to 'our nuptial grace'. Another 'Bridal Song', said in my copy to be by Shakespeare or possibly Fletcher, looks to be perfectly safe, composing a wedding bouquet of assorted flowers, but before long a blighting heavenly body supervenes:

All dear Nature's children sweet
Lie 'fore bride and bridegroom's feet,
   Blessing their sense!
Not an angel of the air,
Bird melodious or bird fair,
   Be absent hence!

Can Donne save the side? Very nearly, but each of his epithalamions lapses at some point into religious references: one would be sunk by a reference to the ark, another by mention of 'the Church Triumphant', while in a third, the 'Epithalamion made at Lincolnes Inne', the final stanza's joyous conflation of the sacrificial and the sensual would certainly be out of order. Even Wordsworth does no better, in terms of team selection: the sonnet written in 1812 for the marriage of his brother-in-law, Thomas Hutchinson, to Mary Monkhouse, has 'angels of love' cruising in its third line.

Perhaps the moderns can help. After all, Dannie Abse's collected poems *White Coat, Purple Coat* (Hutchinson, 1989) has 'Epithalamion' as the second item in the book – a fine singing poem it is, too, but would the registrar run the risk of the reference in the fourth verse to 'you blackbird priests in the field'? Then there is Auden's 'Epithalamium', written for Peter Mudford and Rita Auden, the younger of his nieces, in May 1965. This would have the registrar scurrying for the dictionary or, better still, John Fuller's *W. H. Auden: A Commentary* (Faber, 1998) for clarification about, for instance, 'Jealousy's / teratoid phantasms', or 'with civic spear and distaff / we hail a gangrel / Paleocene pseudo-rat'. But sadly, at the point where '[We] answer the One for Whom all / enantiomorphs / are super-posable', those Upper Cases would probably disqualify the poem anyway. What about Ted Hughes? 'Bride and Groom Lie Hidden for Three Days', from *Cave Birds*, sounds promising and might actually make it through the maze, assuming that no exception is taken to the couple being 'like two gods of mud'. On the other hand, the poem's gristly mechanics of mutual creation (for example, 'He has assembled her spine, he cleaned each piece carefully / And sets them in perfect order' or, later, 'She gives him his teeth, tying their roots to the centrepin of his body') might not be the most obvious choice for the occasion. Patric Dickinson has an epithalamion, but a start with a biblical echo might be sufficient to count it out: 'Each gives: the giving sometimes / Makes the receiving seem / A lesser thing. . . .'. As for C. Day Lewis, 'A Marriage Song' written for his friends Albert and Barbara Gelpi invokes the natural world to enhance 'bright weather / Of inward blessedness' and 'carol our hopes for them', phrases which might provoke a call for the third umpire. Across the water, Richard Wilbur's elegant 'A Wedding Toast', written for his son and new daughter-in-law, isn't even borderline, predicated as it is on St John's account of the wedding at Cana. The fact is that there is not, amongst these eleven poems, one which would be a sure-fire inclusion at a civil ceremony. The only hope might be to have recourse to Scotland again, in the person of Douglas Dunn, in whose 'Wedding', though '. . . no shrubbery / Or abundance of green / Hallows this couple', poverty is outflanked and 'delight / Overlaps all things': though even here 'hallows' would have to be nodded through.

And now another question nags. Is the epithalamiast always or predominantly a male creature? How is it that none of the epithalamions I came across are the work of women? Perhaps convention was against them in the past: perhaps in the present they are too wise to buy into what looks like a niche market, only for poets prepared to become bureaucrat's bards.

# Dealing with Disaster

On 12 October last year, exactly a week after the Paddington rail crash, Andrew Motion's poem about the accident, 'Cost of Life', was printed in some, though not all, editions of the *Guardian*. Two days later, in the same paper, Catherine Bennett compared the poem with McGonagall's 'The Tay Bridge Disaster' , commenting that 'neither poet shrinks from describing the impact of the crash', and taking the Laureate to task on more than one count: 'Even supposing that this horribly recent event is proper material for instant poetry, Motion seemed to have nothing in particular to say about it, other than to urge his readers to imagine (had anyone in this country not done so already?) the agony of the victims.' Three days after this the *Observer*, the *Guardian*'s Sunday sister, carried a leader headed 'People's Poetry', commending Motion for his poems for the TUC Conference and on the Paddington crash. These were, the leader declared, 'well-judged – and, more importantly, popular. They may strike some in the intelligentsia as mawkish, but the mainstream reader finds them comprehensible and enjoyable'.

There are some interesting issues here, beyond the immediate ones of how any reader might find a poem about a lethal rail crash 'enjoyable', or how anyone could know, five days after a poem's first publication, that it was popular. We are constantly alerted to disasters both man-made and natural. The extent to which a poet will take them into account in his or her work must obviously vary with temperament and purpose, though it would require a fairly hermetic existence to be completely unaware of such things. How, if at all, is the poet to deal with them? In the case of Andrew Motion's Paddington poem, Catherine Bennett suggests that he has fallen short in two ways: by publishing his poem too soon after the event, and by having nothing much to say about it anyway. The first point seems a fair one: even if there is no guarantee that longer deliberation always results in a better poem, there is something indecorous about the appearance of the poem in the immediate wake of the accident. However good the poet's intentions, the reader may be left feeling uneasily that misfortune has been too readily appropriated.

Bennett's second criticism, that of not having much to say, looks rather less straightforward, but is also more interesting in its implications. All disaster poems, though tethered to a particular moment, have questions of chance, justification, justice, belief hovering about them: and even a poem which limited itself entirely to describing the detail and circumstance of a disaster would still be likely to raise such issues in the reader's mind. But what, exactly, does Andrew Motion's poem say, and what is its intention? Fair judgement is, it must be admitted, almost put in jeopardy by the muddled layout of the poem as it appeared in the *Guardian*, not to mention several misprints and an unfortunate confusion of the author's name with that of the biographer of a late princess (whose death in an accident was the subject of one of Motion's pre-Laureate poems). Nor is the poem necessarily much helped by the injunction to 'imagine', repeated eight times, and presumably a topical nod in the direction of John Lennon's 'Imagine', voted the nation's favourite pop lyric in the same week as the Paddington accident.

Written in rhyming or near-rhyming couplets (though these break up towards the end of the poem), 'Cost of Life' has in common with many other disaster poems an opening which evokes the time before the accident – almost a time of innocence, for writer and reader, though informed by hindsight. In this case the initial setting is a country station seen at the autumn dawn, a kind of sequel to Adlestrop in its pastoral view, with 'cattle still in their yards, fields lush and empty', and an atmosphere not really dispelled by the realistic details of 'that man there with a Kleenex-snippet stuck / on his shaving cut, this woman here with a fleck / of lipstick on a front tooth . . .'. The poem then describes the packed commuter train approaching the city (producing either consciously or unconsciously on the way reminders of another poem about a train heading for London: Motion's London with 'its slate-acres hammered out like lead' calls to mind 'London spread out in the sun, / Its postal districts packed like squares of wheat' in 'The Whitsun Weddings', and when the train nears the city Larkin's 'walls of blackened moss / Came close . . .' finds an echo in Motion: '. . . the brick terraces crushing closer, their black walls / swirling graffiti, damp dribbles . . .'). It is not until half-way through the poem that the moment of impact is reached: a moment that is extended considerably, a clever embodiment of the tendency for such experiences to stretch time, as victims often testify. Motion evokes tellingly a scene 'where furious quick dust-storms smear a dry dew- / fall on what survives of tables, chairs, head-rests', though it could be argued that some of the details can't help sounding too obviously poetic, at least when read in the close aftermath of the accident: 'the pop of strong wood giving way, the thin fly- / away whip of cables snapping, the reedy phone / still weeping in the ash-mess hiding human bone.' The poem ends with the idea of silence working its way back up the line as a mist, wisps of it dispersing variously. It doesn't make for a strong ending, but evaporation may be the right conclusion for a poem which ends with the numbness of someone who stares 'like everyone alone will stare / and see no more than featureless and wasted air'. Even if it has no philosophical point to make, the poem conveys sympathetically, with its mixture of lyrical airiness, realistic detail and odd moments of clumsiness, the terrifying effect of the crash on 'daily lives doing no more than their best / to stay daily, and continue by daily laws'.

Sympathy wasn't lacking in the author of 'The Tay Bridge Disaster', either, though he was such a connoisseur of catastrophes that the expression of it became somewhat formulaic. Even more than trains, he liked ships, whose passengers would, typically, set off 'on a very beautiful day' and, commendably sensing the need for a rhymed couplet, also 'with spirits light and gay', before coming to grief. Usually the disaster is followed by an evocation of the human suffering involved and, more often than not, by a conclusion briskly wishing the souls of the victims well. McGonagall's poems gather a whole fleet of maritime disasters, including the *Stella*, the *Storm Queen*, the *Dundee*, the *Lynton*, the *Columbine*, the *Forfarshire*, the *London*: boat after boat foundering in the rough swell of his verse, to be bottled in couplets. Water wasn't his only medium: he wasn't averse to the occasional fire, whether in a hairdresser's at Scarborough, the People's Variety Theatre in Aberdeen, 9 Dixie Street, London, or the theatre at Exeter. But, to revert to his most famous poem, it is precisely the poet's inability to match the enormity of the Tay Bridge disaster with anything more than unintentionally humorous bathos, dire rhymes and hiccoughing line-lengths which has guaranteed the poem's survival. Here the inappropriate and the incongruous are memorable catastrophes of their own, ensuring that the poem, like the event it commemorates, 'will be remember'd for a very long time'. It is the only disaster poem I can think of which might, as a rule-proving exception, meet the terms of the *Observer* leader by being 'enjoyable'.

I had forgotten, until re-reading it, the references in the poem to supernatural forces, 'the Demon of the air' and 'the Storm Fiend'. Such powers become central in another poem about the Tay Bridge disaster, Theodor Fontane's 'Die Brück' am Tay'. Fontane visited Britain on three occasions, and his poems also include a short descriptive piece about the Goodwin Sands, as well as a disaster poem set in America, about a heroic helmsman, John Maynard, who stayed at his post aboard a burning lake steamer, thus saving the lives of his passengers but losing his own. In Fontane's Tay Bridge poem, the account of the accident is sandwiched between dialogue involving the three witches from *Macbeth*, who are obviously still at large north of the border and meet again here to wreak further destruction. The collapse of the bridge is told as a ballad focusing on the return home for Christmas of Johnie (*sic*), a passenger on the train. His father, the bridge-keeper, peers out into the night, reassures his wife and tells her to light the Christmas tree candles in anticipation of Johnie's arrival: but to no avail. 'Tand, Tand, / Ist das Gebilde von Menschenhand', chorus the witches before and after doing their worst ('Trash, trash, / Is anything that humans fashion.') The idiom here, reminiscent of Goethe's 'Erlkönig', may be quaint, but it does provide a structured rationale, and a context within which to consider the brute fact of human suffering.

The same is true in a different way of Hardy's 'Convergence of the Twain', whose philosophical, abstracted title at once puts distance between the writer and the event. This impression is heightened by the bracketed sub-title (*Lines on the loss of the 'Titanic'*) and the Roman numerals which separate each of the poem's eleven triplets from one another, and confirmed by the wrought structure and syntax of the triplets themselves, with their final lines

twice the length of the two preceding ones. Such sense of deliberation is in tune with the poem's presiding force, that of 'The
Immanent Will that stirs and urges everything', and the conflict
between human achievement ('the Pride of Life that planned
her') and the ultimate authority of 'the Spinner of the Years': an
apt reminder, indeed, of the struggle of the Titans with the gods.
But this mythical plane in no way inhibits a powerful evocation
of the wreck itself, as observed by the 'Dim moon-eyed fishes'
(stanza five) or colonised, two stanzas earlier, by another creature:

> Over the mirrors meant
> To glass the opulent
> The sea-worm crawls – grotesque, slimed, dumb, indifferent.

The idea of the iceberg ('A Shape of Ice') developing as a dark
*alter ego* to the ship under construction, so that they are 'twin
halves of one august event' in the making, provides as clear a
framework as the witches in Fontane's Tay Bridge poem, while
similarly steering clear of any complex teleological questions.

One end of a scale measuring the slant of disaster poems to the
incidents which trigger them might be represented by another
famous shipwreck, that of the *Deutschland*. Here, too, there is a
clue right at the outset, with Hopkins's dedication of the poem
'To the *happy* memory of five Franciscan Nuns . . . drowned
between midnight and morning of Dec. 7th, 1875' (my italics).
And the shipwreck itself is not so much contained between the
hymn of praise to God of the poem's first part, and the triumphal
invocations at the poem's conclusion, as entirely subsumed by
the poet's affirmation of faith which not only annexes the disaster but recasts it as a rich hosanna. Here, despite the onslaught of
'the widow-making unchilding unfathering deeps', the divine
soars above everything:

> in thy sight
> Storm flakes were scroll-leaved flowers, lily showers – sweet
> heaven was astrew in them.

What makes this such an astonishing poem is its sheer energy
and the high-tension possibilities that Hopkins discovers for

structure and language: they become in themselves a storm which magnificently dramatises the fury of the sea, while at the same time dissolving it in 'a mercy that outrides / The all of water, an ark / For the listener'. It is hard to think of any other disaster poem which succeeds in describing the circumstances of a disaster so startlingly, even as it commandeers it for the poet's own beliefs.

Almost at the other end of the scale stands a poem like Larkin's 'The Explosion', the final poem in *High Windows*. Here the instant of a pit explosion is embedded in a calm, seemingly casual account of everyday routine and early morning pleasures such as chasing rabbits or the chance discovery of a nest of lark's eggs. As in many disaster poems there is a prelude, and we reach the mid-point of the poem before, briefly:

> At noon, there came a tremor; cows
> Stopped chewing for a second; sun,
> Scarfed as in a heat-haze, dimmed.

Yet even this muffled report leads to a little epiphany well short of apotheosis but which, as so often with Larkin, mitigates the bleakness: a haunting of hope. This is conveyed in a second, more defined explosive instant, with the vision of the miners' wives, in which the men seen earlier as 'Coughing oath-edged talk and pipe-smoke' are transformed:

> . . . and for a second
> Wives saw men of the explosion
>
> Larger than in life they managed –
> Gold as on a coin, or walking
> Somehow from the sun towards them,
>
> One showing the eggs unbroken.

Here the fragile eggs with their promise of incipient life, though unhatched, become emblems of hope, however uncertain the vision ('Somehow') or transitory ('for a second'). If the mist which evaporates at the end of Andrew Motion's Paddington poem seems less hopeful than this, it may just reflect the difficulty, for many, of finding a context of belief to counterbalance mischance and disaster. The worst of these may all too easily call to mind Voltaire's depiction of men and their planet, in his poem about the Lisbon earthquake of 1755, as tormented atoms stranded on a pile of mud: 'Atomes tourmentés sur cet amas de boue'.

# Goldberg Variations

Goldberg, one of the two bullying interlopers in Pinter's *The Birthday Party*, demands of the wretched Stanley, whose birthday it is: 'Is the number 846 possible or necessary?', then dismisses his own suggested answers (first, 'Neither': then 'Both') with an exhilarating piece of philosophical obfuscation: 'It's only necessarily necessary! We admit possibility only after we grant necessity. It is possible because necessary but by no means necessary through possibility. The possibility can only be assumed after the proof of necessity.' In a different but similarly playful vein Charles Simic, writing in *PN Review 131*, wittily characterises the poet through the ages as Proteus, in one way or another always able to give the slip to officialdom and even death. There may be, he suggests, any number of idioms for what is done in the name of poetry, from protest to praise, passion to politics, pilgrimage to philology.

This is not just a matter for the critics and biographers. Most writers have at some point faced the challenge of the possible and the necessary: the need for a personal definition of the art of the possible, and an answer to the wartime postcard which asked, with an implied accusation, 'Is your journey really necessary?' You don't have to be a disciple of Malrow to know that all artistic endeavour is in a practical sense superstructural, predicated more often than not on the assumption of at least a garret in which to starve. Yet there are sufficient well-known examples (and not only Romantic ones) to show that writing can articulate an imperative by no means confined to recording the history of the tribe or to purifying its language, and circumstances which can elicit a response as stubbornly ineluctable as Luther's speech at Worms ('Hier stehe ich. Ich kann nicht anders') or Beethoven's epigraph to his F Major string quartet ('Muss es sein? Es muss sein.') The same is true of the writer's relations with the world. If on the one hand we have Goethe's Tasso declaring that seclusion is the necessary condition for developing a talent (and along with it Emerson's retort: 'Talent alone cannot make a writer. There must be a man behind the book'), on the other hand we have such instances as the challenge issued to Akhmatova by the woman in the prison queue in Leningrad, or the fate of Mandelstam.

Even where necessity is not defined by historical imperatives, it still often forms part of the writer's dialogue with him- or herself. In Clive Wilmer's Radio 3 interviews with poets, for instance (collected in *Poets Talking*, Carcanet, 1994), a number of the writers bring the subject to the surface. Michael Longley asserts: 'I write poetry because of an inner compulsion. Deep down I believe it's very important, but I think I'm rather shy about saying how important I think it is, not just for me but as an important way for humanity to redeem itself.' James Fenton, with his quick riposte to the possible identification of some of his work as 'jeux d'esprit' ('There is an element of the game in poetry, there is certainly an element of the spirit in poetry') offers a timely reminder of the claim which playfulness may stake in the whole enterprise: and Ted Hughes, in the final piece in the book, conveys a powerful idiom of personal necessity, seeing art as a manifestation at the psychological level of 'our constant struggle to pull ourselves together and to deal with difficulty and with injury and with illness and with threats and fears.' Again, to read a book like *Anthony Hecht in conversation with Philip Hoy* (Between The Lines, 1999: one of an excellent series of wide-ranging interviews with poets) is to be made aware of the way in which a life has in the living enacted the epicentral position of poetry, an experiential proof of its necessity.

One element conspicuously absent from most contemporary views of poetic necessity is the kind of loftiness displayed by Eliot in his 1932–33 Norton Lectures, where it is deployed to ring-fence the whole business of writing and secure it against what he perceives as democratic dilution. Remarking in the opening lecture that 'the part of society to which Dryden's work, and that of the Restoration comedians, could immediately appeal constituted something like an intellectual aristocracy', he proceeds without hesitation to the universal, asserting that 'when the poet finds himself in an age in which there is no intellectual aristocracy, when power is in the hands of a class so democratised that whilst still a class it represents itself to be the whole nation; when the only alternatives seem to be to talk to a coterie or to soliloquise, the difficulties of the poet and the necessity of criticism become greater.' In one of the later lectures, 'The Modern Mind', the reason for transferring this sense of necessity to the critic becomes clear: 'I should say that the poet is tormented primarily by the need to write a poem – and so, I regret to find, are a legion of people who are not poets: so that the line between "need" to write and "desire" to write is by no means easy to draw.' And the concluding lecture, with its well-known comment that 'poetry is not a career, but a mug's game', though it insists on the variety of poetry and its ability to 'make people see the world afresh, or some new part of it', ends by looking not out but in: 'It [poetry] may make us from time to time a little more aware of the deeper, unnamed feelings which form the substratum of our being, to which we rarely penetrate; for our lives are mostly a constant evasion of ourselves, and an evasion of the visible and sensible world.'

The inward focus of this final comment carries a strong echo of Rilke, and in particular of his ten *Letters to a Young Poet* (the recipient was Franz Xaver Kappus), all but one written in 1903 and 1904 but not published until 1929, a date equidistant from Rilke's death and Eliot's American lectures. Even allowing for the gap between Rilke's time and our own, not to mention the very particular circumstances of his life and the patronage he enjoyed, these letters still make fascinating reading. The material world, Rilke suggests in the opening letter, is more cryptic and less open to ready articulation than is generally assumed: 'Most events are unsayable, and occur in a space whose threshold no word has ever crossed, and more unsayable than any are works of art, mysterious existences whose life, alongside our transitory one, persists.' For the young poet, the initial response must be self-examination, a questioning of what is seen as a serious and absolute calling:

This above all else: ask yourself in your deepest night hour: *must* I write? Dig deep down into yourself in search of an answer. And if this should come in the affirmative, if you are permitted to respond to this serious question with a resonant and direct 'I *must*', then lead your life according to this necessity: your life down to its most trivial and insignificant moment must become emblem and evidence of this urge.

Again and again Rilke emphasises the qualities required in the quest for artistic truth – humility, attentiveness, patience and, above all, an acceptance of loneliness ('. . . Rilke, whom die Dinge bless, / The Santa Claus of loneliness' is one of the judges of Auden's tribunal of poets in the first part of *New Year Letter*). This willed apartness is to include a shunning of literary criticism and aesthetics, seen as 'either factional views set in stone and bereft of sense in their lifeless petrification, or else clever word games, in which today one view prevails and tomorrow the opposite. Works of art are limitless in their loneliness and accessible to nothing less than to criticism.' In the final letter, written more than four years after the others, Rilke is still keen to put criticism in its place, referring to 'the unreal half-artistic professions which, while they feign a closeness to art, effectively deny and attack the existence of all art, as does more or less all journalism and almost all criticism and three-quarters of what is called literature or claims its name.'

Irony is similarly suspect: a concentration on serious things will result either in its falling away, or its adoption as another tool for serious work. For Rilke the mission of the artist (and his outlook lends itself readily to religious terms of reference) involves the suffering locked up in patience: 'to be an artist means: not to calculate and count; to mature like the tree, which does not pressurise its sap and stands confidently in the spring storms without worrying that no summer might follow them. Come it will. But it will come only to those who are patient . . .' And this is especially so for the young artist, whose lack of experience leaves him with no answers to the questions he asks.

There is a nostalgic side to Rilke's view that the isolation of the artist can reproduce that of childhood 'when the adults went round embroiled with things that seemed important and grown-up because the grown-ups appeared so busy and because none of their conduct made any sense to you.' In the absence of common ground between the artist and those around him, the natural world is still at hand as directly as for the child, he argues: 'the nights are still there and the winds that traverse the trees and many lands; in the world of objects and animals all is still activity in which you may participate; and children are still as you were when a child, just as sad and happy, – and to think of your childhood is to live among them again, amongst the lonely children, and the grown-ups are nothing, and their dignity has no value.'

Over against this summoning of the child we might set Rilke's admiration for Cézanne, expressed in letters dating from 1907 which give a picture of a stubborn, enraged old man who 'sits in the garden like an old dog, the dog of this work that is calling him again and that beats him and lets him starve', and whose still-lifes are 'wonderfully preoccupied with themselves'. What both the old man and the child appear resistant to (and again the religious pattern asserts itself) are the temptations of the world, the flesh and the devil. If the devil in *Letters to a Young Poet* is the critic or the journalist, the world is all that has conspired to debase the physical and the sensuous elements of creation, so that it is perceived as fragmented and dispersed rather than as composed of interconnected components. Even the simple act of eating, Rilke suggests, has been made into something else: 'deprivation on the one hand, abundance on the other have clouded the clarity of this basic need, and a similar blurring has affected all the deep, simple bare necessities by which life renews itself.'

If this strikes a note still topical, so even more does Rilke's view of love and the role of women. In this realm, too, the young poet must expect more questions than answers: true love, like poetry, demands a long apprenticeship of loneliness and gradual maturing. All too often, since young people are unready for such demands, love falters and fails, taking refuge in social conventions and lacking any prospect of real growth. Yet if we have the courage to take on the challenges of love 'as a burden and an apprenticeship, instead of losing our way in the whole facile and foolish game, in which men have taken refuge from all that is most seriously serious in their existence – then a degree of progress and alleviation might be perceptible to those who come long after us: that would be no mean thing.' Above all, Rilke foresees a time when men and women might find true equality in their attitudes to one another, seeking each other out 'not as objects . . . but as brother and sister and neighbours and getting together as human beings, in order to bear in common, with simplicity, gravity and patience the burden of gender that is imposed upon them.' He goes further, suggesting that after a transitional phase in which women might imitate the ways of men, they will one day come into their own and be the highest expression of human love.

Finally, it is perhaps their insistence on patience which gives Rilke's letters their relevance, even to poets of a post-heroic age – at any rate to those who, by temperament or circumstance, find that there are no easy or immediate returns on their impulsion to write. Rilke's own life, whatever its privileges, demanded perseverance enough, as Auden recalled in one of his 'Sonnets from China':

> Tonight in China let me think of one
>
> Who for ten years of drought and silence waited,
> Until in Muzot all his being spoke,
> And everything was given once for all.

That triumphant resolution may momentarily obscure what the *Letters to a Young Poet* make very clear – that poetry itself is Protean and that, in some instances at least, its claims can extend well beyond the literary or the merely fashionable. Goldberg, in *The Birthday Party*, may first have made his speech about the Necessary and the Possible in Bayswater, but it was at the Ethical Hall.

# The Muse Militant

At the time of writing, in mid-March and with the budget yet to come, the subject of education has dominated the headlines for several weeks. Issue after issue has mushroomed into prominence, including the resignation of super-heads appointed to save failing schools; government proposals to lengthen the school day; the amendment or repeal of Section 28; changes to A Levels; the future of grammar schools; the creation of special academies in problem areas; and performance-related pay for teachers. Meanwhile, a *Guardian* poll showed that some 200,000 teachers, worn down by workload, stress and bureaucracy, were said to be seeking retirement or other employment. The poll's findings were greeted by a blocking defensive stroke from a spokesman for the Department for Education and Employment ('Our reform of teachers' pay and proposals for their professional development will transform teaching and make it more attractive than ever'), while union leaders warned that the government would ignore them at its peril. Some pundits thought there should be less government interference, others that there should be more, not fewer, government initiatives: and a renewed focus on the disparities between private and state education helped to keep the flames of debate merrily leaping.

Amid all this, at the end of February the *Times Educational Supplement* ran a piece under the bold headline LAUREATE CALLS UP THE TROOPS FOR POETRY WAR. The article announced that 'an army of poets is to be sent into teacher-training colleges', in a project which was 'the result of relentless lobbying by Andrew Motion, the Poet Laureate . . . [who] has said he is troubled by children's lack of interest in poetry and pledged to make promoting verse in schools a priority.' The distinguishing feature of the plan was that 'previous projects have taken poets into the classroom, but this initiative aims to reach more children by enthusing teachers'. Furthermore, 'the initiative, to be run by the Poetry Society and funded with £83,000 from the Department for Education and Employment, will include a website with advice on how to bring poetry to life as well as offering teachers in-service training'. This seems a very worthwhile scheme, not least because it addresses the needs of teachers: needs which have been too often depicted almost as if they were opposed to the interests of children. Teachers find themselves at the confluence of every pressure – lack of parental support, underfunding, deprivation, curriculum changes, bureaucratic oppressiveness: they deserve all the support they can get. The Laureate's campaign might even, with luck, turn out to be a stepping-stone on the way to showing teachers greater respect, and to a better understanding among planners and bureaucrats of the benefits for students of making room for teachers' own autonomous creativity. But the wording of the *Times Educational Supplement* headline is instructive: its martial idiom seems only too appropriate for the confrontational character of much of the current debate. It has an almost Arnoldian ring to it, like a battlecry for the republic of letters superseding the hymns of the church militant. Or is it really an acknowledgement of the fact that poetry is always likely to find itself in conflict with any system of rules and regulations, other than those of its own making?

At this point it is the face of Robin Williams which looms up, relaxed and smiling, in his portrayal of a teacher of literature, John Keating, in Peter Weir's 1989 film *Dead Poets Society*. Keating arrives as a replacement for 'our beloved Mr Portis' at a highly traditional American boarding school whose iron conformity rests proudly on 'the four pillars' of 'tradition, honor, discipline, excellence'. Keating, an old boy of the school and so ideally placed for subversion, enters the classroom for the first time in his new guise whistling the *1812 Overture*, and is soon cheerfully instructing his pupils to 'Seize the day, boys – make your lives extraordinary': more specifically, to open their text books and rip out page 21 of Dr J. Evans Pritchard's introduction, *Understanding Poetry*, then all the others. (Pritchard's critical method involves a graph which purports to measure the success of a poem, with one axis for 'technical perfection', the other for 'importance'). There is an interesting hesitation on the boys' part before they assault the authority of the printed word, but with no suggestion that this is due to any historical awareness of how sinister the destruction of books can be, rather than just the tenacity of conformism and the difficulty of daring. Keating has no doubts about the enterprise he is embarked on: 'This is a battle, a war, and the casualties could be your hearts and souls . . . You will learn to think for yourselves again, you will learn to savour words and language'. His great ally is Whitman, first conjured by his somewhat immodest suggestion that his pupils might address him as 'O captain, my captain', and the word 'yawp' which he writes excitedly in bold capitals on the board. The belief that he wants to impart is the answer which Whitman offers, in 'O Me! O Life!', to the question raised by life's perpetual injustices and struggles: 'That you are here – that life exists and identity, / That the powerful play goes on, and you may / contribute a verse.'

In some ways the film's approach is facile, generating an atmosphere which crosses a hot adolescent flush with mildly Orphic rituals. As so often with portrayals of schools, the stereotypes prevail: the rigid conformists versus the Romantic rebels, the middle-aged versus the young. The same could be said to an extent of other films about school life, such as Vigo's *Zéro de Conduite* or the film which owes something to it, Lindsay Anderson's *If . . .*, with its altogether more knowing take on boarding school and sex. There the only possible ending is revolution, but one that itself seeks refuge from despair in the surreal. In *Dead Poets Society*, by contrast, the rebels remain clean-living American boys, their innocence hardly compromised by falling giddily in love with a drum majorette, or by the occasional cigarette. *If . . .* ends with the headmaster being shot through the head: the final sequence of *Dead Poets Society* has the boys merely repeating the homage of a gesture of freedom taught them by Keating, standing on their desks as he leaves in disgrace. Above all, Keating never seems really pressurised (the real pressure is on his pupils), whether happily supervising a football match while the soundtrack swells with the *Ode to Joy* from Beethoven's Ninth, or encouraging one of his charges, Neil Perry, to defy his intolerant father's veto and pursue his desire to act (this time it's the slow movement of the 'Emperor' Concerto in the background). Anderson's school rebels turn the guns on the oppressors: here Neil chooses suicide (with his father's pistol) in preference to conformity. But the school's demand for obedience is only partly to blame: the inflexible disapproving father (another stereotype) is also culpable.

A few other writers are called in evidence, rather predictably, with Frost's untaken road and Thoreau's lives of quiet desperation, but again and again it is Whitman to whom Keating returns. However well this may serve the purposes of the film, it represents a somewhat lopsided view of the poet. While it is true that much of his work is combative, predicated on abiding memories and images of the Civil War, he repeatedly subsumes conflict by enclosing it in the broadest possible embrace, as in 'Song of Myself', where conflation begins on an earthly plane ('With music strong I come, / with my cornets and my drums, / I play not marches for accepted victors only, I play marches / for conquer'd and slain persons') but finally assumes overtly cosmic proportions:

> Before I was born out of my mother generations guided me,
> My embryo has never been torpid, nothing could overlay it.
>
> For it the nebula cohered to an orb,
> The long slow strata piled to rest it on,
> Vast vegetables gave it sustenance,
> Monstrous sauroids transported it in their mouths and
>     deposited it with care.

And while the poet celebrates the 'latent right of insurrection! O / quenchless, indispensable fire!' ( 'Still though the One I sing') and, most obviously in 'Song of the Open Road', his readiness to meet any challenge ('My call is the call of battle, I nourish active rebellion, / He going with me must go well arm'd'), elsewhere it is this same sense of inclusiveness which prevails. It is as if, faced with the clamour of misfortune, Whitman seeks to drown it out with the kind of indiscriminate relish suggested by 'Each moment and whatever happens thrills me with joy' ('Song of Myself') or declarations like the one in 'I Sing the Body Electric': 'All is a procession, / The universe is a procession with measured and perfect motion'. One of the most direct expressions of this attitude is 'On the Beach at Night Alone', which appeared as 'Clef Poem' in the second edition of *Leaves of Grass* (1856) and was revised for the fourth edition of 1867, the year of Arnold's 'Dover

Beach'. Convinced that 'A vast similitude interlocks all', the poet recites a litany of inclusion that begins with 'All spheres, grown, ungrown, small, large, suns, moons, planets' and culminates in 'All lives and deaths, all of the past, present, future'. He concludes: 'This vast similitude spans them, and always has spann'd, / And shall forever span them and compactly hold and enclose them.' This has, almost, a lawyer's anxiety about the possibility of some loophole being left: the price of opting for inclusiveness. Like much of Whitman, it could also be seen as the noisiest imaginable version of quietism.

If, for films such as *Dead Poets Society*, the revolutionary aspects of Whitman have the greatest potential, in educational terms it is the prefaces to *Leaves of Grass* which might still resonate, whether the 1855 Preface, ('take off your hat to nothing known or unknown or to any man or number of men, go freely with powerful uneducated persons and with the young and with the mothers of families, read these leaves in the open air every season of every year of your life, re-examine all you have been told at school or church or in any book . . .'); or that of 1876, which he wrote after illness, and wanted to be seen as a preface to all his work. Here he declares that

> a man is not greatest as victor in war, nor inventor or explorer, nor even in science, or in his intellectual or artistic capacity, or exemplar in some vast benevolence. To the highest Democratic view, man is most acceptable in living well the average, practical life and lot which happens to him as ordinary farmer, sea-farer, mechanic, clerk, laborer, or driver . . . and especially where and when, (greatest of all, and nobler than the proudest mere genius or magnate in any field), he fully realizes the Conscience, the Spiritual, the divine faculty, cultivated well, exemplified in all his deeds and words, through life, uncompromising to the end – a flight loftier than any of Homer's or Shakspere's – broader than all poems and bibles – namely, Nature's own, and in the midst of it, Yourself, your own Identity, body and soul.

This may not be as pithy or practical as what Milton wrote over three hundred years earlier in 'Of Education' ('I call therefore a complete and generous education that which fits a man to perform justly, skilfully and magnanimously all the offices both private and public of peace and war'), but it does connect with some of our current dilemmas. These, to come back to the news highlights of recent weeks, are well put in an article by A. C. Grayling in the *Guardian* (11 March 2000) which suggests that, in contrast to Aristotle's view that 'we educate ourselves so that we can make use of our noble leisure', 'the contemporary view distorts the purpose of schooling, by aiming not at the development of individuals as ends in themselves, but as instruments in the economic process.' Going on to make a distinction between education and training, Grayling writes:

> Above all, education involves refining capacities for judgment and evaluation; Heraclitus remarked that learning is only a means to an end, which is understanding – and understanding is the ultimate value in education. . . . But a school can only educate as well as train if the circumstances for doing so are right . . . In the case of so-called 'sink' schools in problem areas, part of the solution is surely . . . to do the opposite of congregating children together during school hours; it is to have many smaller units with high staff-to-pupil ratios, where children can be treated and taught as individuals, and given an opportunity to experience the kind of intellectual space needed for assimilating what is learned, and connecting it with the wider educational experience.

It would be hard of think of a better practical argument for the importance of including not just poetry but the arts in general more fully in educational planning and thinking. In this context, Andrew Motion's proposal could be a valuable tactic. On a strategic plane, it offers real potential for the General Teaching Council chaired by David Puttnam to play its part. On any level, it is likely to involve some tough campaigning.

# The P-word

I once found myself stranded, along with my fellow passengers, in a snowbound train north of Birmingham, during an over-ambitious journey aiming at Edinburgh. An eerie atmosphere settled upon us, in which the unwrapping of a sandwich would have been a major acoustic event. Despite the occasional hushed remark, the general silence became intent: not a drum, not a cellular phone. It represented the stoicism of people resigned to nothing going on happening. What finally broke it was not an official announcement, but one by a passenger who must have been asked a question. 'I am,' he declared with some pride, 'One of Britain's forty remaining glass eye makers'. You could feel the air clench: and even more when he went on to say that, before technology enabled an improvement in materials, the old glass eyes would sometimes explode if subjected to sudden changes of temperature, and you would have to go down to the chemist's and choose a new one from a tray. Looking out at the snow, it was hard not to conjure a vision, so to speak, of popping eyeballs. Everyone in the carriage seemed to be concentrating on the middle distance.

The same embarrassment might have been produced by substituting 'poet' for 'glass eye maker' (and what should be substituted for 'forty'?). To claim the title of 'poet' is not only, often, to kill a conversation stone dead, but is actually considered improper by many poets, as I was reminded when reading Louise Glück's highly enjoyable collection of essays, *Proofs and Theories* (first published by the Ecco Press, and by Carcanet in 1999). She makes the point clearly in the opening essay, 'Education of the Poet': 'I use the word "writer" deliberately. "Poet" must be used cautiously; it names an aspiration, not an occupation. In other words: not a noun for a passport.' Robert Graves, for one, would have agreed with her: in *Goodbye to All That* (notwithstanding the blurb of the Penguin Modern Classics edition loftily announcing that 'his principal calling is poetry') he reveals that for him, when it came to passports, even 'writer' was best avoided. 'In my passport I am down as "University Professor". That was a convenience for 1926, when I first took out a passport. I thought of putting "Writer", but passport officials often have complicated reactions to the word. "University Professor" wins a simple reaction: dull respect. No questions asked. So also with "army captain (pensioned list)".' As for 'poet', to Graves it was 'a praise word', allowable when used by others, but impermissible for any poet worth the name to apply to himself or herself. A similar and characteristically forthright repudiation is to be found in Edwin Brock's autobiography, *Here. Now. Always.* (Secker & Warburg, 1977): 'It occurred to me after I'd published several books that I could call myself a poet. But I dismissed this idea – I'd hate to be the kind of shit who gives himself a title like that'. But when outed by the *Daily Express* as a policeman who also wrote poetry, he did acknowledge that if he had been only one without the other he would hardly have been considered newsworthy.

Such disavowals have a long pedigree, and consort with Keats's view of the poet as having no identity, because he is forever 'filling some other body', as they do with the modesty which seems to shadow pride in the same poet's famous comment, 'I think I shall be among the English Poets after my death'. But the situation is not always so simple, or so simply explained. If, as Glück asserts, 'the poetic vocation is felt to be dramatic, glamorous', how is it that it can also be, in a wide social context, impossible to mention without apparent unease for speaker and listener? Is it partly because of the difference Glück notes (in 'The Idea of Courage') between oppressive societies where poets can be defined by the circumstance of opposition (though this has dangers of its own), while 'the free society, the society that neither restricts speech nor values it, ennervates (*sic*) by presenting too few obstacles'? Or is it a measure of the self-consciousness which, in the aftermath of Romanticism, still seems to make of the poet a being apart? It's an apartness which poets themselves have not always discouraged. As Randall Jarrell noted in *Poetry and The Age* (1953), 'We are accustomed to think of the poet, when we think of him at all, as someone Apart; yet was there – as so many poets and readers of poetry seem to think – *was* there in the Garden of Eden, along with Adam and Eve and the animals, a Poet . . .?' Or consider David Gascoyne's somewhat uneasy answer, for 'an enquiry' published nearly twenty years earlier in *New Verse 11*, to the question – 'As a poet what distinguishes you, do you think, from an ordinary man?':

> I believe that the poet is distinguished from the 'ordinary man' by his attitude towards experience. This attitude, as far as I am concerned, is one of continual expectancy, which may at times become a state of hyperæsthesia. At the same time I am very doubtful as to whether the 'ordinary man' exists at all. Everyone probably has some sort of attitude towards experience, though perhaps neither so constant nor so consciously developed as that of the poet. (Reprinted in *Selected Prose 1934–1996*, Enitharmon, 1998.)

Of course the statement 'I am a poet' may be unacceptable not just because of the afflatus it suggests, or a shamanistic residue clinging to it. Very precisely it conceals the implication it carries, and which perhaps accounts in part for the non-response it elicits. 'I am a poet': that is, 'I am a recognised/successful poet'. In the ensuing silence hovers the question, 'Says *who*? Who has granted this status?' It implies a sense of accepted value no longer perceived as generally available. And questions which might validate or simply socially follow this assertion seem harder than those attending the other arts. For instance, 'I am a painter', once any possible ambiguity involving decoration has been cleared, isn't a statement that people seem to find as daunting. ('Oh really? What do you paint – landscapes? Abstracts? And in what medium – watercolours? Acrylic?') In the case of a poet, the same kinds of questions sound inescapably trite ('What do you write about? Do you use a word processor? A sharp pencil? Rhyme? Have you had anything published?'). I wonder how much this is to do with having only words with which to confront someone who has claimed them as his or her particular currency. At all events, to take refuge in the word 'writer' seems little better than a delaying tactic, given that the follow-up is likely to be 'What kind of writing?', and so to lead back to 'poetry'. There may be another distinction: at least a painter, like a novelist, could conceivably make a living from what he or she does, and so is spared causing a further embarrassment, the suspicion born of the work ethic that being a poet isn't a proper job anyway. Enter the shade of Blake, sitting in his print shop at 27 Broad Street waiting for customers, and getting on with his own work at night.

How much has any of this to do with the natural isolation of the poet in an age of what Montale called 'mass solitude', a time which he pinpointed (in *Poet in Our Time*, Marion Boyars, 1976) as the change from *homo faber* to *homo destruens*? Glück writes convincingly of the insulation of the writer during 'active composition' – from the world, from self, from the past. And, post-composition, from the work composed. For her, writing is not only 'an act, or condition, of ecstatic detachment' but also 'a revenge on circumstance' that allows 'control of the past', and she concludes: 'No process I can name so completely defeats the authority of event.' Yet she also records ('The Dreamer and the Watcher') the need that she has felt for her own writing to connect with the world:

> What had to be cultivated, beyond a necessary neutrality, was the willingness to be identified with others. Not with the single other, the elect, but with a human community. My wish was to be special. But the representative life I wanted to record had somehow to be lived.

Elsewhere her essays provide sharp reminders of how difficult this might be, given the dominant roles the times have assigned to polarisation, confession, competition. 'We live in an age of dogma: this encourages readers to mistake representation for advocacy' ('On Hugh Seidman'); '. . . dark truth has become unnervingly popular, a literary convention which seems oddly incompatible with its experiential precursors: anguish, isolation and shame' ('The Forbidden'); and, from 'Introduction to The Best American Poetry 1993', 'Hierarchy dissolves passionate fellowship into bitter watchfulness'. (This last comment is an example, by the way, of Glück's concisely expressed wit, a feature of these essays. On the whole she admirably avoids the weakness of the epigram, its tendency to draw attention to itself rather than the idea it encapsulates. Two of my favourites are her neat observation that 'the function of an ideal is to compel, in our behavior, its approximation' ('Disinterestedness'), and her summary, in

'Education of the Poet', of her own situation in mid-adolescence:
'I had great resources of will and no self').

On balance, though, Glück locates the uncertainty of the contemporary artist as much in the artist's love of truth as in society.
Since 'there is, unfortunately, no test for truth' there is also 'no
possible security. The artist, alternating between anxiety and
fierce conviction, must depend on the latter to compensate for the
sacrifice of the sure' ('Against Sincerity'). That mention of anxiety
brings to mind another book from America which also has much
to say about the contemporary poet's situation, Harold Bloom's
*The Anxiety of Influence*, first published in 1973 (Second Edition,
Oxford University Press, 1997). For Bloom the poet of today is
very much a latecomer who, measuring himself against the past,
is in danger of seeming sadly diminished. He traces a Viconian
view of poets as prophets, and of the first poets as 'the anthropo-
logical equivalents of wizards, medicine men, shamans, whose
vocation is survival and teaching others to survive.' In this perspective, 'we need to begin again in realizing for how long and
how profoundly art has been menaced by greater art, and how
late our own poets have come in the story.' Developing an argument of considerable subtlety which he himself summarises
towards the end of the book, he suggests that:

> the covert subject of most poetry for the last three centuries
> has been the anxiety of influence, each poet's fear that no
> proper work remains for him to perform . . . Did the anxiety
> of style change also even as the anxiety of influence began?
> Was the burden of individuating a style, now intolerable for
> all new poets, so massive a burden before the anxiety of
> influence developed? When we open a first volume of verse
> these days, we listen to hear a distinctive voice, if we can,
> and if the voice is not already somewhat differentiated from
> its precursors and its fellows, then we tend to stop listening,
> no matter what the voice is attempting to *say*.

In so far as this situation can be remedied at all, Bloom sees every
poet's (and critic's) struggle and challenge as a necessary
skewing and distortion of his precursors, with the strongest poets
able ultimately to absorb them, new work claiming the old like
bindweed running up a hedge, and making of the past a shape all

its own. This contest with the dead exacts its price, however, in the form of a solipsistic narrowing on the part of the poet, 'a sacrifice of some part of himself whose absence will individuate him more, as a poet.' Yet there can be no avoidance of the issue: 'The precursors flood us, and our imaginations can die by drowning in them, but no imaginative life is possible if such inundation is wholly evaded.'

And what of the future? Part of an antidote to despair, a way of grappling with the burdens of self-consciousness and the past, might be what Louise Glück characterises in her final essay as 'an intensity of awareness'. This, she suggests, 'is impoverishment's aftermath, and blessing: what succeeds temporary darkness, what succeeds the void or the desert, is not the primary gift of the world but the essential secondary gift of knowledge, a sense of the significance of the original gift . . .'. Grounded in her own experience, this viewpoint aims beyond it. It also sits well with Randall Jarrell's modest assertion that 'if poets write poems and readers read them, each as best they can – if they try to live not as soldiers or voters or intellectuals or economic men, but as human beings – they are doing all that can be done.' Yet wariness of the P-word remains: and that such a simple notion – a word to describe the maker of a made thing – retains the power to describe gaps, as well as sometimes to bridge them, ought to reassure us that there are still plenty of bracing challenges.

# Informing Silences

At the start of the second week in November last year I found myself in a late fifteenth-century underground passage beneath Exeter's High Street. The atmosphere was a little dank but, surprisingly, not very cold. The darkness was complete and, as it seemed at first, so was the silence. Later in the month I found darkness and silence in alliance again, at a Buddhist monastery (despite the title, in fact a community of nuns) deep in the Devon countryside, where the meditation with which the day formally began and ended took place in the context of the winter night.

I have the Poetry Society to thank for these and eight other locations, the upshot of a suggestion I had made that, alongside the numerous residencies and placements for poets involving, for instance, solicitors, shops, financiers and oil rigs, it would be interesting for a poet to spend some time in places where silence had a part to play. After all, 'the common of silence', in Emerson's memorable phrase, surrounds us despite the world's cacophonies. Yet it is far more than the blank margins surrounding words or music, and far more complex: there are, as Thomas Cromwell says in *A Man for All Seasons*, many kinds of silence. Many poets have been aware of the adjacency of silence, and of its variety: it can be 'the perfectest herald of joy', as in *Much Ado about Nothing*, Wordsworth's 'eternal silence' contrasting with 'our noisy years', 'more musical than any song' as Christina Rossetti suggested, or Keats's 'icy silence of the tomb'. In Emily Dickinson's poems, it is often silence which seeds the dashes that punctuate her poems. There are contemporary examples, too, in the work of writers such as R. S. Thomas, whose poems often seem to balance on the cusp of silence. 'Via Negativa' (from the 1972 collection *H'm*) is just one of many possible examples. Here '. . . God is that great absence / In our lives, the empty silence / Within, the place where we go / Seeking, not in hope to / Arrive or find. . .'.

The influence of silence or near-silence depends on its location and its nature: it is sometimes willed, sometimes simply an absence of language or human sound. Its effects can range from the unnerving to the spiritual, from tension to profound calm: and it can powerfully inform the world of sound and noise that it surrounds. In this perspective it is, as Thomas Merton wrote, 'the silence of the world which is real'.

So my aim was to experience and write about silences of widely varying origin and impact: and inevitably, since total silence is such a rarity, to consider as well the inter-relations of silence and sound. If this seems an oxymoronic notion, by the time I went down into the underground passages it had doubled, with the idea that poems informed by my locations might be set to music by Isabelle Ryder, a young composer with whom I had already worked, and then be performed in five counties of the South West. For this development of the project funding was sought from and generously offered by The Year of the Artist / South West Arts, Exeter Arts Council and The Arts Council of England. But first of all the poems had to be written.

I decided at the outset that, while not excluding the possibility that a poem might spring fully armed, I would as a rule not attempt to write any poems until I had visited all the locations I had chosen, though I would allow myself to take brief notes *in situ*. Likewise, any notes that I did take would not be re-read until all the visits were over. In the underground passages, the brevity of my notes was assured by the need to write with the notebook balanced on one knee, and by the circumscribed beam of a head torch. In any case, what I learned from those first two visits was invaluable but hardly a matter of notetaking. In the passages, I discovered the variety which the mind gives to silence as it works upon it, as it seizes on any interruptions, such as the occasional morse of faint but precise footsteps somewhere overhead. In the monastery, I began to learn something of the possibilities of letting go, of detachment even from the tendency of the conscious mind to colonise each facet of its surroundings. And in both places there were details which, barely defined at the time, assumed importance when it came to writing the poems.

It was February when I spent two days in Exeter's Royal School for the Deaf – not that silence and deafness are by any means close companions, as Oliver Sachs reminds the reader in *Seeing*

*Voices* (Picador, 1990): 'The congenitally deaf do not experience or complain of "silence". These are our projectors, or metaphors, for their state. . . . Those with the profoundest deafness may hear noise of various sorts and may be highly sensitive to vibrations of all kinds'. It is also the case, as he points out later in the book, that 'the deaf may inhabit a world of silence without *being* silent'. Nor, with signing (a highly expressive language in its own right) and lip-reading, is communication as limited as might be thought. At the Royal School, what struck me above all was the extraordinary, unforgettable patience and dedication required both of teachers and students in the effort to overcome the effects of deafness, and I hope that something of this response may have informed the poem that ensued. At the suggestion of the principal, John Shaw, I took an audiology test during the course of my visit. On the wall of the audiologist's room was a chart which gave examples of what became inaudible with progressive deafness: first, the rustling of leaves, birdsong, quiet conversation; later, the sound of cars; later still, pneumatic drills, a plane taking off; finally, a rocket. Once again, without my being especially aware of it at the time, though I did make a note, it was detail which turned out to harbour the germ of the poem.

My visit to the Royal School for the Deaf also caused me to re-read the poems of David Wright, who came to England from South Africa at the age of fourteen in order to attend the School for the Deaf in Northampton, having become deaf seven years earlier. Two of his lines seemed particularly suitable as an epigraph to the poem I eventually wrote: 'Oh silence, independent of a stopped ear, / You observe birds, flying, sing with wings instead' ('Monologue of a Deaf Man'), and this led me to have an epigraph for each of the poems in the cycle, none of which has an individual title.

It wasn't hard to find an epigraph for the next place I visited, Sainsbury's branch in the centre of Exeter, where I spent the late evening of 14 February beneath a variety of hanging cardboard signs, included a heart-shaped one with the injunction DON'T FORGET VALENTINE'S DAY. I was allowed to have the place to myself, with even the shelf-stackers gone. The silence was compromised, of course, by the assorted flutings and groanings of ventilation and refrigeration, but the atmosphere was powerful, as was the effect of being surrounded by more words than the busyness of shopping usually allows you to consider fully. Across the screens at each check-out there tracked endlessly the retailer's message of love: *Goodbye hope to see you again soon.* From time to time the words would come to a halt, arbitrarily and abruptly. At one moment, I found myself staring at nothing more or less than *soon Goodbye hope.*

In March I had a fine variety of places to visit: the Mecca Bingo Hall in Exeter out of hours (formerly the Gaumont Cinema, and one of Britain's thirty-two listed cinemas), the Teign Valley close to Castle Drogo at dawn, Belstone Tor on Dartmoor at night, and St David's Church in Exeter, which celebrates its centenary this year and is to be the venue for the first performance of the settings of the poems. It turned out that Belstone and the Teign Valley, geographically within a few miles of one another, became a single poem, while to my surprise the balloon which was to be my final 'location' put in an early appearance in the poem about the Bingo Hall – where, incidentally, I also found a card advertising a promotional offer of truly philosophical resonance: *Even if you don't win you can't lose.* In St David's I spent seven hours or so, during which time five people came in – one simply passing through the church, one to fetch something from the organ loft, two elderly ladies looking round, and an Irish gentleman who said that he had a deal of information about Athens and wondered whether I would be interested.

My last two locations were to be a day of drifting in an open boat off the coast of East Devon in April, and a balloon flight in the vicinity of Bath. Both took place, though weather insisted on its say: on the water, three hours of dry weather preceded five of rain; the balloon flight, twice postponed, had to wait until 14 May and, as I had set myself a deadline of 31 May, became the rule-proving exception in my resolve not to write any of the poems until I had completed my fieldwork. At sea silence is nearly always prelude or aftermath, and there is almost always the trickle of water under the bows, so I was surprised when this setting produced one of the most intense silences of any. The weather had already deteriorated to the point where the horizon was blotted out by the oncoming fret and drizzle. Sky and sea were a single grey wall. And there came a few minutes of utter stillness, with not even the sound of the waves against the clinker hull, before the rain began, water pooling on water . . . The balloon flight manifested intensity of a different kind, the intermittent roar of the main burner alternating dramatically with silence. I was intrigued to learn that there was also a second and much quieter burner, the cow burner, for use when passing over sheep and cattle.

One other location, which originally formed no part of my plan, is included in the cycle. In July 1999 my wife and I visited Oradour-sur-Glane, a Limousin village made famous for the worst possible reason, the massacre of over six hundred of its innocent inhabitants perpetrated by the Germans in June 1944. As the Guide puts it: 'The name of Oradour . . . indicates that from the Roman period there was an *oratorium* there, i.e. an altar and a place to offer prayers for the dead . . . Alas, it could never have better deserved the name it received!' The village has been preserved as it was in the aftermath of the killings, and silence is enjoined on all visitors. To visit Oradour is to be appalled and moved – but also, of course, to court all the risks of disaster tourism, and to be reminded of Wittgenstein's injunction to remain silent about things that cannot be spoken of. I had no intention of writing about it after our visit. Yet – and this became clear to me when I was staying with the Buddhists – it began to seem impossible to write about silence and to leave out of consideration one of the most telling silences I had encountered. To have done so would have seemed an evasion. The difficulty, as always with such subjects, was in trying to avoid trespass and the wrong kind of elaboration. One attempt at an answer was the placing of the poem about Oradour at the centre of the cycle: another was the formulation of the poem as a simple litany. Another, with the agreement of the composer, was the decision not to set the poem to music: when it came to the concerts, it would simply be spoken.

When I sat down to write the first draft of the poems, in the first week of May, I found that they were to hand. The advantage of waiting till then had been six months of hatching: the advantage of writing them at the same time was the unity of the cycle, with links between the poems which seemed to emerge quite naturally, as did contrasts of tone and structure. At the time of writing, Isabelle Ryder, unfazed by the shadow of John Cage at her shoulder, is undertaking the setting of the poems. The challenges and fruit of collaboration are ahead. But I can say already that this has been a highly enjoyable undertaking, ranging as it has from the dark stillness of those underground passages to the exhilaration of a balloon printing its pear-drop shadow across the land on a brilliant May morning, and taking in earth and sea along the way. And although, to quote the wonderful lines by Emily Dickinson which are the epigraph to the ballooning poem, 'You cannot solder an Abyss / With Air', the people I have encountered or talked to in connection with the project have, without exception, engaged very readily with it. If, as the psalmist suggests, 'The dead praise not thee, O Lord: neither they that go down into silence' (Psalm 115), there is still interest among the living in retrieving silence's informing gifts.

2001

# Rocks of Ageing

'Old age,' Emerson wrote in his *Journals*, 'brings along with its uglinesses the comfort that you will soon be out of it – which ought to be a substantial relief to such discontented pendulums as we are. To be out of the war, out of debt, out of the drouth, out of the blues, out of the dentist's hands, out of the second thoughts, mortifications, and remorses that inflict such twinges and shooting pains, – out of the next winter, and the high prices, and company below your ambition, – surely these are soothing hints.' Such relative cheerfulness, in which Lethe washes the slate clean, is hardly characteristic of writers taking the measure of their mortality. From Bacon ('I am too old, and the seas are too long, for me to double the Cape of Good Hope') to Christina Rossetti's 'Mirage' ('. . . and now I wake, / Exceeding comfortless, and worn, and old') to Dylan Thomas ( 'Old age should burn and rave at close of day') or Eliot's Gerontion ('I an old man, / A dull head among windy spaces'), few have been able to muster the apparent insouciance of the same poet's Prufrock ('I grow old . . . I grow old . . . / I shall wear the bottoms of my trousers rolled'). Too often, for the poet whose destiny it is to live into old age, duration seems to mean a durance of greater or lesser vileness.

Historically, morale can hardly have been helped by the 'half in love with easeful death' tendency, the Romantic wager by which some poets seemed to trade an early death for the consideration of posterity. 'Most poets are dead by the end of their twenties', Robert Graves observed in a 1962 *Observer* interview. And perhaps there was only ever limited solace to be had from grafting the poet's own wish for immortality onto the beloved, 'That in black ink my love may still shine bright'. Commuting from dream to history, old poets never die, they simply rave away: or else, as Yeats writes in 'The Coming of Wisdom With Time', they 'may wither into the truth'. In 'The Spur' he confesses to some of the common vices of old age:

> You think it horrible that lust and rage
> Should dance attention upon my old age;
> They were not such a plague when I was young:
> What else have I to spur me into song?

Other poets, in answer to the same question, could legitimately add disappointment, envy and disbelief to the list of impelling forces: though in the case of 'The Spur', at least one of Yeats's biographers takes a generous view, writing that 'lust and rage are here not the lasciviousness and irascibility of an old man's brain grown febrile, as some critics have said, but pure passions, spontaneous and complete as peasant life.' (Richard Ellman, *Yeats: The Man and the Masks*, Penguin, 1987).

If some succeed in avoiding dole, it is often by opposing soul to body, as Yeats himself did in 'The Gift of Harun al-Rashid', in which 'The soul's own youth and not the body's youth / Shows through our lineaments'. The real exemplar here, though, is not Yeats but Eliot, whose *Four Quartets* are seamed through and through with the quest for an answer to the diminishments wrought by time. Here the 'enchainment of past and future / Woven in the weakness of the changing body' of 'Burnt Norton', leads in 'East Coker' to a view of old age as a time not of serenity, but active disturbance:

> Do not let me hear
> Of the wisdom of old men, but rather of their folly,
> Their fear of fear and frenzy, their fear of possession,
> Of belonging to another, or to others, or to God.

Ageing is seen in itself as a process of elaboration rather than simplification, one in which 'The world becomes stranger, the pattern more complicated / Of dead and living' – and the conclusion is the challenge that 'Old men ought to be explorers', though the exact force of that 'ought' is unclear. Moral imperative, or thoughtful wishing? A demand, or a dodge? 'The Dry Salvages', with its meditation upon the nature of experience, the unchangeable rock of what is and what has been, takes its momentum from the notion of the changes which overtake time-travellers as they journey ('You are not the same people who left that station / Or who will arrive at any terminus'), and culminates in a conclusion which sees us as overcoming time by striving for 'right action', and 'only undefeated / Because we have gone on trying'. But it is the final quartet, 'Little Gidding', which has the most unblinking view of 'the gifts reserved for age', in words given to the 'dead master' whom the poet encounters:

> First, the cold friction of expiring sense
> Without enchantment, offering no promise
> > But bitter tastelessness of shadow fruit
> > As body and soul begin to fall asunder.
> Second, the conscious impotence of rage
> > At human folly, and the laceration
> > Of laughter at what ceases to amuse.
> And last, the rending pain of re-enactment
> > Of all that you have done, and been; the shame
> > Of motives late revealed, and the awareness
> Of things ill done and done to others' harm
> > Which once you took for exercise of virtue.

The force of these lines is, perhaps, only partly subsumed at the end of 'Little Gidding', with its vision of a transfiguration beyond or out of time, in which memory is no longer a burden, but 'a liberation'. Reading like a gloss on 'Behold, I make all things new' (Rev. 21:4), the closing lines posit the achievement of 'A condition of complete simplicity / (Costing not less than everything)'.

That horror of the time when 'body and soul begin to fall apart', somehow held at tongs' length by Eliot, finds its wry counterpoint in one of D. J. Enright's 'Low-key Haiku', in which 'A kind of Velcro / Barely holds them together / Your body and soul.' This comes from *Old Men and Comets* (OUP, 1993), which a better than usual blurb describes as being about 'the peculiar preoccupations of age, its fears and its reactions, cantankerous, incredulous, sorrowful; and some evidence of the licence that age avails itself of as *amour propre* ebbs away.' Thus 'Sweet Tooth' is a craving for 'Something to sweeten the sourness of age, / Its waning appetites', while 'Memory' suggests memorably that 'When little is left of the flower / You revisit your roots'. For

Enright, wit and self-deprecation seem the best weapons for coping with age, which he categorises in one poem as 'a side-effect of youth'.

Altogether different perspectives inform the poems about ageing to be found in the work of the late R. S. Thomas, poems that attend on silence and absence, and which sound the huge dark parishes of time and history, of science and love, in which God possibly might be. A poem such as 'Senior' (from the 1981 collection *Between Here and Now*) moves out from the span of a single life ('At sixty there are still fables / to outgrow, the posses-siveness / of language') to a cosmic bleakness:

> A man's shadow
> falls upon rocks that are
> millions of years old, and
> thought comes to drink at that dark
> pool, but goes away thirsty.

Thomas often displays, too, disenchantment with the world, whether as in 'Postscript', in which industrial society has shut out the poet ('Was there oil /For the machine? It was / The vinegar in the poets' cup'), or as in 'Taste', where he lightly concedes the worth of Shakespeare, Donne and Wordsworth, then dismisses the claims of Tennyson, Browning and Hardy, before looking to his own time:

> And coming to my own century
> with its critics' compulsive hurry
>
> to place a poet, I must smile
> at the congestion at the turnstile
>
> of fame, the faceless, formless amoeba
> with the secretion of its *vers libre*.

But can Tennyson be so easily dismissed, at least when it comes to the matter of old age? For all its flourishes, the dramatic mono-logue of 'Ulysses' is a bold apologia for making the best of what is left:

Old age hath yet his honour and his toil;
Death closes all: but something ere the end,
Some work of noble note, may yet be done,
Not unbecoming men that strove with Gods.

Who, in growing older, would not hope to assent to the poet's assertion that 'Tho' much is taken, much abides', or to the rhetoric that can characterise even those 'made weak by time and fate' as nonetheless 'strong in will / To strive, to seek, to find, and not to yield'? Well, Larkin for one, who thought Tennyson silly and sentimental ('The Most Victorian Laureate', *Required Writing*, Faber, 1983 – and he repeated the opinion in several letters), but also ascribed to him tenderness and 'a gruff ability to hit the nail on the head in matters of common concern'. Many of Larkin's own poems, such as 'The View' or, even more, 'The Old Fools', read like a riposte to 'Ulysses', rewriting 'made weak by time and fate' in the idiom of contemporary experience:

Not knowing how, not hearing who, the power
Of choosing gone. Their looks show that they're for it:
Ash hair, toad hands, prune face dried into lines –
How can they ignore it?

Here the lights which, in 'Ulysses', 'begin to twinkle from the rock' and invite departure, appear only in 'days of thin continuous dreaming / Watching light move' with, later in the poem, the idea that 'Perhaps being old is having lighted rooms / Inside your head, and people in them, acting.' As for the rock itself, in Larkin's poem it looms threateningly as 'extinction's alp'. And while Ulysses scorns a dull existence, the mere accretion of days, 'As tho' to breathe were life', for Larkin's old fools it is the only life they have, 'the constant wear and tear / Of taken breath'. No poet renders more vividly, with fear disguised as contempt, the indignities of old age: and as another poem, 'The Winter Palace', suggests, the only relief in prospect is blankness: 'Then there will be nothing I know. / My mind will fold into itself, like fields, like snow.'

Much of the same sense of futility and emptiness going hand in bony hand with age informs C. H. Sisson's poems. *In the Trojan Ditch* and *Anchises* (Carcanet, 1974 and 1976) already have much

211

of retrospect and remorse about them, for all their energy, but it is the later work in the *Collected Poems* (Carcanet, 1998) which comments particularly on the life lived from the viewpoint of old age. Regret there certainly is, as in 'Et in Arcadia ego' ('The living days are over, and I remember / Only where I have failed, as any might, / On this or that occasion, with him or her'), and disillusionment too ('We stand impeccably aloof / At last, and see the empty plate', Sisson writes in 'On living rather long'), as well as the knowledge that the world has moved on, a world 'Which will refuse our gifts and run / From us . . .' ('Triptych'). Many elements combine in Sisson's work, and many echoes, from classical stoicism to points of comparison with Eliot, R. S. Thomas and Hardy. These affinities involve imagery as much as outlook and subject matter: for instance, the images of the sea deployed by both Eliot and Sisson to convey the continuum of life going on; or references to landscape and the natural world, common to Sisson and Hardy, to evoke longing or regret. But when it comes to what one poem ('Necessity') defines as 'the ultimate stone paths of age', Sisson conveys in a manner and diction entirely his own the material weight of that burden. 'Finale', the last of the *Collected Poems*, gives us the husk living on:

> There is the work I did
> – Paper and ink –
> I have no part in it:
> There is no link
>
> Between the man who wrote
> – And more, was once alive,
> And this relic for whom
> The end does not arrive.

If bleakness can be bracing, it is also good that differences of experience and temperament ensure other responses to our ineluctable greying. A distinctive recent example is Roy Fuller, who adopted quite early on the guise of old bufferdom as a defensive bulwark, and lived to convert this into the fully realised measures of his fine last collection *Available for Dreams* (Collins Harvill, 1989). Here the curtailments of age are salted with humour and real delight. A poem such as 'Art in Old Age' may repeat the biliousness of Yeats's 'The Spur', but the approach is altogether lighter:

> Minginess and vanity of age!
> One almost comes to feel no work of art
> Is good if by some other than oneself.
> What in the end will we be forced to read
> To gain aesthetic satisfaction free
> From irritation?

Another, 'Matter', seems explicitly to cast doubt on the Yeatsian escape route of soul from body ('I'm deeply unhappy bodies should disappear; / And wish the soul's quickness were a better bet'). Yet the dominant note of the book is the liberated one of its final lines, which offer up the stuff of a life: 'Available for dreams: a mighty cast / Of all the dead and living of my life'. Taking stock, the poet refuses to be browbeaten, and Fuller is even able to contemplate with lighthearted envy the achievement of those who resisted the temptation to go on writing: 'Ah, to destroy one's stuff and still survive; / To keep quite silent in gaga later life!' Tellingly, every poem in the book is a sonnet: and the sense of crafted achievement is inseparable from the finally grateful tone.

Gratitude likewise permeates another last collection, that of Auden, whose *Thank You, Fog* (Faber, 1974) flags the note of praise which carries through to the final poems. One of these, 'Lullaby', suggests that 'Narcissus is an oldie' and paraphrases the song which the poet had sung thirty-five years before in honour of Yeats: 'In the prison of his days / Teach the free man how to praise' becomes 'Let your last thinks all be thanks'. But there is also a retreat into the world of a second infancy in which the poet sees himself 'snug in the den of yourself' and where dreams, even if nightmares, are banished as 'jokes in dubious taste, / too jejune to have truck with'. This lullaby, with its nursery refrain (*Sleep, Big Baby, sleep your fill*) is an anaesthetic, babying the poet to oblivion.

Meanwhile, behind the old, the young press forward. And given the increased longevity which the demographers and doctors promise us, there comes the prospect of a growing army of pensioner poets, all rhythmically tapping their feet and demanding attention, their mutual envy sharpened by a diminishing number of publishers and readers. Following the example already set by some gifted elders (among whom Edwin Morgan is surely one to rank), they may have to seek new dreams, subjects beyond the measure of their own decline.

# Triplex

I remember a survey in which people were shown a set of photographs and asked to identify which of them were poets. The results, thought to be surprising, suggested that the public at large had a clear, if inaccurate, idea of what a poet ought to look like. I wonder how it would have gone with the three photographs of writers which have haunted me since my schooldays, when I first saw them. The first is one of Nadar's portraits of Baudelaire: head and shoulders, with features of extraordinary intensity; the face deeply lined, the mouth thin but wide; dark hair straggling forward over one side of the domed forehead; the whole expression suggestive of a knowledge acquired through suffering, a man bearing the scars of being put through the mill. Then, a picture of Kafka, cropped perhaps from a picture of the writer standing beside a seated Felice Bauer: the appearance of knowledge turned inwards, with a secrecy about the honed features even though the subject is looking directly at the camera. And thirdly, the famous picture of Rimbaud taken by the poet and photographer Étienne Carjat in December 1871. In each of these photos it is above all the eyes which make the strongest impression: Baudelaire's, darkly ringed with fatigue or exhaustion, the pupils with a pinpoint of light at their centre and huge, virtually flooding the sockets; Kafka's, clear and precise, again very dark though the whites are clearly defined; and, most compelling of all, in the Rimbaud photo eyes seared to blankness, the pupils almost with the same suggestion of translucency as in Picasso's 1923 portrait of his two-year-old son Paul. Here is something even more hypnotic than Man Ray's painted eye attached to a wagging metronome, which provoked more than one viewer to vandalism. Carjat's picture gives a real clue to the remarkable quality of the poet's eyes, and (even though black and white) to their colour, likened by his contemporaries to forget-me-not and periwinkle.

Of course even such brief descriptions already imply the complexity of the photographic image beyond the simple chemical process of its creation. What we might bring to our understanding of these pictures is inseparable from what we know of the writer's life, or even from what we wish to make of it. For instance, Enid Starkie, one of Rimbaud's most devoted biographers, writes (in *Arthur Rimbaud*, 1961): 'In the midst of depravity and vice, his face kept the look of extraordinary purity which we see in the photograph taken by Carjat at this time: the eyes and brows have in them an astonishing and spiritual beauty.' In a different way, to have read *Les fleurs du mal*, *der Prozess* or *Une Saison en Enfer* would also make it impossible to look at these pictures innocently. Then there is the matter of the writer's self-image, or the photographer's own desire to project a particular version of the subject. As Susan Sontag writes in *On Photography* (1978), 'In the normal rhetoric of the photographic portrait, facing the camera signifies solemnity, frankness, the disclosure of the subject's essence. That is why frontality seems right for ceremonial pictures (like weddings, graduations) but less apt for photographs used on billboards to advertise political candidates. (For politicians the three-quarter gaze is more common: a gaze that soars rather than confronts, suggesting instead of the relation to the viewer, to the present, the more ennobling abstract relation to the future).' There is something of that soaring gaze in the Rimbaud picture, in which the sitter is looking slightly to the left of the camera. It is a look sufficiently abstracted, elevated even, to call to mind Rimbaud's declaration, in the famous letter of 15 May in the same year to Paul Demeny: 'Je dis qu'il faut être *voyant*, se faire *voyant*'.

But most of all, as Sontag points out, the photograph as a medium has a power denied to painting because

> . . . [it] is not only an image (as a painting is an image), an interpretation of the real; it is also a trace, something directly stenciled off the real, like a footprint or a death mask. While a painting, even one that meets photographic standards of resemblance, is never more than the stating of an interpretation, a photograph is never less than the registering of an emanation (light waves reflected by objects) – a material vestige of its subject in a way that no painting can be.

But what kind of vestige? And if our reading informs our view of a writer's picture, how does the picture then also inform our reading?

The December 1871 photograph of Rimbaud was not the first Carjat took. Nor, suggests Graham Robb in a new biography of the poet (*Rimbaud*, Picador, 2000), is it necessarily the most informative one, famous as it is:

> This is a photo of Rimbaud pretending to be a poet. Critics, like parents, do not always prefer the most realistic image of their darling. The puffy little face of the October photograph stares straight back at the lens and looks far too young to have written a masterpiece like 'Le bateau ivre'. In the December photograph, the diverted eyes allow the fantasy to slip past their radar: 'His eyes are stars', drooled Jean Cocteau in 1919. 'He looks like an angel – a materialization.'

The October picture, Robb tells us, was considered by two of the poet's friends to be 'the most lifelike image of Rimbaud at any age'. 'Interestingly', comments Robb, 'it is also the least well-known. Perhaps it was too lifelike.' Certainly it stands in striking contrast to the later photograph: the face pudgy, as Robb notes, the eyes shadowy, the mouth and chin suggesting a petulance bordering on sulkiness. An altogether less alluring, less dangerous presence. If Robb here dispels something of the mythopoeic suggestiveness of the better-known picture, his book also dismantles many of the Rimbaud myths created by the poet's family and friends as much as by early biographers such as Berrichon. In documenting the well-known facts of the poet's life, including his involvement with Verlaine ('his weak and lyric friend', as Auden describes him in his sonnet 'Rimbaud'), Robb succeeds in conveying brilliantly Rimbaud's restlessness, his sheer elusiveness – to himself as well as others: characteristics which the still camera is perhaps least able to catch. His scrupulously researched account of Rimbaud's time in Aden and Africa is particularly telling. Not only has he spent time in East Africa and established a number of new facts, but he also considers Rimbaud's involvement with gun-running and slavery with an objectivity not skewed by any *parti pris*.

Here the picture of the poet which emerges from the life is a temperament as much self-denigrating as contemptuous of others, and a mind that seethes, working at extraordinary speed, riffling through a catalogue of possibilities only to discard item after item almost as soon as it is considered or tried out. Above all, while insisting on the verifiable details, Robb resists the biographer's (and photographer's) temptation to pin his subject down, allowing the reader to appreciate Rimbaud's elusiveness and untying a number of loose ends which legend had previously conjoined. His biography has an airiness due in part to the wit of the writing, which makes the most of some of the farcical as well as poignant elements in the story. There is a splendid description, for example, of Verlaine meeting his wife and her mother in a Brussels park: 'At 4 p.m., Mathilde and her mother saw a gloomy alcoholic swaying towards them through the park. Verlaine had been saying goodbye to Rimbaud. He followed them to the station, clutching a roasted chicken, lurched on to the train and collapsed into his seat. There was no sign of his evil friend.' Elsewhere Robb writes with aphoristic neatness, as in his observation that 'anyone who left home as often as Rimbaud inevitably spent a great deal of time there': or his definition of the work of an insurance salesman as 'a legal confidence trick requiring an ability to inspire fear of sudden damage.' French Soho is seen as 'a society that was held together, like Rimbaud's poems, by destructive urges', while in depicting Rimbaud's time in Africa the poet's biographers 'have sometimes appeared to gather the threads of European civilization about him like policemen escorting a nudist.' Just occasionally the phrase-making becomes over-heated, as in the evocation of Rimbaud's caravans which 'set off for the coast like long, repetitive poems in four-legged stanzas. . .'.

Perhaps the most difficult task facing any biographer of Rimbaud is to do proper justice to the texts themselves – texts which can move as elliptically and swiftly as their author, and which can suffer from being quoted in less than full. Robb chooses to quote from the poems in English in the body of his book, with the French originals at the back in an appendix. 'If space permitted', he comments, 'it [this appendix] would contain all the original texts. I hope that this deficiency will be construed as an encouragement to acquire a copy of Rimbaud's poems'.

This seems a reasonable way of hoping to convert a constraint into a virtue. But the December 1871 Carjat photograph – which features on the cover of Robb's biography – may also play its part in sending the viewer to the poems, posed and self-conscious though it may be. We might consider alongside it the anecdote related in Gustav Janouch's *Conversations with Kafka* (quoted by Susan Sontag). Janouch had multiple exposures of one person on a single print, the work of an automatic machine recently installed in Prague:

> When I took such a series of photographs to Kafka I said light-heartedly:
> 'For a couple of krone one can have oneself photographed from every angle. The apparatus is a mechanical *Know-Thyself.*'
> 'You mean to say, the *Mistake-Thyself,*' said Kafka with a faint smile.
> I protested: 'What do you mean? The camera cannot lie!'
> 'Who told you that?' Kafka leaned his head toward his shoulder. 'Photography concentrates one's eye on the superficial. For that reason it obscures the hidden life which glimmers through the outlines of things like a play of light and shade. One can't catch that even with the sharpest lens. One has to grope for it by feeling . . .'

Baudelaire's view of photography was no better: its invention was divine retribution for the public desire for a form of art which would exactly reproduce Nature, the act of a vengeful God whose Messiah was Daguerre. 'And now the public says to itself: "Since photography gives us every guarantee of exactitude that we could desire (they really believe that, the idiots!), then photography and Art are the same thing." From that moment our squalid society rushed, Narcissus to a man, to gaze at its trivial image on a scrap of metal . . .'. But for Rimbaud, as much an outlaw unto himself as ever, there would be no such confrontation with what might be an excellent opportunity. At one particularly restless point in the early 1880s, as Graham Robb reports, he '. . . set his sights on Harar again and then on the distant kingdom of Choa: he would load up a camel with photographic equipment, travel 450 miles into the interior, and turn himself into the Étienne Carjat of Abyssinia. Photography, Rimbaud observed, 'is unknown there and it will make me a small fortune in very little time'.

# The Very Thing

Objects or, rather, references to them are everywhere: and once you've begun to notice them, they seem to multiply endlessly. Objects as clues, objects as emblems, as triggers, as secrets, as irreducible quiddities, as reminders of absence, as impervious, unsheddable, Dinge an sich. Objets d'art, objets trouvés, object lessons, objects of exercises and attention, objects as proof of André Breton's claim that the ambition of Surrealism was to rehabilitate the object: even, in one broadsheet, an 'Object of the Week' column. On every side, objects fulfilling the etymology of their name by being thrown in front of the mind.

I know exactly where I contracted a heightened sensitivity to the word: it was on a first visit to Tate Modern at Bankside, a building that is itself a formidable and indeed rehabilitated object. Scarcely less formidable is the handbook to the gallery, an object described as 'more than simply a guide', being also 'a flexible tool for the understanding of modern art'. The book, like the gallery, is arranged thematically, tracing the development of the nude, landscape, still-life and history painting through the last century, and 'their re-emergence in modern art as the body, the environment, real life and society'.

The texts which discuss these transformations have plenty to say about objects. Thus, while the human figure has always been a preoccupation for artists, 'In the modern period . . . it has been increasingly animated, ritualised and deconstructed, as artists have made the body both subject and object.' Landscape as a term derives much of its resonance 'from the often uncertain boundary between nature and culture, the objective and the subjective.' But, unsurprisingly, it is in the section on Still-Life, written by Paul Moorhouse and titled 'Still-Life / Object / Real Life' that objects really come into their own, an introductory chapter having already asserted that 'it is the ubiquity, and on one level, the timelessness

221

of foodstuffs and vessels that make them both immediate and economical for artists to work with, and at the same time capable of evoking a universal chord of recognition.' We are reminded that Cubism, Dada and Surrealism all played their part in promoting the object: 'To the artistic resonance of inanimate objects these movements in turn added the subversion of aesthetic values, shock tactics and fetishism, and the seductive appeal of mass-produced consumer items.'

In the voyage towards the present bearings of art, various sea-marks are sighted. An early one is Duchamp, for whom '. . . an actual object functions as art, removing any need for representation. The implication is that the boundary between art and real life has been dissolved.' For all that, it is conceded that 'Duchamp's readymades could rarely – if ever – be mistaken for everyday objects . . . the context in which these things are displayed, and their strangeness, mark them out as functionless objects for contemplation.' With a nod to the persistence of the still-life tradition in the work of artists such as Bonnard, Derain and Patrick Caulfield, the handbook gallops quickly on to the non-representational work of, for instance, Anthony Caro and Bridget Riley, then to those who have made use of 'real objects as the stuff of art', Robert Rauschenberg, Christo, Jasper Johns among others, and so to conceptual art, represented by Michael Craig-Martin's 'An Oak Tree', a glass of water on a shelf about which the handbook comments that 'the notion that ephemera could embody and evoke complex conceptual content is central to the resurgence of interest in much object-based art today'. Rachel Whiteread, Susan Hiller and Damien Hirst are all cited as having 'in their different ways provided exemplars of this sensibility'. The conclusion is that 'having abolished virtual reference to other things, the concern among many artists now is that the objects they make should take their place in the real world *and* that these things should be charged metaphorically, embodying symbolic meaning.' Reinforcing quotations at the end of the section come from, amongst others, Matisse ('The object is an actor: a good actor can have a part in ten different plays: an object can play a different role in ten different pictures. The object is not taken alone, it evokes an ensemble of elements'), Donald Judd ('There is an objectivity to the obdurate identity of a material'), Tony Cragg ('It is about time we stopped, started clarifying and re-evaluating the objects we have put into the world') and Susan Hiller ('Objects embody meanings'). One of the presiding spirits, mentioned but perhaps not sufficiently acknowledged here, would seem to be Kurt Schwitters and his Merzbau project, essentially the conversion of random objects into art (commemorated in a recent touring exhibition, *Aller Anfang ist Merz*, which opened in his home city of Hanover).

The second half of the handbook, an A–Z of 100 selected artists, pays its own homage to objects, with the inclusion of Ian Hamilton Finlay's 'interactions of word, image and physical material' and, above all, the work of Cornelia Parker, whose ways with objects are chronicled with a seriousness which borders on the comic. 'In 1988 Parker laid out a large number of domestic silver objects in the path of a steam roller: these flattened objects were then suspended by transparent wires in the Hayward Gallery, London. In 1991 a garden shed, assembled in the Chisenhale Gallery, London, and filled with objects bought from local car boot sales, was taken away and blown up by the British School of Ammunition. The fragments of the shed and its contents were then brought back to the gallery and suspended from the ceiling by wires and illuminated by an ordinary household light bulb.' The handbook suggests what such treatment of the artist's materials might mean: 'their flattening or being blown up does not mark an end, but is actually the beginning of their transformation in which meaning is found in their subsequent suspended state. The garden shed can be identified as a place of refuge whose symbolic resonance is enhanced by having been destroyed. . . . Parker's process is akin to that of an alchemist – turning base metal into gold.' This passage, as others like it throughout the handbook, comes close to sounding prescriptive in its interpretation, while trying to sustain a note of humble tentativeness.

I wonder what Magritte would have made of any of this. Few artists can have undertaken a more dogged search for the true nature of the object. He saw his own work as the attempt to describe, 'insofar as I can, by means of painted images, objects and the coming together of objects, in such a light as to prevent any of our ideas or feelings from adhering to them. It is essential not to confuse or compare these objects, these connections or encounters between objects, with any "expressions" or "illustrations" or "compositions".' He believed that by dislocating objects from their generally accepted contexts, or by combining them in bizarre jux-tapositions, it might be possible to discover their essential and poetic meaning. Intriguing and witty as many of the resulting paintings are, there are times when the quest can seem perhaps too obsessively playful. 'Les mots et les images', an essay by Magritte in *La révolution surréaliste* (December 1929) illustrated with his own drawings, begins with the proposition that 'An object is not so pos-sessed of its name that one cannot find for it another which suits it better' [followed by a sketch of a leaf labelled 'le canon'], cart-wheels along through assorted statements such as 'Everything tends to make one think that there is little relation between an object and that which represents it' [followed by two identical drawings of a house, one labelled 'l'objet réel', the other 'l'objet représenté'], to end with 'Sometimes, the names written in a paint-ing designate precise things, and the images vague things [fol-lowed by the word 'canon' in a balloon beside an ill-defined sketch which might or might not be a cabbage] or the contrary' [followed by the word 'brouillard' in a rectangle, next to a precisely drawn object which might be a capstan].

At this point I find myself recalling one of Auden's 'Shorts,' an admonition which no Surrealist painter or poet would assent to: 'No, Surrealists, no! No, even the wildest of poems / must, like prose, have a firm basis in staid common-sense'. (I wonder whether he knew Magritte's 1945-46 painting *Le bon sens*, which nicely shows still-life objects on a table, four apples beside a dish of pears, all standing on a blank, framed canvas, as if on a tray). Auden's own view of the world of objects is summed up in the 1969 poem 'I am not a camera', with its epigraph from Eugen Rosenstock-Huessy, 'Photographic life is always either trivial or already sterilised.' The poem itself establishes at the outset the distinction perceived between the human and the mechanical:

> To call our sight Vision
> implies that, to us,
> all objects are subjects.

The implication of the human perspective is precisely that regard, that capacity for the moral and for human sympathy which is not available to the world of machines. 'Instructive it may be to peer through lenses', goes a later verse of the poem, yet this can never be more than a process of neutral inspection and recording, so that 'each time we do . . . we should apologise / to the remote or the small for intruding / upon their quiddities'.

In 1956 Auden wrote a sonnet actually called 'Objects', which makes the same kind of distinction in a different way. On one hand are 'Those wordless creatures who are there as well, / Remote from mourning yet in sight and cry', on the other the human capacity for feeling and the weighing of experience. The 'creatures' are seen as 'tearless', justified simply by existing on their own terms – 'If shapes can so to their own edges keep, / No separation proves a being bad.' The first line of the sestet, on which the poem pivots, draws from this the generalised conclusion that 'There is less grief than wonder on the whole', even though this assertion is qualified by the admission that 'of course we care / Each time the same old shadow falls across // One Person who is not.' The note of elegy on which the sonnet closes is mysterious and may even seem to establish some common ground for the mortal human condition and, from the opening line, the mute integrity of 'All that which lies outside our sort of why.'

Some ninety years earlier, a poet admired by the young Auden had had her own say about the relations between objects and the human mind:

> Perception of an object costs
> Precise the Object's loss –
> Perception in itself a Gain
> Replying to its Price –
> The Object Absolute – is nought –
> Perception sets it fair
> And then upbraids a Perfectness
> That situates so far –

Here Emily Dickinson suggests that consciousness is a price worth paying for the loss of the object's autonomy, even though it is that same consciousness which finds duality and distance regrettable concomitants of perfection. Her poem seems to foreshadow the more extended quizzing of the interplay between the mind and the objects of its attention which threads through much of the work of Wallace Stevens, in poems such as 'Notes Toward a Supreme Fiction' and 'An Ordinary Evening in New Haven', with its courting of 'the eye's plain version' and 'the poem of pure reality' homing 'straight to the transfixing object'. In 'Credences of Summer' the poet tries to concentrate on the specificity and fullness of the world as it is, almost, as it seems, to blot out any Platonic perspective which might see any object as an instance of the ideal – 'Let's see the very thing and nothing else', he enjoins. Thus the rock that inhabits sea, land and air is seen as irreducible, nothing more or less than itself, one thing among 'Things certain sustaining us in certainty', as the season of summer also does. Yet resolution is not so easily achieved, as the singers of the poem's seventh section discover, for whom (they are described in the past) 'It was difficult to sing in face / Of the object. The singers had to avert themselves / Or else avert the object.' The possession of the object by 'the thrice concentred self' is depicted as a 'savage scrutiny', in fact a triple assault –

> Once to make captive, once to subjugate
> Or yield to subjugation, once to proclaim
> The meaning of the capture, this hard prize,
> Fully made, fully apparent, fully found.

The last three sections of the poem attempt to work their way beyond the duality of subject and object, putting forward the possibility that 'the arranged and the spirit of the arranged' might be superseded by 'another complex of other emotions. . .'. In the final section, 'the personae of summer play the characters / Of an inhuman author', to whom they appear 'part of the mottled mood of summer's whole' and who find themselves 'Completed in a completed scene, speaking / Their parts as in a youthful happiness'. This is less a resolution of the issues raised in the poem than an agnostic hope expressed as the freedom of summer that releases the protagonists 'for a moment, from malice and sudden cry.'

For some contemporary artists it is their own body which has become the medium of expression, the object becoming subject as in Monica Hatoum's video explorations of her body, or actually providing the materials of art, witness the sculptor Marc Quinn's frozen cast of his head made with eight pints of his blood, or the 'carnal art' of the French artist Orlan. Innovation, detachment or reflexive self-absorption? Such procedures may conjure a nightmare compounding the worlds of Narcissus, Bosch and Frankenstein, yet they also seem unnervingly appropriate to a time when body parts are removed by pathologists, sometimes without consent, and when astonishing scientific advances make the news alongside appalling stories of inhumanity and disaster. Perhaps they also lend weight to a bleakness of outlook, a sense of the object in isolation, which could be represented by Francis Bacon's remark in a 1966 interview with David Sylvester: 'Of course, we are meat, we are potential carcasses.' Meanwhile, the novelist Giles Foden writes (*Guardian*, 5 February) in praise of the rapper Eminem, comparing him with Browning and castigating the singer's critics for failing to consider his angry and provocative lyrics as 'a detached aesthetic object'. Ah.

# Under the Eye of Apollo

On 13 March 1818, in a letter to Benjamin Bailey, Keats wrote that: 'the truth is, it is a splashy, rainy, misty snowy, foggy, haily floody, muddy, slipshod County – the hills are very beautiful, when you get a sight of 'em – the Primroses are out, but then you are in – the Cliffs are of a fine deep Colour, but then the Clouds are continually vieing with them . . .'. Reading this in Exeter 138 years to the month after it was penned, it seems to embody a recurrent if not a permanent truth. For Keats, waterlogged in Teignmouth with his ailing brother Tom, the Devon climate was a continuing source of amazement. The letter to Bailey develops the theme: '. . . I think it well for the honor of Brittain that Julius Cæsar did not first land in this County – A Devonshirer standing on his native hills is not a distinct object – he does not show against the light – a wolf or two would dispossess him'. The next day, in a letter to his friend John Reynolds, the lightness of tone has become the frustration of being cooped indoors. 'Being agog to see some Devonshire, I would have taken a walk the first day, but the rain wod not let me; and the second, but the rain wod not let me; and the third; but the rain forbade it – Ditto 4 ditto 5 – So I made up my Mind to stop in doors, . . . mais! but alas! the flowers here wait as naturally for the rain twice a day as the Muscles do for the Tide. – so we look upon a brook in these parts as you look upon a dash in your Country – there must be something to support this, aye fog, hail, snow rain – Mist – blanketing up three parts of the year – This devonshire is like Lydia Languish, very entertaining when at smiles, but cursedly subject to sympathetic moisture.'

A week later things were no better, and even three weeks on '. . . Devonshire continues rainy. As the drops beat against the window, they give me the same sensation as a quart of cold water offered to revive a half drowned devil – No feel of the clouds dropping fatness . . .'. Reynolds gets a further report the next day

('The Climate here weighs us [down] completely – Tom is quite low spirited – It is impossible to live in a country which is continually under hatches – Who would live in the region of Mists, Game Laws indemnity Bills &c when there is such a place as Italy?') and again as the month nears its end, Keats writing on 27 April that '. . . We are here still enveloppd in clouds – I lay awake last night – listening to the Rain with a sense of being drown'd and rotted like a grain of wheat – There is a continual courtesy between the Heavens and the Earth. – the heavens rain down their unwelcomeness, and the Earth sends it up again to be returned to morrow. . . .'

March 2001 has also offered the full range of deluge: cloudbursts, stair-rods, buckets, cats and dogs and even, to commandeer the French idiom, ropes. Compounding the great difficulties of a countryside which, for all the official protestations to the contrary, seems largely closed by the foot and mouth epidemic, this year has notched up the wettest March on record. If there are any small hopes to be salvaged from the situation, one might be that the effect on the habit of reading might be as fructifying as that of New York power cuts on the birthrate (in Teignmouth Keats read Milton and Wordsworth). It was certainly instrumental in giving me the chance to re-read the selection of Keats's letters edited by Robert Gittings (OUP, 1970). In doing so I was struck again by the note of idealism and altruism which runs through them, from time to time surfacing explicitly, as in his assertion to his publisher John Taylor (in his letter of 24 April 1818) that 'I find there is no worthy pursuit but the idea of doing some good for the world', or again in a letter to the lawyer Richard Woodhouse written in October of the same year – '. . . I am ambitious of doing the world some good: if I should be spared that may be the work of maturer years – in the interval I will assay to reach to as high a summit in Poetry as the nerve bestowed upon me will suffer.' The startling suggestion that poetry might fill in the time between now and a later vocation compares interestingly with his declaration, writing to Reynolds in August 1819, that 'I am convinced more and more day by day that fine writing is next to fine doing the top thing in the world; the Paradise Lost becomes a greater wonder – '. The debate with himself proceeds for a time on levels ranging from the philosophical to the practical, in search of a point of balance between order and disorder, brute savagery and 'great Nature'. In particular, there was for a time the possibility of medicine as a career.

The facts of Keats's time as a dresser at Guy's Hospital have been well documented – the appalling scenes he would have witnessed, the clumsy incompetence of the surgeon Lucas for whom he worked for a time, a routine as ruinous as that inflicted on today's junior doctors – and both Robert Gittings and Andrew Motion in their biographies of the poet (Heinemann, 1968: Faber, 1997) write interestingly about the possible influence of such experience on his work as a poet. Gittings sees his choice of medicine as entirely natural, recalling Keats's devoted nursing of his mother during her fatal illness, and considers that 'hospital experience . . . gave a new reality to Keats's poetry', while Motion comments that both Keats and Astley Cooper, the senior surgeon at Guy's, 'set the need for compassion at the centre of their work.' Even when Keats decided to relinquish medicine for literature (a move that Chekhov, had he been alive at the time, might have characterised as abandoning his wife for his mistress), he kept his medical text-books, as both biographers point out, suggesting that the subject left its mark on his writing. 'The best of his poems have an objective exactness which undoubtedly developed through the study of medicine' writes Gittings, citing as instances 'the wreath'd trellis of a working brain' from the 'Ode to Psyche' and the ending of 'Endymion', whose 'picture of the hospitals restoring their patients to friends and relatives, cured without the aids of medicine, is perhaps a symbol of his own final rejection of medicine as a way in which he was to serve life.' Motion agrees that 'quitting the hospital did not mean rejecting medicine altogether', and notes that in the opening lines of 'Endymion' '"Beauty" is not an escape but a medicine (promoting "a sleep / Full of sweet dreams, and health, and quiet breathing")'. He also writes eloquently of medicine's more diffuse afterlife in the poems: 'While we read his work and notice its consoling luxuries, its healthy and unhealthy airs, its medicinal flowers, its systems of nervous sensibilities, its working brains, its ethereal flights, its emphasis on "sensation", its fluctuating temperatures, its marvellous chemical transformations, and its restorative sleeps, we realise that these things are not just incidental details, but the components of a selfless and moral imagination.' He is surely right to link the specifics of the medical training with the less readily quantifiable features of Keats's temperament. 'There have,' he adds, 'been many other doctor poets, but few apart from Chekhov have made their apparently divided lives as whole as Keats did': and in a note he gives Smollett, Crabbe, Maugham, Bridges and Dannie Abse as examples.

The evidence seems to suggest that either medicine has been tried out by some poets as a possible avenue, then discarded for one reason or another; or that, where it has been pursued, it is hard to isolate as an influence. The first category would certainly include Crabbe, whose attempts to set up as a surgeon in Aldeburgh did not thrive, even though Maskill, the surgeon to whom he had been assistant, had by then left the town. His own departure for London in 1780, 'with a box of surgical instruments, £3 in cash, and some manuscripts', seems to have been the beginning of the end, and his admission to Deacon's Orders on 21 December the following year, the end of the end. A more colourful example is Oliver Goldsmith who, after the beginnings of a picaresque non-career (career, in his case, was always more a verb than a noun), arrived in Edinburgh in 1752 to study medicine. 'He sang Irish songs, told good stories, made many friends, and wrote letters which already show his characteristic style,' notes the *Dictionary of National Biography*. There followed various wanderings abroad, and the possible taking of his MB at either Louvain or Padua, before he reached London without funds and became a chemist's assistant. At one point he hoped to work as a surgeon in a factory on the coast of Coromandel, but failed to gain the necessary qualification. Later, when the publication of his essays had 'proved the growth of his fame', he attempted to return to medicine and set up as a physician but, as the *DNB* reports, 'One of his patients preferring the advice of an apothecary to that of her physician, Goldsmith declared that he would prescribe no more.' The case of Robert Bridges (who, like Keats, had a younger brother to whom he was devoted, and who died prematurely) is somewhat different. Even though he declared that he 'had no intention of making it his lifelong profession', he studied at Barts, and after graduating worked there as a casualty physician for two years. In 1878 he became assistant physician to the Great Ormond Street Hospital for Children, then to the Great Northern Hospital in Holloway. His medical career was ended in 1881 by an attack of pneumonia and empyema.

What of those who continued with the practice of medicine? One well-known instance is William Carlos Williams, whose poems are often said to have benefited from a medical man's acute focus on the particular and the detailed. There is not much direct evidence, in the work, of his profession as a paediatrician, but the reader of his *Selected Poems* (recently re-issued as a Penguin Classic, and edited by Charles Tomlinson) will find in poems such as 'At the Ball Game', 'A Portrait of the Times' or 'Journey to Love' an outlook tempered by an awareness of poverty and pain. Just occasionally there are reminders of his profession, as in the opening of 'Spring and all' ('By the road to the contagious hospital') or book 2 of 'Paterson', with its description of walking taken directly, as Tomlinson points out in his introduction, from an article ('Dynamic Posture') in the *Journal of the American Medical Association*. But the relation of paediatrics to poetry may be no more exactly knowable than it appears in Lowell's discussion of Williams's use of language:

> Of course, one cannot catch any good writer's voice or breathe his air. But there's something more. It's as if no poet except Williams had really seen America or heard its language. Or rather, he sees and hears what we all see and hear and what is the most obvious, but no one else has found this a help or an inspiration. This may come naturally to Dr Williams from his character, surroundings, and occupation. I can see him rushing from his practice to his typewriter, happy that so much of the world has rubbed off on him, maddened by its hurry. Perhaps he had no choice.

A less-known example, perhaps, is that of Hans Carossa, an almost exact German contemporary of Williams, who worked in the field of that most poetical of diseases, tuberculosis. Again, it would hardly be possible to know this from the poems themselves, any more than they give much indication of the times through which Carossa was living (he was born in 1878 and died in 1956): though, as with Williams and Keats, there is the sense of a need to measure the world's woes. In Carossa's case this led to a lyrical subsumption which encouraged his admirers to compare him with Goethe, and his detractors to complain that he had not taken enough account of the times.

There is a clear human, as well as literary, interest in the conjunction of poetry and medicine, though we tend to ask how the doctoring affects the poetry rather than the other way about. It's possible to see both worlds as a kind of fraternity, and they have in common the interplay of feeling and technical detachment. Sickness and cure have also long been metaphorical as well as literal commonplaces of the writer's condition: in this sense, there has been no shortage of wounded surgeons plying the steel. Medicine and mortality have perforce occupied the same ward in our consciousness, and the link has been reinforced in our own time with the spread of information (even when it has to work against the secrecy induced by specialisation and the fear of litigation), not to mention the work of poets such as Sharon Olds and Thomas Lynch. And as Gittings reminds us in his Keats biography, Apollo is the god of healing as well as of poetry – a point that chimes with another of Keats's letters written in Teignmouth in early 1818, in which (perhaps making the best of the weather) he advocates receptivity rather than busyness: '. . . let us not therefore go hurrying about and collecting honey-bee like, buzzing here and there impatiently from a knowledge of what is to be arrived at: but let us open our leaves like a flower and be passive and receptive – budding patiently under the eye of Apollo and taking hints from every noble insect that favors us with a visit . . .'.

If 'passive and receptive – budding patiently' is likely to remind the reader of the situation of any medical sufferer, in March 2001 it was also true that 'buzzing here and there', or at any rate up to London, was one way to escape the continuing west country deluge. On the 29th of the month it was largely dry in the capital, with only a short shower accompanied by a crackle of early evening thunder and a snap of lightning to threaten the pedestrian victims of a day-long tube strike. None of this deterred Dr Dannie Abse, who was speaking at the Royal Society of Literature on 'The Two Roads Taken'. With two uncles, four cousins and his brother Wilfred all involved with medicine, it was hardly surprising that Abse should have found himself studying anatomy and physiology at King's College Hospital in 1944. He has admitted to finding it difficult at times to follow both roads, and once described himself on a radio programme as 'a dilettante doctor and a professional poet'. But he has changed his view since then, seeing the two roads as very close. For him poetry is an escape into, not out of, reality: and he believes in the value of experience, doctoring being central to his. (Incidentally, he has also quoted Hugh Kenner as saying of William Carlos Williams that 'he had the toughness and irritability of a physician').

Many of Abse's poems, amongst them some of the most memorable, arise directly from his experience as a doctor. In this he is greatly aided by a gift for fluent narrative which enables him to balance without strain positive and negative, the intimacy of pain and celebration, death and life, what he describes in 'The Stethoscope' as '. . . the sound of creation / and, in a dead man's chest, the silence / before creation began.' From opposite ends of his experience he can draw on the sublime smile of a woman who has just given birth, as he does in the fine poem 'The smile was', and the 'bloodless meat' of the corpses described in 'Carnal Knowledge', which Abse and his fellow students are called upon to dissect:

> you, threat,
> molesting presence, and I in a white coat
> your enemy, in a purple one, your nuncio'

And, rounding the circle of experience, 'Tuberculosis' raises the ghost of Keats, who long ago acknowledged the reach of Apollo, in one of his mighty letters to George and Georgiana in America: 'The great beauty of Poetry is, that it makes every thing every place interesting'. This evolving belief, along with his own apprehension of the centrality of beauty, was what enabled him to make the right choice between, as he put it when writing to Mary-Ann Jeffery, the daughter of his Teignmouth landlady, 'despair & Energy'.

# Sodium, the Black Sausage and Witless Nature

The discussion about specialist schools in recent months is nothing new. Like some others of my generation, I followed the regime of a one-year sprint to O levels, followed by four years of concentration on A, then S, level subjects. This had timetabling consequences from the outset: since I had opted for German, this meant that science would occupy just one or two lessons a week until O level, with no question of sitting the exam in science subjects, and thereafter would entropy altogether. Such minimal attention to such a huge field made systematic husbandry virtually impossible, as the physics teacher discovered to his cost when he tried to capture our interest and understanding with endless note-giving. A more memorable approach was adopted by the other science masters we had during the year. One (who had known Dr Spooner at New College, and who alleged that the prodigal son had had the strength to return home because he had gone further than the bible's report and had actually eaten the husks fed to the swine, thus ingesting a good helping of energising Vitamin B) entertained us by lobbing lumps of sodium into the school swimming pool, where they crackled and exploded gratifyingly as he had said they would: another promised, and eventually performed, the Black Sausage Experiment. This, probably involving sugar and concentrated sulphuric acid, produced an unlikely black pillar which shot upwards and outwards, as if to compensate for every indoor firework that had ever failed. No doubt we were taught other worthwhile things, but it is these two occasions which persist, exotic outcrops in a landscape as seemingly ordered as the Addison hymn sometimes sung in the school chapel, the spacious firmament and spangled heavens proclaiming their great Original and rejoicing in reason's ear, 'For ever singing as they shine, / "The hand that made us is divine."'

With no examination looming, we were able to treat science as at best an amusing diversion, at worst a dull interlude. This gave it the edge over maths, a nightmare world of blocks and pulleys, bluebottles hitting express trains and C's vindictive sabotaging of A's attempts to fill a bath. Worse still, the answers were given in the back of the book, but between the idea and the reality fell the shadow, in the form of the lugubrious and mildly suggestive rubric *Show your workings*. Whatever the original problem, the real one became the attempt to find a plausible route from the given question to the given answer: work in which the imagination proved an inadequate substitute for logic.

Given this deplorable hinterland, it was with particular relish that I pounced on *A Quark for Mister Mark: 101 Poems about Science*, edited by Maurice Riordan and Jon Turney (Faber, 2000). Acknowledging the 'pioneering and historically oriented' 1984 anthology *Poems of Science*, compiled by John Heath-Stubbs and Phillips Salman, the editors make no claim to be comprehensive, but note 'more responses to science and scientific ideas in contemporary poems'. As they also admit, 'the 101 pieces here are not, of course, strictly about science. They are about love and death, frailty, grief, mischief, moments of recollection and introspection, about the sorts of things one expects to find in poems anyway. Science may cast such themes in a different light, but its use in poetry is often oblique, glancing, wry or sardonic'. Their enjoyable selection ranges from an extract from Thomson's 'The Seasons', which rounds to 'The full-adjusted harmony of things', to Albert Goldbarth's properly scientific 'Arguing Bartusiak', and includes Richard Wilbur and Peter Redgrove (the only writers with three poems each in the book). Astronomy, anatomy and physiology are prominent throughout, along with atoms, minerals and evolution – as the editors note, 'poets are good, it seems, on heavenly bodies and lower life forms'. But they also point to the relatively narrow range of scientific subjects, and confess to finding rather little to read about technology, commenting that 'perhaps only certain kinds of news from science can get through clearly.'

This is a frontier which has been quite regularly patrolled in recent years, and from which reports differing widely in emphasis have been brought back. This year a fascinating addition to the 'one-way traffic' has become available in the form of Primo Levi's choice of his favourite books, *The Search for Roots*, translated, edited and introduced by Peter Forbes, with an afterword by Italo Calvino (Calvino/Allen Lane, 2001). The poetry / science divide was a subject Levi returned to several times in *Other People's Trades*, where (in 'News from the sky') he contrasts the traditional view of the heavens as they appeared to poets and lovers ('with the word "stars" Dante ended the last three verses of his poem') with today's stars: 'They are atomic furnaces. They do not transmit messages of peace or poetry to us, but quite other messages, ponderous and disquieting, decipherable to a few initiates, controversial, alien.' He concludes that 'the scientist-poet is not yet born and perhaps never will be born who is able to extract harmony from this obscure tangle, make it compatible, comparable, assimilable to our traditional culture and to the experience of our puny five senses made to guide us within terrestrial horizons.' In 'The Moon and Us', published just before the first moon landing on 21 July 1969, he emphasises the gap between science and poetry: 'It is a pity, but this time of ours is not a time for poetry: we no longer know how to create it, we do not know how to distil it from the fabulous events that unfold above our heads.' He does not think it likely that 'the poet of space' will come along – 'The flight of Collins, Armstrong and Aldrin is too sure, too programmed, not "wild" enough for a poet to find nourishment in it. Of course, it is asking for too much, but we do feel cheated.'

When it comes to technology and its influence on society, it is another Italian poet, Eugenio Montale, to whom we might look. In *Poet in our Time* (first published in 1972) he suggests that the ambition of contemporary artists is 'to imitate nature in its perennial flux, its continual process of creation and dissolution'. Even though 'there is nothing diabolical about the construction of machines. Man is a constructor by nature: he was one when he was sharpening stones and discovering the fusion of metals. . . . The machine in itself is neutral', in the technological age 'speed and self-transformation are the characteristics of the marketable idea.' In such a context art becomes anti-art, whose adept 'knows that the three-dimensional nature of objects is a provisional victory which has already been outstripped by science, and he also knows that the only reality is the perennial flow of vital energy.' About contemporary poetry he observes merely that 'you cannot trust the words since the words are of today, but their meaning must be sought between the lines.' Astute in his analysis, Montale concludes rather limply that 'I love the age in which I was born because I prefer to live in the stream rather than to vegetate in the marsh of an age without time . . . a poet must not turn his back on life. It is life which contrives to elude the poet.'

'To live in the stream' is given a particular focus in Richard Dawkins's *River out of Eden* (Weidenfeld and Nicolson, 1995), though it is hardly seen as a matter of preference. For Dawkins, Darwinian theory has not only a 'superabundant power to explain' but also 'a poetic beauty that outclasses even the most haunting of the world's origin myths'. 'There is,' he affirms, 'more poetry in Mitochondrial Eve than in her mythological namesake.' Though he writes with infectious enthusiasm, for instance about the truly amazing bee dance, the underlying rhythm is clear enough: 'DNA neither knows nor cares. DNA just is. And we dance to its music.' Amongst those called in evidence is Housman ('For Nature, heartless, witless Nature / Will neither know nor care.'). In the final chapter, Dawkins traces evolutionary progress across a number of thresholds of which the seventh, the Language Threshold, is a major one 'which may or may not be crossed on a planet'. Then comes the Cooperative Technology Threshold; the Radio Threshold, already crossed here on earth: then, 'the only further step we have imagined in the outward progress of our own explosion. . . . Threshold 10, the Space Travel Threshold.' Dawkins's reminder of the message that we have already sent into space, a picture of a naked man and woman with hands raised in a gesture of peace, would not displease believers in extropy, but the sense of human isolation in a world where 'nature is not cruel, only pitilessly indifferent' is reasserted at the end of the book, with Wordsworth's glimpse (from Book Three of *The Prelude*) of Newton's statue in Trinity College, Cambridge:

> The marble index of a mind for ever
> Voyaging through strange seas of Thought, alone.

Dawkins's deterministic world picture, with its note of persistence almost *malgré tout*, can read like a form of chemical Calvinism. Others have come up with a less bleak view, or at any rate one which aims specifically at a sense of value. Peter Forbes, in his editorial for a 'Poetry and Science' issue of *Poetry Review*

(June 1987), insisted that 'Science has not usurped anything: what it has done is to open up previously unknown worlds – the micro-worlds of atom and gene, the macroworlds of quasars and black holes. Subjects like these abound in fascinating concepts and par-adoxes, and as such are ripe for poetry. . . . This issue constitutes a plea for a metaphysical poetry. . . . The spiritual and physical are intertwined. Separated, one shrinks to an empty trammelling creed, the other to stark brutality.' And Peter Redgrove, in an interview with Neil Roberts which is one of the centrepieces of the issue, argues against behaviouristic principles, complaining that 'the scientists have given us a picture of nature which is com-petitive, alien, empty, mechanical, and a universe in which we are complete strangers, and in which – talking about continuums – there is no continuum between ourselves and nature'.

An informative discussion of poetry and science is to be found in the introduction to *The Faber Book of Science* (1995), an excellent anthology: to read Carl Sagan on a grain of salt, or Primo Levi on the story of a carbon atom, leaves the black sausage experiment standing. The collection is edited by John Carey, who sees science-writing as tending 'towards one of two modes, the mind-stretching and the explanatory. In practice, of course, any partic-ular piece of science-writing will combine the two in various proportions. . . . The mind-stretching, also called the gee-whizz mode, aims to arouse wonder, and corresponds to the Sublime in traditional literary categories.' He goes on to remark that 'given the boundless human implications of science, it seems strange that poets have not used it more'. He wonders why, with science's 'dominant position in contemporary culture', the majority of con-temporary poets are 'science-blind', and recalls Auden's pro-fessed discomfiture when in the company of scientists ('I feel like a shabby curate who has strayed by mistake into a drawing room full of dukes'). Historical assumptions about the inherent super-iority of the poetic imagination to the scientific are part of the story, but in the end it is language which Carey sees as the deci-sive issue. The increasingly specialised language of scientists offered 'freedom from the vast cloud of associations, nuances and ambiguities that ordinary language carries along with it, and on which poets depend', while for poets 'the new technical language seemed a sterile sea of jargon, in which the imagination would freeze and drown'. Yet Wordsworth's vision encompassed a world in which 'the remotest discoveries of the chemist, the botanist, or mineralogist, will be as proper objects of the poet's art as any upon which it can be employed', and even Coleridge could spot some common ground: 'The first man of science was he who looked into a thing, not to learn whether it could furnish him with food, or shelter, or weapons, or tools, or ornaments, or *play-withs*, but who sought to know it for the gratification of knowing.'

Among the few poems in the book are extracts from Erasmus Darwin and from Alfred Noyes's epic about the march of science, 'The Torch-Bearers'. There is also a typically combative MacDiarmid poem, 'Two Scottish Boys', which compares the poet William Sharp (who wrote as Fiona Macleod) and the physician Sir Patrick Manson (whose work in tropical medicine led to the nickname 'Mosquito Manson'), very much to the advantage of Manson. The poem ends by quoting Sainte-Beuve on Flaubert, as a parallel instance:

Sainte-Beuve was right – the qualities we most need
(Most of all in sentimental Scotland) are indeed
'*Science, esprit d'observation, maturité, force,*
*Un peu de dureté,*' and poets who, like Gustave Flaubert,
(That son and brother of distinguished doctors) wield
Their pens as their scalpels, and that their work
Should everywhere remind us of anatomists and physiologists.

Poet and therefore scientist the latter, while the former,
No scientist, was needs a worthless poet too.

As for contemporary poets, James Kirkup and Dannie Abse get a look-in, as does Lavinia Greenlaw with her poem 'The Innocence of Radium', which is included in *A Quark for Mister Mark* as well. The two books also have in common Tennyson ('In Memoriam' LIV and LV) and Donne ('Of the Progress of the Soul' – 'Knows't thou how blood, which to the heart doth flow, / Doth from one ventricle to the other go?') – Donne, for Carey 'the first and last' English poet not to feel alienated by the language of science, 'being born at just the right time (1572), after the beginning of modern science but before its specialized technical vocabularies had really taken off'.

Only one recent poet, Miroslav Holub, features in both Faber anthologies and in the 'Poetry and Science' issue of *Poetry Review*. In *The Faber Book of Science*, Carey includes 'Shedding Life', a wonderfully vivid piece about the cellular death of a muskrat shot dead, from Holub's 1990 collection of essays, *The Dimension of the Present Moment*. It is a pity that, for whatever reason, he did not also include the final essay in that book, 'Poetry and Science', which brings together many elements of the discussion. Holub is critical of the attitude of artists to science: 'They content themselves on the one hand with a subnormal understanding, of the present sciences in particular, and with a pretended general understanding of 'Science' on the other, albeit they mix up science, technology and the application of both – which is rather the consequence of the given social structure than the responsibility of science.' This is particularly reprehensible given the centrality of science, and that 'no one of goodwill can fail to perceive current scientific events and their eminent role in our intellectual life.' In words echoed by Carey in his introduction, Holub sees an important feature of the gap between poetry and science to be linguistic, with greater affinities to be found between scientists and painters: 'There is no common language and there is no common network of relations and references. Actually, modern painting has in some ways come closer to the new scientific notions and paradigms, precisely because a painter's vocabulary, colours, shapes and dimensions are not congruent to the scientist's vocabulary. Their vocabularies are not mutually exclusive, but complementary.' In the end, for Holub 'the basis of poetry is the unpronounceable, the basis of a picture is the unpaintable, the basis of music is the unplayable and the basis of a drama is hidden beyond the action. Perhaps art is based on the immanent inadequacy of its means, while science insists on the adequacy, or at least the temporary adequacy, of its means.' In terms of language, this again contrasts the rich ambiguities of poetry with the sparse clarity of science with its words 'chosen so as to bar all possibilities except one.'

Yet the poetic and scientific modes do have things in common: 'both kinds of communication involve a definite time of the full intellectual or intellectual-emotional presence. In addition, both are concerned with the establishment of a lasting memory. . . . And both . . . are a function of condensation of meanings, of the net weight of meaning per word, of inner and immanent intensity.

Opposed to other written communications, they are – at their best – concentrates, time-saving devices.' Much of the remainder of the essay is concerned with articulating the tensions which divide or, sometimes, connect the two realms. One side of the argument is represented by the kind of approach to which Richard Dawkins would be sympathetic, where feelings and ethics are seen as epiphenomenal: 'human approaches do not count in science. The moral and aesthetic values emerge at the very beginning and at the very end of the scientific activity, not in its mechanism'. In this perspective the distinction between poetry and science is clear. 'The basic difference between the emergence of the scientific theme and the poem theme is the notion and necessity of purification, definition and linearity in the former, and the notion of necessity of the openness, ramification-potential and multilevel interaction in the latter. The scientific theme implies as much light as possible, the poetic one as many shadows as possible'. At the same time, there is a similar excitement to be had from both, 'the experience of the little discovery, which is virtually identical when looking into the microscope and seeing the expected (or at times the unexpected but meaningful) and when looking at the nascent organism of the poem. The emotional, aesthetic and existential value is the same.' At its conclusion, the essay draws back to a world picture reminiscent of Montale, artist and scientist alike operating 'in a world and in an age dominated by the giants of management and manipulation, by untamed autonomous superstructures which look down at us as if at an easily manageable microbial culture.

'And this is the last aspect of reality where there is a total amalgamation of science and poetry: some sort of actual or potential hope in the world of autarchic actions.'

Something of the same tentative optimism can be seen at work in some of Holub's poems, such as 'Landscape with Poets' (from *Vanishing Lung Syndrome*, Faber, 1990). Here, hedging his bets, the poet imagines 'some day' when poets will commandeer the landscape with their verses uttered in succession, like a kind of Orphic Mexican wave, and:

> Orpheus underground will sound
> the upper harmonic registers
> and the words will float like clouds,

across the information threshold,
up to the shallow sky,
like proteinoids and oligonucleotides,
words as honest as chemical bonds,
words with the autocatalytic function,
Genomic and decoding words,

and there will be
either a new form of life
or, possibly,
nothing.

Meanwhile, I wonder whether we have yet had time to assimilate fully the implications of having crossed the nuclear threshold, or the power of the famous photograph of the earth seen from space, that image of simple unity pocketed by the lens.

2002

# Bridge Passages

The murderous attack on the World Trade Centre and the New York air crash a month later, though very different in nature, both raise obvious ontological, even theological issues of a kind which often surface in the wake of catastrophe, whatever its cause: justice; mercy; providence; free will; evil. When the everyday is torn apart, the great abstractions soon show. There is nothing new about this, as Voltaire's stories constantly remind us, with their nagging attempts to find a tenable perspective short of despair which could account for a world in which natural disasters, inhumanity and futile sacrifice seem more the rule than the exception. More recently, Thornton Wilder's short novel *The Bridge of San Luis Rey*, though it may have lost something of the renown that it enjoyed in the years following its publication seventy-five years ago, addresses the same questions, as the titles of its first and last parts signal – 'Perhaps an Accident' and 'Perhaps an Intention'. The opening sentence of the book plainly describes the incident in question: 'On Friday noon, July the twentieth, 1714, the finest bridge in all Peru broke and precipitated five travellers into the gulf below.' Brother Juniper, a 'little red-haired Franciscan from Northern Italy [who] happened to be in Peru converting the Indians', comes to the conclusion that 'if there were any pattern in a human life, surely it could be discovered mysteriously latent in those lives so suddenly cut off. Either we live by accident and die by accident, or we live by plan and die by plan. And on that instant Brother Juniper made the resolve to inquire into the secret lives of those five persons that moment falling through the air . . .'.

In Wilder's story, even the name of the bridge carries an implicit metaphysical question: and the whole idea of a bridge seems so obvious in its connotations of communication and connection that you might think it hardly usable as an image or metaphor. It seems odd, though I am not quite sure why it should be, to find no mention of bridges in the bible: certainly Young's *Concordance* has no entry for them. And in *The Pilgrim's Progress*, there is no bridge over the deep river which lies between the pilgrims and the gate of the Celestial City. When it comes to poems, most of the bridges to be found in them are of sighs (or of Sighs, in the case of Byron and Hood) and few are the equal of 'le pont Mirabeau', with its hypnotic refrain – 'Vienne la nuit sonne l'heure / Les jours s'en vont je demeure'. Apollinaire's poem, full of music and artful ease, encapsulates magically much of the poetry written about rivers and its themes of the flux of time passing, and the fate of love within it (though we might also bear in mind the cheerful singing of the lover under the railway arch in Auden's 'As I walked out one evening' – 'Love has no ending'). A clattering bridge almost as famous as Apollinaire's is McGonagall's 'Beautiful Railway Bridge of the Silv'ry Tay', while past generations of British schoolchildren brought up to admire heroic actions were encouraged to con by rote Macaulay's version of 'How well Horatius kept the bridge / In the brave days of old', though the lines which perhaps stick in the memory longest come at the beginning of the tale rather than the end – 'Lars Porsena of Clusium / By the nine gods he swore / That the great house of Tarquin / Should suffer wrong no more.'

Kipling and Hardy also have ballads involving soldiers and bridges, though each displaces Macaulay's epic centrality in its own way. In 'Bridge-Guard in the Karroo', set in South Africa at Blood River Bridge, Kipling at first seems to echo Macaulay's heroic tones in describing the scene at sunset:

> Royal the pageant closes,
>    Lit by the last of the sun –
> Opal and ash-of-roses,
>    Cinnamon, umber, and dun.

But the perspective is soon brought down to that of the soldiers changing the guard on the bridge, stumbling on empty tins of rations as they come on duty. When the majestic note is sounded once more, it is to celebrate the night sky, the bridge and the approaching train, while the soldiers themselves have become in every sense a detail, parenthetical witnesses of little apparent consequence:

> (Few, forgotten and lonely,
>   Where the white car-windows shine –
> No, not combatants – only
>   Details guarding the line.)

In Hardy's 'The Bridge of Lodi', a song title as well as the site of one of Napoleon's battles, the poet visits the scene and is pleased to let his imagination work on it – 'In the battle-breathing jingle / Of its forward-footing tune / I could see the armies mingle / And the columns crushed and hewn'. But to his dismay he finds that the locals whom he encounters have forgotten the battle altogether:

> Not a creature cares in Lodi
>   How Napoleon swept each arch,
> Or where up and downward trod he
>   Or for his outmatching march!

Debating whether the local forgetfulness isn't perhaps admirable, a refusal to glorify war, he concludes that personally he likes the song well enough to go on singing 'that long-loved, romantic thing'.

One of the most unusual poems about bridges must be Burns's 'The Brigs of Ayr', 234 lines in energetic couplets which have at their heart a debate between 'The Sprites that owre the Brigs of Ayr preside'. Auld Brig 'seem'd as he wi' Time had warstled lang', while 'New Brig was buskit in a braw new coat'. The hundred lines of bickering which follow, with each bridge allowed three speeches, are good roistering stuff covering religion, politics, and tradition and experience versus innovation and reform. The Auld Brig accuses the New of upstart conceit: it might learn in time to be more modest, though it probably won't last long enough for that. The Auld Brig, ripostes the New, is a 'poor narrow footpath of a street', a pathetic 'ugly Gothic hulk'. The Auld Brig: just wait till you've had two or three winters, when '. . . crashing ice, borne on the roaring speat, / Sweeps dams, an' mills, an' brigs a' to the gate'. This will be 'a lesson sadly teaching, to your cost, / That Architecture's noble art is lost!' The New Brig: good riddance, too, given what gothic architecture had to offer – 'Forms like some bedlam statuary's dream, / The crazed creations of misguided whim', or 'Mansions that would disgrace the building taste / Of any mason reptile, bird or beast'. The Auld Brig broadens the argument, lamenting the passing of worthy men and the rise of 'staumrel [half-witted], corky-headed graceless gentry, / The herryment [plundering] and ruin of the country'. The New Brig will have none of this, seeing much that is established as also corrupt, and 'As for your Priesthood, I shall say but little, / Corbies and Clergy are a shot right kittle'. At this point the dispute is dissolved, rather than resolved, by the entry of 'a fairy train' led by the Genius of the stream, at the head of the Seasons, then assorted Virtues, and ending with Peace and Agriculture. A good time, the reader feels, is had by all, and most of all the poet, who rounds it all off with nods to assorted ladies and patrons.

More usually bridges feature in poems as atmospheric locations conducive to contemplation of one kind or another: often commanding a topographical view, they invite philosophical ones. The natural human tendency to pause on a bridge, to look out or down, has its share of representations, from Wordsworth on Westminster Bridge (two hundred years ago next September) to Hardy on Sturminster Foot-Bridge, with many later poets following in something of the same vein. Thus Douglas Dunn, contemplating the Tay Bridge in a poem of that title in *Northlight* (Faber, 1988), tellingly evokes Dundee seen at dusk ('Pale, mystic lamps lean on the river-road / Bleaching the city's lunar after-image'), seems at one point simultaneously to conjure and transmute McGonagall ('The rail bridge melts in a dramatic haze') and at the poem's end satisfyingly offsets the local against the cosmic:

> Conjectural identity's outdone
> By engineering, light and hydrous fact,
> A waterfront that rises fold by fold
> Into the stars beyond the last of stone,
> A city's elements, local, exact.

Farther south on the same coast lies the Humber Bridge, its opening celebrated in a cantata composed by Anthony Hedges, for which Larkin wrote the words under the title 'Bridge for the Living'. Beginning with a description of Hull which carries an echo of Wordsworth ('Behind her domes and cranes enormous skies / Of gold and shadows build; a filigree / Of wharves and wires, ricks and refineries' sits comfortably alongside 'Ships, towers, domes, theatres, and temples lie / Open unto the fields, and to the sky; / All bright and glittering in the smokeless air'), the poem goes on to evoke the city's hinterland in a manner reminiscent of early Auden, before homing to the bridge itself. Here the poem opens out from the local to the emblematic, striking a soft note of hope rare in Larkin in its view of individual lives 'All resurrected in this single span' and the bridge itself as representative of human reaching out 'that we may give / The best of what we are and hold as true: / Always it is by bridges that we live.'

Norman MacCaig, in the short poem 'By Achmelvich Bridge', concentrates on capturing the mood of the place, which seems to have its own power to alert the senses: a place where 'A floating owl / Unreels his silence, winding in and out / Of different darknesses . . .', and the mosses '. . . smell of wells, / of under bridges and of spoons'. At the end of the poem, 'owl goes off. / His small soft foghorn quavering through the air'. Similarly, in Ruth Fainlight's translation of a Jean Joubert poem, 'Wooden Bridge over Drac Torrent', there is silence counterpointed by the cry of a bird, but here the atmosphere is more desolate, a cold landscape provoking the poet to question human identity:

> What are we, lost
> beyond limits or memory –
> transparent, immobile?
>
> while somewhere else
> water slides between arches
> and the bird blindly
> follows its flight.

Both MacCaig's alert sense of wonder and Joubert's opening into unease have a delicacy that sets them apart from the more brutal encounters with which some bridges have been associated. Quite apart from the traps and trolls which folklore has frequently located on or under them, bridges are always likely to be places of challenge, of the way barred as much as access granted, witness the incident in Malory's *Le Morte d'Arthur* when Sir Launcelot 'rode over a long bridge, and there start upon him suddenly a passing foul churl, and he smote his horse on the nose that he turned about, and asked him why he rode over that bridge without his licence.' In the ensuing confrontation the churl 'lashed at him with a great club shod with iron' whereupon Sir Launcelot, as is the way of these things, calmly drew his sword 'and clave his head unto the paps.' Then there is Sir Gawain, in *Sir Gawain and the Green Knight*, who finds himself at one point 'on the main highway, / Which brought the brave man to the bridge's end / With one cast. / The draw-bridge vertical, / The gates shut firm and fast, / The well-provided wall – / It blenched at never a blast.' Equally unnerving, and no less dramatic, is the narrative of Edmund Blunden's 'A Bridge', in which the poet is directed to the bridge by a 'greybeard' who, by the poem's end, has become 'the grey ghost'. The old man's false promise of a peacefully slow river turns out to be pure nightmare, a Bosch-like ferment of swarming creatures:

> And congregate in sharkish hate
> Hundreds of demon slayers basked
> In the mid gulf, scaled thunder-bronze,
> And their swift brains one victim asked.

Edward Thomas seems to have been more fortunate: finding himself (in 'The Bridge') 'on a strange bridge alone' at dusk, he is taken out of time to a place where 'The dark-lit stream has drowned the Future and the Past': what ensues is a vision of 'the moment brief between / Two lives' which, though unreal, is still powerful and consoling, an apprehension of 'Things goodlier, lovelier, dearer, than will be or have been.'

Even avoiding a bridge can't always keep you out of trouble, though you may learn something from doing so, as Seamus Heaney relates in a poem in *Death of a Naturalist* (Faber, 1966), 'An Advancement of Learning' (with its title nodding to Bacon). 'As always, deferring / The bridge', the poet finds himself having to confront an old terror on the embankment path, in the form of a rat: 'I stared him out // Forgetting how I used to panic / When his grey brothers scraped and fed / Behind the hen-coop in our yard, / On ceiling boards above my bed'. In overcoming his fear he has undergone a minor rite of passage, and when finally he crosses the bridge he does so with a new strength.

Is there safety in numbers? MacNeice's 'The Burnt Bridge' is set in a haunted dreamscape with a quest which won't quite behave itself – the dragon fails to appear, but things look up for the protagonist when, after safely getting through a dark wood, he emerges into sunlight and 'a shining river caught his eye / With a bridge and a shining lady.' They waste no time, for only three lines on 'He took her hand and they struck a light / And crossed that bridge and burnt it' – but find themselves on an unreal and hallucinatory shore from which only daylight and the end of dreaming can rescue them. In the far more down-to-earth setting of Weymouth, Hardy, in 'The Harbour Bridge,' makes of the bridge so carefully described at the outset the little stage on which one of his human shows is played out: we eavesdrop with him on the fraught encounter between a sailor and his wife, as she vainly attempts to persuade him to leave his lover and come home. They go their separate ways again. Here the bridge is the locus of division, not connection and soon, as the poem concludes, 'White stars ghost forth, that care not for men's wives, / Or any other lives.' The girls in Derek Mahon's 'Girls on the Bridge' seem at first to be relaxed enough, having paused where the road comes to the bridge, 'perhaps the high road south', and are 'content to gaze / At the unplumbed, reflective lake' – though the reader will already have been alerted to unease by seeing 'Munch, 1900' beneath the poem's title. At ease now, the girls are nonetheless 'Grave daughters / Of time' and cannot ultimately avoid the point described at the poem's end, where time will ambush them. The bridge, though a pause for calm, is also where the road leads on:

> The road resumes, and where it curves,
> A mile from where you chatter
> Somebody screams.

That scream might serve as a reminder of the intimate connection between bridges and death, as for instance in the fourth of John Ash's 'Five Macabre Postcards' in *The Branching Stairs* (Carcanet, 1984), where 'I reach the bridge over the river. How splendid it is! Adorned with iron statues of river-gods no one believes in; it presents a selection of vistas ideally suited to doomed lovers or ironic suicides . . .': or, more directly, as in a short poem in *Autumn*, Patricia Beer's last collection (Carcanet, 1997), 'Looking Down at Clifton Suspension Bridge'. The view of the bridge has been shrunk by distance to the scale of a model, with the ant-like humans on it so small as to be invisible, though the imagination knows what they are up to:

> We cannot see God's tiny creatures going
> On to the middle of the bridge to drop,
> And not a single toy Samaritan
> Bustles about persuading them to stop.

Here is a view close to despair, given the mockery implicit in that 'toy Samaritan' who 'bustles about'. It leads full circle back to Wilder's Peruvian bridge, and the attempt to salvage some kind of sense from the world's insanities. At the end of *The Bridge of San Luis Rey*, it is clear that no discernible ethical logic dictates life and death: and though the five who perished when the bridge fell are still more or less remembered by those nearest to them, these survivors realise that 'soon we shall die and all memory of those five will have left the earth, and we ourselves shall be loved for a while and forgotten. But the love will have been enough; all those impulses of love return to the love that made them. Even memory is not necessary for love. There is a land of the living and a land of the dead, and the bridge is love, the only survival, the only meaning.'

# Reach and Grasp

Acting as master of ceremonies at the Turner Prize award ceremony in December, as his initials neatly suggest he should, Matthew Collings began by asking us television viewers whether glamour could be a way of making art accessible. The rhetoric of this question hung like a defining cloud over all that followed, as assorted celebrities were paraded in pairs to express a brief opinion about the four shortlisted contenders, Richard Billingham, Martin Creed, Isaac Julien and Mike Nelson. One of the first on was Zadie Smith, who spoke up for Richard Billingham, photographer, as the only one of the four to celebrate the human in his work. She thought the others all showed, in comparison, a marked poverty and operated in the realm of 'the fatuous artspeak of the art scene'. Zadie was thanked both for her opinion and 'for being so glamorous' – clearly we were not intended to lose sight of this issue.

We were swept on to be told about Martin Creed, creator of a work consisting of a light going on and off in a room (M. C. again, I noticed – a trite coincidence, of course, but somehow noticing it seemed in keeping with the tone of the occasion). He is 'a modern version of the minimalist', according to Collings: and whereas sixties minimalists were inexplicable, their successors are funny as well as inexplicable. Creed has a band, we were informed, and one of their numbers is called 'Nothing'. His art works include *blue tac* (a blob of it stuck onto a wall, sticking nothing; the means become the end). Then there is work No. 88, *A sheet of A4 paper crumpled into a ball*. Comments about his work included 'a play on doubt' and 'funny and interesting'. Creed himself thought 'the real problem is that you have to make decisions if you want to do anything': his credo was, he divulged, the equation '$0 + 1 - 1 = 0$', but the point is that 'something happens on the way'. Over to a member of another band, Blur, and the singer Sophie Ellis-Bextor:

she turned out to share Zadie Smith's liking for Richard Billingham's work. Then to an art historian, who said that Creed was 'playing with the idea of insubstantiality'.

And so on, in galloping précis through Mike Nelson's installations, typified perhaps by an October 2001 installation at the ICA titled *Nothing is true. Everything is permitted* (Collings: 'installations are the new oil paint, and what artists have to do to be noticed'. Nelson described his work as 'narratives which undulate between different time periods, different locations') and, after a commercial break (Collings: 'Coming up next, Madonna's arrival among the mortals . . . Meanwhile, enjoy the well-directed ads . . . Hey, welcome back!'), the film work of Isaac Julien. This included *Vagabondia*, set in the Sir John Soane museum, a location whose complexities offered, according to Julien, the chance for 'a reading of the space, but it's not something you automatically have access to.' The final duo of commentators was Adrian Searle, who distinguished Julien's work from commercial cinema, seeing its compressed nature as a suspended moment able to generate a story in the viewer's head: and Zadie Smith, again talking real sense in suggesting that while it was a good idea to see what could be done with film in a manner distinct from commercial cinema, the real question ought to be whether the resultant art was *good* art.

By now the programme had provided a vivid reminder of what a poor medium television is for considered discussion, so it was unsurprising that after a brief mention of the judges, a final bout of speculation involving Matthew Collings moving model horses and riders and weighing up the odds for who might be 'Turner Prize top dude 2001', followed by a quick appearance by the chairman of the judges, Sir Nicholas Serota (the Turner Prize 'exists in part so that we may make up our own minds,' he said somewhat delphically), here at last was Madonna (*née* M. C., for heaven's sake). There is no such thing as 'the best' anyway, she opined, only opinions. Art was always at its best when there was no money involved, because art has to do not with money but love. She emphasised the point by referring to a four-syllable form of family activity not usually to be found on the daytime side of the watershed, and announced Martin Creed the winner. The audience whooped, the camera gave an aerial view of Creed, he came up to collect his cheque for £20,000 and uttered a single vapid sentence of thanks ('to almost everyone'), and Collings expressed his delight that the Turner Prize had again created debate, as this must be good for art. Roll end credits, voice-over apology for swearing on live show: end.

*Must* it be good for art? Even after allowing for the demands of television, and such virtues as snappiness, self-deprecation and humour, the fact is that one or two exceptions notwithstanding, those who appeared on the programme succeeded in steering clear of anything which might suggest much by way of significance or seriousness, or anything less or more than irony of one kind or another. What the programme lacked in pomposity it made up for in superficiality: and there was something strikingly old-fashioned about the jokiness of it all, which seemed little more than a variant on the supposed need to *épater le bourgeois*, a diet thin enough after all this time and in danger of reducing the avant-garde to an anorexic *arrière-pensée*. Was this art at its most corrupt and knowing, another ceremony of innocence drowned, or could the approach really be justified in the terms Matthew Collings suggested at the outset, as glamour working in the interests of access?

Access, accessible, accessibility. Verb, adjective and noun have had a good run in our time, whether as 'the principle of making education available to those who might normally be excluded from it' (*Oxford Dictionary of New Words*, 1997), or signifying 'to get in touch with (one's deepest inner feelings or subconscious desires), to experience at a deep level' (ibid.), quite apart from the established meaning of 'accessible' as something or somewhere capable of being entered, reached or used as an access. On the physical or material plane the need for access and accessibility is self-evident, whether in the provision of ramps and lifts for wheelchair users, the maintenance of a decent public library system or in widening access to education, something which Estelle Morris as Secretary of State said in an interview at the start of the year we are 'lousy at' as a nation. More broadly, the accessibility of any artistic experience must depend, like many others, on the time available, on employment and social structures as well as individual interest and preference. The trouble is that all too often the matter of access seems to become a validation in itself, as if getting the wheelchair into the building was the end of it, whatever the building might be. At worst this can result in an over-simplification as wilful as any obscurity could be, with complicity and condescension dancing attendance.

The world of poetry has the makings of a good litmus test for the whole business of 'accessibility', as I was reminded when reading *Troubled Thoughts, Majestic Dreams* (Gallery Books, 2001), a selection of prose writings by the Irish poet and critic Dennis O'Driscoll. The word itself surfaces from time to time, as in an interview with Michael Garvey in which, answering the question 'How do you draw people to poetry, how do you move people to be open to it? How do you get people to try it?', O'Driscoll declares that 'I'm not in the least bit proselytising about the art; I have nothing of the salesman in me when it comes to poetry. I am particularly sceptical about the idea of trying to offer people so-called accessible poems as a lure. I don't believe in accessible poems, I only believe in good poems.' Again, in 'A Map of Contemporary Irish Poetry' he observes that 'some of Ciaran Carson's verse, much of Paul Muldoon's and most of Medbh McGuckian's has proved to be less limpid and accessible than that of their elders in Northern Ireland, Seamus Heaney, Derek Mahon, Michael Longley and James Simmons' – but an observation is what it is, not a judgement. Elsewhere he writes of Marianne Moore, 'an ambitious and determined perfectionist, her move with her mother to New York City in 1918 provided what her beloved Henry James called – in a phrase she cited at the end of her poem, 'New York' – "accessibility to experience"'. This phrase must have a particular resonance for O'Driscoll, who works in the Stamp Duty Office in Dublin Castle and is perfectly aware of 'the penalties to be paid for attempting to serve both Muse and Mammon'. Though there are some advantages in this situation, such as the insights it allows into other worker-poets such as Larkin, it also means that his work as poet and critic is corralled into evenings and weekends, with the survival of ideas threatened by a heap of files. Yet, characteristically, he sees both sides of the argument: 'If, at indulgent intervals, I allow myself to worry about the effect my job has on my writing, I also wonder how, were I to retire, my writing would cope with having me around the house all day. With a full-time job, I may be treating my poetry too lightly; without a job, I might take it too seriously.' In such a perspective, which is not without its pride, it is possible to see America's published poets as 'more likely to be found drafting applications for tenure-track teaching posts than drawing up manifestos' ('The Best American Poetry 1997'), and at the same time still to maintain (in the Michael Garvey interview) that 'the aspiration of poetry is always towards the creation of something permanent in language: in our era of the disposable, the ephemeral, this is counter-cultural – as, indeed, is the fact that genuine poetry transcends the blinkered vision of the journalistic present; it inhabits the present, but it is also very much in dialogue with the inherited forms and the great voices of the past.' O'Driscoll may not proselytise, but it is his powerful sense of how poetry might be defined which makes these essays and reviews more than the sum of their parts. This has nothing to do with accessibility any more than what he sees as 'today's preference . . . for poetry that hovers between the oblique and the obscure, that is knowing but not revealing, that hints at significance without doing anything as old-fashioned as delivering any' ('Obiter Poetica').

The best consequence of O'Driscoll's relative apartness from the literary world is the clear-eyed independence of his judgements: and his range is considerable, from the aphorisms collected in 'Obiter Poetica: *From a Poetry Sketchbook'*, which continue the idiom of Wallace Stevens's 'Adagia', (sometimes explicitly, as in 'All poetry is experimental; some poetry is "experimental". The "experimental" kind is about nothing except the "experiment". It is like the play in which the set is the star, or the opera in which the costumes upstage everything else.'), to individual Irish, American, English and other European poets, to more general appraisals of, for example, contemporary Irish poetry, or poetry in translation. O'Driscoll's highly readable, indeed accessible approach stays close to the primary texts and is often witty, his liking for the aphoristic moment not confined to 'Obiter Poetica': of Milosz's *Facing the River*, for example, he writes that 'wise poets cannot be imitated the way that clever poets can: wisdom is not for the workshops; it is a gift – bestowed or earned.' The landscape that such assertions bring into view has interesting parallels with the world of the Turner Prize. Thus 'poetry doesn't move at a speed measurable by journalists. Hence, the media's focus on poems which are political or, better still, "controversial"' ('Obiter Poetica'), while in 'Troubled Thoughts: *Poetry Politics in Contemporary Ireland'*, 'becoming a poet in Ireland is a matter not so much of apprenticeship as audition. Successful poets need to be seen and heard; and (as it is claimed of beauty pageants) "personality" counts for a great deal if you are to win the star prizes. . .'. And 'R. S. Thomas: *The Poetry of Paintings*' allows for a direct comparison between words and works of art:

> Reversing the natural order of things, some poems could be said to be made of images and some visual art to be made of words. In conceptual and installation art, it is almost true to say that the words *are* the work of art far too often; bombastic texts written to accompany trivial exhibits read like attempts to justify verbally what disappoints visually. It is as if the manifesto and not its manifestation was what finally counted.

O'Driscoll's own manifesto, or the core of it, could be said to inhere in a single sentence from 'Pen Pals', where he writes: 'The standard of poetry written cannot be divorced from the ethical standards of poets, who should adopt their own Hippocratic oath – to use language at all times as an instrument of truth.'

It is translation, though, which confronts accessibility with its most direct challenge, and O'Driscoll weighs the matter carefully in the final section of his book, both in a general piece ('In Other Words: *Poetry in Translation*') and in considerations of individual writers. He points out that 'whatever is inevitably lost in translation, far more is to be gained from reading Feinstein's Tsvetaeva or Reid's Neruda or Hamburger's Celan than from wasting time on mediocre and imitative talents in our own language,' and he understands the importance of translation for minority languages, while also seeing that it is hard to outflank the uncompromising attitude of such as John Weightman, who 'writes of translators as if they were engaged in some kind of reverse alchemy, turning gold into dross' and thinks it (in Weightman's own words) 'one of the bitter truths of life that all poetry, whether great or less great, is untranslatable. Whereas music is universal, each good poem is ultimately shut off inside its particular language, and there is no way of appreciating its unique effect apart from knowing that language, and knowing it well . . .'. In another piece ('Sylva Fischerová') O'Driscoll makes the good point that 'abstruseness in translated poetry is troubling because one is unsure whether its source lies in local cultural and linguistic nuances or is merely an instance of that universal phenomenon – obscurity masquerading as profundity.' Then there is the case of Celan ('Seeing Red'), whose poems 'are of the kind that communicate before they are understood or, rather, which communicate without ever being understood.'

Reading this called to mind Eliot's conclusion to his 1932–33 Harvard lectures, *The Use of Poetry and the Use of Criticism*, where he chews over the supposed difficulty of modern poetry, ascribing it to a number of possible causes such as personal ones which 'make it impossible for a poet to express himself in any but an obscure way', or novelty, or the reader's anticipation of difficulty, or even 'the difficulty caused by the author's having left out something which the reader is used to finding'. Two paragraphs later, Eliot is led to this conclusion:

> To return to the question of obscurity: when all exceptions have been made, and after admitting the possible existence of minor 'difficult' poets whose public must always be small, I believe that the poet naturally prefers to write for as large and miscellaneous an audience as possible, and that it is the half-educated and ill-educated, rather than the uneducated, who stand in his way: I myself should like an audience which could neither read nor write. The most useful poetry, socially, would be one which could cut across all the present stratifications of public taste – stratifications which are perhaps a sign of social disintegration. The ideal medium for poetry, to my mind, and the most direct means of social 'usefulness' for poetry, is the theatre.

Quite apart from the tone of *de haut en bas*, and the debatable view that the theatre is the most socially efficacious medium (nowadays it would have to be the internet, television or, just conceivably, the re-emerging cinema) there is something incongruous about the picture of Eliot, book in hand, confronting an audience composed, as he imagines, of patches and rude mechanicals. Time, perhaps, to bring on a volume of Browning, in the hope that it might fall open at 'Andrea del Sarto': 'Ah, but a man's reach should exceed his grasp, / Or what's a heaven for?' Well known

261

as these lines are, they surely only have their full sense when considered in the light of what follows: '. . . all is silver-grey / Placid and perfect with my art: the worse!' This suggests that true glamour, and an altogether more interesting view of the avant-garde, are to be found in the challenges of work predicated not on media appeal, the market or a stale bohemianism, but on real respect for the intelligence of readers or viewers, as well as on the need to pioneer beyond established limits – the desire, in a term noted in the *Oxford Dictionary of New Words*, to push the envelope.

# Polyglots and Pedigree

The Abbey of Thélème, planned and built by Rabelais' enlightened giant Gargantua, was a kind of dream Renaissance comprehensive school true to the derivation of its name (from the Greek θελημα, wish, desire). In pointed contrast to medieval antecedents, the Abbey would have no surrounding walls and no clocks, and there were to be women as well as men, with both alike free to leave at will: and the vows of chastity, poverty and obedience would be replaced by the possibilities of marriage, wealth and freedom. Hexagonal in design, with towers at each turn, the Abbey was to include 'libraries in Greek, Latin, Hebrew, French, Tuscan and Spanish', and inscribed over the main entrance was the Thélémites' sole rule, FAY CE QUE VOULDRAS. 'So nobly were they instructed', Rabelais reports, 'that there was not one amongst them, man or woman, who did not know how to read, write, sing, play tuneful instruments, speak five or six languages and to compose in any of them as much in verse as in prose.' Later in the century Montaigne, too, acknowledges the place of languages in education (in 'De l'institution des enfans'), recommending foreign travel partly to study the character and customs of other nations, and so 'to rub up and hone our brain against that of others': but also 'in order to kill two birds with one stone' by beginning from earliest childhood with visits to 'neighbouring countries where the language is most removed from our own and which, unless you speak it early on, you cannot get your tongue round.' And at the turn of the century, in a play whose alternative title is *What you will*, there is Sir Andrew Aguecheek who, as Sir Toby Belch informs us, 'plays o' the viol-de-gamboys, and speaks three or four languages word for word without book . . .'.

The question of how best to acquire a second language, and at what age, has remained an educational issue on and off right up

263

to the present, when the emergence of the European Union has heightened its relevance. It is given edge by the perceived self-consciousness of the British (or the English?) when it comes to speaking any language other than their own. Historically this has been accompanied by the kind of arrogance exemplified in Walter Bagehot's assertion (in the *National Review* of January 1856) that 'French is the *patois* of Europe, English is the language of the world', an attitude faithfully reflected in the xenophobia of today's tabloids and the tendency to talk of 'going into Europe', as if the United Kingdom were located on an altogether different continent. Nor has the dominance of English in the world of computers and information technology helped linguistic perspectives.

Another historical angle which has cast shadows of its own is the residual impact of Latin and Greek as they used to be taught, trapped in the ghosts of generations past who, like Miss Blimber in *Dombey and Son*, found themselves 'dry and sandy with working in the graves of deceased languages'. Latin had (and continues to have) its own virtues, both in itself and as a kind of meccano set enabling the user to find out about language and about many of the patterns and derivations underlying, for instance, English and French: yet its influence on approaches to modern language teaching has at times seemed baleful. Though the situation has improved enormously over the last thirty years, it is sobering to think how many potentially fluent speakers of an earlier time might have been deterred or inhibited by too gruelling and isolated an insistence on grammar and written work. Witness Goethe, who writes in *Dichtung und Wahrheit* of having to wrestle with Latin grammar, whose rules seemed to him 'ridiculous, since they were contradicted by so many exceptions that I had to learn each one specially.' Like many before and since his time, he relied on rhyming *aide-mémoires* which he enjoyed singing to himself. Better still, his father taught his sister Italian in the same room, and that proved much more interesting than learning Latin by heart: 'I listened from behind the book and picked up the Italian, which struck me as a delightful digression from the Latin, very quickly.'

Now the government has announced a new plan for modern languages, in the wake of the Nuffield Languages Enquiry chaired by Sir Trevor MacDonald. Among the Enquiry's conclusions were that 'there is no rational path of learning from primary school to university and beyond, and investments in one sector are rarely exploited in another': and that 'there is a widespread public perception, backed by research, that learning another language needs to start earlier if the next generation is to achieve higher standards. An early start to language learning also enhances literacy, citizenship and intercultural tolerance.' The government proposes that every child of seven shall be entitled to learn a foreign language, and that from the age of fourteen languages shall no longer be compulsory. The response has been mixed, with on the one hand real enthusiasm for the spread of language teaching in primary schools (one in five already teaches a foreign language), and on the other alarm at the proposed dropping of modern languages from the core curriculum at Key Stage 4 (along with Design and Technology). Then there is that word 'entitled', which certainly doesn't suggest compulsion and even sounds a little evasive, almost an admission that it is a right in principle rather than a sure commitment. Yet the implied wariness may be prudent and necessary, given the likely difficulties of staffing, and of finding extra time in an already packed curriculum.

With the consultation period for the government's green paper relating to education for the 14–19 age group ('Extending Opportunities, Raising Standards') ending on 31 May, the current debate focuses very much on practicalities. The government's plans have been condemned as a devious way of trying to solve the problem of teacher shortages, while the Nuffield Enquiry team has suggested that the removal of languages from the core curriculum would be a blow to national competitiveness. In a letter to the *Times Educational Supplement* (22 February 2002) Steven Fawkes, a past president of the Association for Language Learning, acknowledges that 'flexibility in the curriculum is a good thing' but asks, 'how can any serious proposal at the start of the 21$^{st}$ century even hint that languages might not be an essential part of that flexibility? . . . As the government develops its welcome skills agenda in the 14–19 sector, how can it possibly overlook the huge gap the country currently accepts as a norm in its language skills, at a time when global communication is at a premium?' In an article in the same issue, Helen Ward sees 'finding time in the day and trained staff' as the two major stumbling-blocks in the way of the government's hope of achieving its plan by 2012, and points out that, according to the Nuffield Languages Enquiry, 'just 5.3 per cent of language graduates went into education in 1998'. At the time of writing, responses on the internet are overwhelmingly in favour of an earlier start to language teaching, and enthusiastic about the potential for integrating languages with other subjects and activities, from dance and music to PE. One or two teachers express doubts about their own competence: many more, about staffing and timetabling. One contributor points to the existing role of languages such as Urdu and Gujerati in a Britain that is already multilingual. The argument is not a simple one: and it may also be worth remembering that, at present, it is not uncommon for pupils starting a second foreign language (often German or Spanish) at the age of fourteen to find success and enjoyment in doing so, frequently in contrast to what is perceived as the slog of doing French up till then. On the other hand, it has also been suggested that starting a language earlier can be the basis for a more durable interest. At all events, there is a striking absence from the discussion of reference to literature or the imagination, let alone enjoyment. The emphasis is very much on 'operational competence', with the occasional genuflection to 'intercultural skills' and tolerance.

When it comes to linguistic competence, it does seem that the case for starting earlier is powerful. It is cogently put by Steven Pinker in *The Language Instinct* (Penguin, 1995) – and although he is writing predominantly about the acquisition of a first language, much of his argument would seem to hold equally for a second one (although some would say that learning a second language in childhood can impair acquisition of the first one, the evidence here seems very mixed). Discussing the superiority of children over adults when it comes to language learning, Pinker rehearses the commonly held explanations – that children 'make errors unselfconsciously, are more motivated to communicate, like to conform, are not xenophobic or set in their ways, and have no first language to interfere', but comments that recent evidence is against them, and suggests that 'holding every other factor constant, a key factor stands out: sheer age'. Arguing that 'acquisition of a normal language is guaranteed for children up to the age of six, is steadily compromised from then until shortly after puberty, and is rare thereafter', he cites 'maturational changes in the brain, such as the decline in metabolic rate and number of neurons during the early

school-age years, and the bottoming out of the number of synap-
ses and metabolic rate round puberty' as 'plausible causes',
together with the fact that 'the language-learning circuitry of the
brain is more plastic in childhood'. He concludes that 'language
acquisition might be like other biological functions. The linguistic
clumsiness of tourists and students might be the price we pay for
the linguistic genius we displayed as babies, just as the decrepi-
tude of age is the price we pay for the vigor of youth'.

A concern for precision, a sensitivity to linguistic origins, the
playful enjoyment of the inter-relations of language, an awareness of linguistic contexts – these are matters of moment to
writers as much as to linguists, and no one underlines this more
clearly than Ezra Pound, in his literary essays. In 'The Serious
Artist' (1913) he declares that 'the touchstone of an art is its precision', and sees this as implying a sense of control particularly
pertinent for poetry with its highly energised use of language. He
also sees knowledge of more than one language as an essential
qualification, not only for writers but for critics as well:

> Every critic should give indication of the sources and limits
> of his knowledge. The criticism of English poetry by men
> who knew no language but English, or who knew little but
> English and school-classics, has been a marasmus. When we
> know to what extent each sort of expression has been driven,
> in, say, half a dozen great literatures, we begin to be able to
> tell whether a given work has the excess of great art. We
> would not think of letting a man judge pictures if he knew
> only English pictures, or music if he knew only English
> music – or only French or German music for that matter.

In a later essay, 'How to Read', Pound reiterates that exactness is
the truly human measure, and defines great literature as 'simply
language charged with meaning to the utmost possible degree',
while 'different languages – I mean the actual vocabularies, the
idioms – have worked out certain mechanisms of communication
and registration. No one language is complete.' More tenden-
tiously, perhaps, he argues that

> one does not need to learn a whole language in order to
> understand some one or some dozen poems. It is often

enough to understand thoroughly the poem, and every one of the few dozen or few hundred words that compose it.

This is what we start to do as small children when we memorize some lyric of Goethe or Heine. Incidentally, this process leaves us for life with a measuring rod (a) for a certain type of lyric, (b) for the German language, so that . . . we never wholly forget the feel of the language.

When Pound writes about language, he does so with passionate curiosity, holding in his mind both the variety and the universality of humanity's 'most efficient registering material', as he calls it in 'Date Line' (1934). 'Language is not a mere cabinet curio or museum exhibit . . . You cannot govern without it, you cannot make laws without it'. In one sense, of course, language *is* a museum exhibit, as Penelope Lively reminds us in her 1987 novel *Moon Tiger*: 'We are walking lexicons. In a single sentence of idle chatter we preserve Latin, Anglo-Saxon, Norse; we carry a museum inside our heads, each day we commemorate peoples of whom we have never heard.' As to the relation of language to governance, it is instructive to consider what has happened in the two generations since Pound wrote, as recorded for instance by a commentator such as George Steiner. *In Bluebeard's Castle* (Faber, 1971) still reads pertinently. Steiner amply shares Pound's respect for language – 'an explicit grammar is an acceptance of order: it is a hierarchization, the more penetrating for being enforced so early in the individual life-span, of the forces and valuations prevailing in the body politic': yet his view is bleaker. He doubts the continuing primacy of the word in a world increasingly dominated by 'the new sound-sphere', in which 'the vocabularies, the contextual behaviour-patterns of pop and rock, constitute a genuine *lingua franca*, a 'universal dialect' of youth. Everywhere a sound-culture seems to be driving back the old authority of verbal order.'

More recently, Steiner has spoken and written about the undesirability of English acquiring too much authority as a global language, at the expense of other languages. Stephen Pinker would agree with him: he sees 'the wide-scale extinction of languages' as 'reminiscent of the current (though less severe) wide-scale extinction of plant and animal species'. Enter Dr Johnson, who observed: 'I am always sorry when any language is lost, because languages are the pedigree of nations'. Quite so – and wouldn't it also be a pity if we were to lose sight of the pleasure, as well as the insights, to be had from learning languages? For instance, isn't there enjoyment to be had from Johnson's remark by discovering that 'pedigree' comes from the French *pied de grue*, a crane's foot, bearing witness to the shape of the symbol once used to show descent on genealogical tables? Languages help us to enjoy language, as well as to deploy it more effectively in the interests of truth and precision. And in granting us access to the literature of other tongues, they also bear out the force of Wittgenstein's comment that 'the limits of my language mean the limits of my world.'

# The Long Home

It is Ennius, best known for his *Annals*, who provides the first of two epigraphs for Geoffrey Hill's *Speech! Speech!* (Penguin, 2000) – AT TUBA TERRIBILI SONITU TARATANTARA DIXIT ('And the trumpet in terrible tones went taratantara'). The second, from Günter Grass, reinforces a sense of finality as well as theatre: VORHANG, BEVOR DU DEN BEIFALL BEGREIFST ('Curtain, before you comprehend the applause'). Taken together, they introduce the perspectives of mortality and oblivion which are two amongst many presences in Hill's 'theatre of voices', to use his own phrase from the poem. From time to time they surface explicitly, whether as 'simple bio-degradation, a slather / of half-rotted black willow leaves / at the lake's edge', or in the context of the contemporary world and its values:

> POSTERITY I how daring! Waste of effort?
> You may conclude so. I do not
> so understand it. Yoú may
> write this off I but it shall not be read so.

Or the subject becomes part of a direction to an actor: 'Act through a few poor mime faces; pose late / reflexion. As not unreflecting try / posterity.' Ennius is a particularly appropriate choice for an opening shot, when it comes to durability. Born in Calabria in 239 BC, he was the author of tragedies, comedies and satires, as well as the *Annals*, to which he devoted the last fifteen years of his life, and which he began with a claim that he was Homer reincarnated – a truth revealed to him in a dream by the ghost of Homer himself. Yet all that survives of a work which may have exceeded 20,000 lines is 600 lines: and even their survival is due, according to the *Oxford History of Classical Literature*, to the fact that 'they were quoted by later authors, often to illustrate a linguistic point or an Ennian reminiscence in Virgil'.

There is no more forceful essay on oblivion than Ecclesiastes, with the Preacher's constant emphasis on vanity and the little-ness of an existence in which 'there is no remembrance of former things'. As for justice, 'the race is not to the swift, nor the battle to the strong, neither yet bread to the wise, nor yet riches to men of understanding, nor yet favour to men of skill; but time and chance happeneth to them all.' As for perspectives, 'all are of the dust, and all turn to dust again', and 'man goeth to his long home, and the mourners go about the streets.' As for writers and readers, 'of making many books there is no end; and much study is a weariness of the flesh.' Even the injunction 'to eat, and to drink, and to be merry' sounds like a minimal consolation in this context, proferred 'because a man hath no better thing under the sun'. Yet, as if by way of a riposte, Ecclesiastes is followed by 'The Song of Solomon', with its delight in the quick of life. Here, 'the winter is past, the rain is over and gone; the flowers appear on the earth; the time of the singing of birds is come'. It is the season of renewal, in which 'he brought me to the banqueting house, and his banner over me was love'. Singing the senses, the writer concludes that 'love is as strong as death', and that 'many waters cannot quench love, neither can the floods drown it'.

Writers down the ages have weighed *now* against *always*, beauty against Lethe, reminding their readers that nothing lasts for ever yet sometimes hoping, like Horace in the fourth book of his *Odes*, that 'the man worthy of praise the Muse forbids to die'. In English literature a *locus classicus* for the stark contest between love and oblivion is the world of Shakespeare's sonnets and the tradition underlying them. As in Ronsard and Du Bellay, it is specifically the power of poetry, even more than that of outwitting death by breeding, which is the antidote to the depredations of time, the possible miracle 'That in black ink my love may still shine bright' (Sonnet 65). Again and again the hopeful note is sounded, often in a sonnet's closing lines, as in these examples:

> So long as men can breathe or eyes can see,
> So long lives this, and this gives life to thee.     (18)

Yet do thy worst, old Time; despite thy wrong,
My love shall in my verse ever live young.     (19)

His beauty shall in these black lines be seen,
And they shall live, and he in them still green.  (63)

To subsume the conflict of 'Omnia mors poscit' and 'Omnia vincit
Amor', the poet conjures the conceit of words. In doing so, he
treads the border of two territories, immortalising himself as well
as the object of his attention in the process. 'Your monument shall
be my gentle verse' (Sonnet 81): his own monument too.

Even when society sidelines poets, the afterlife of words and
the odds of their survival remain a perennial concern for them, as
Ian Hamilton points out in the introduction to *Against Oblivion*
(Viking, 2002), a title whose poignancy is supplemented by his
own death last December. In the twentieth century, he observes,
'. . . poets continued to write poems, and continued also to insist
that what they had to offer was, potentially, of world-altering significance. In practice, as they could all too clearly see, the world
did not have much use for them.' (The book is somewhat oddly
subtitled *Some Lives of the Twentieth-Century Poets,* with *Some* suggesting a metampsychotic multiplicity, and *the* a comprehensive
finality, surely neither an impression intended.) Hamilton takes
Johnson's *Lives of the Poets* as his model although, as he mentions,
Johnson's selection covered two centuries, while he confines
himself to one. He has selected 45 poets, all dead, 23 of them
American, the rest mostly English. Even this selection is, as
Hamilton sees it, unlikely to live up to the book's title *en bloc*: by
analogy with earlier anthologies such as Harold Monro's *Some
Contemporary Poets* (1920) or, fifteen years on, Michael Roberts's
*Faber Book of Modern Verse*, 'it does seem a fair bet that in, say, one
hundred years from now, about half the poets I have chosen . . .
will have become lost to the general view'. Yet if poets are at the
mercy of fashion (nicely described as 'one of oblivion's most reliable lieutenants'), fashion can also help reputations to last for a
time. Hamilton might also have alluded to the opposite case of
poets such as Blake, Clare or Emily Dickinson, fully appreciated
only after their time. But he does make mention of the afterlives
of the poets in the light of their biographers, whether Lawrance
Thompson's vengeful life of Frost or the 'serious dent in Larkin's

Betjeman-like image' made by the appearance of Larkin's letters (edited by Anthony Thwaite) and Andrew Motion's biography. Four poets, however, are excluded on the ground that they have already outmanoeuvred oblivion. For Hardy, Yeats, Eliot and Auden, seen as tetrarchs of the twentieth century, 'oblivion presents no threat', though they may themselves feature as models or, threateningly, 'giant-sized inhibitors' for other poets struggling along in their shadow.

There comes to be a certain predictability about the book's format: some three or four pages mingling critical comment and biographical detail, often including the text of a poem or part of a poem, and ending with one or, more usually, two poems (nearly a quarter of these poems have death as their subject). And the brevity of the entries can tend to cursoriness, for instance in the downbeat assessment of Louis MacNeice. Very occasionally Hamilton allows himself to range more widely, as in interesting excursions about what Wilfred Owen might have become, or about the Beat Generation. Surprisingly often, the poem at the end of an entry is the one already discussed and set out in part, which doesn't do much for the book's liveliness. But there is plenty of energy in Hamilton's characteristic judgements, his natural conciseness reinforced by the summary nature of the undertaking. Thus Edward Thomas is 'a self-lacerating moaner', while 'Pound was always at his best when he stopped thinking . . .'. In the case of Graves, 'a knowledge of the life does tend to undermine one's admiration of the work.' Betjeman is seen as the author of 'slick, sociological light verse' whose rhythms are essentially mechanical and whose verse autobiography *Summoned by Bells* is dismissed as 'a work both tedious and twee.' Hugh MacDiarmid is condemned for his 'glum dicta', and for being 'more concerned with programmes than with actual poetry', and when it comes to the work of R. S. Thomas, 'the reader doesn't read: he listens in.' Hamilton evinces a firm dislike of the dour, the decorative and the dionysiac, and put-downs are considerable in number and degree. Hilda Doolittle, Robinson Jeffers, Allen Tate, Stephen Spender, Randall Jarrell and Dylan Thomas fare no better, and in some cases worse, than MacDiarmid, R. S. Thomas and Betjeman. Presumably intended in part to validate the praise given to others, often qualified though that may be, such instances also raise the awkward question of why they are included at all in a book which must itself afford some sort of stay, however temporary, against oblivion. On the other hand Hamilton can be sympathetic as well as tough: Edna St Vincent Millay, Ginsberg and Larkin are among the beneficiaries.

The interest of the book is not, however, limited to the individual choices and judgements it makes: it is impossible not to be struck by the repeated examples of high ambition, aggressive disappointment, instability and sheer self-consciousness, and the more or less extreme outcomes of what Hamilton calls, with reference to Larkin, 'strands of aspiration and defeat'. The Faustian bargaining of the soul, in return for fame as much as knowledge, seems close to the core of some of these lives and can exact a heavy price: alcohol and suicide feature. 'Sub specie aeternitatis' can come to seem like a quest for the I of eternity. The whole matter of oblivion (with its two meanings, of forgetting as well as of being forgotten) raises the issues of memory, collective and individual, and of value. And of perspectives, from Hamilton's century on to the fiery end of the planet (or, to revert to a Shakespeare sonnet, '. . . the eyes of all posterity / That wear this world out to the ending doom').

Is this nothing more than vanity, at best the kind of pathetic version of it encapsulated in Alfred de Musset's wish to have a weeping willow hanging over his grave in the Père Lachaise (the tree has regularly to be replanted)? Is it even peculiar to poets, rather than a fundamental yearning of the species, a feature of the human imagination? What does come across strongly in the book is the intensity and scope of poets' ambitions, their desire to enact the presence of the grain of sand and the world, but also to cheat mortality. They want the wild flower and heaven: hæcceity and eternity, or its *Ersatz* version, posterity. And the thought of being denied this seems to breed in some poets a real rage, a sense of injustice which may spin out of control or bring on complete disillusionment.

In Hamilton's book, the struggle for artistic fulfilment often comes up against the demands of relationships as well as the longing for recognition, and the interplay of biography and the work, though compressed here, is crucial. A similar emphasis on relationships is evident in many of James Fenton's lectures given as Oxford Professor of Poetry, collected as *The Strength of Poetry* (Oxford, 2001). Fenton has in common with Hamilton the poetry of Frost, Owen, Lawrence, Moore, Bishop, Larkin and Plath and, on a lesser level of allusion, Millay, Pound, Lowell and Hughes. Questions of influence, development and the nature of artistic endeavour are often considered in the context of encounters of one kind or another: Michelangelo and Giambologna, Wordsworth and Keats, Larkin and his father, Marianne Moore and her mother, Shakespeare and the young man and dark lady of the sonnets, Auden and Kallman. Some relationships are political rather than personal – Heaney and the British, Indians and Fijians, imperialists and those they seek to dominate, the effects of war, Britain and Ireland: and the political dimension is an important element of the book.

'Why', asks Fenton in the opening lecture, 'should a sculptor, a poet, feel the need to be the unique object of admiration, to create around himself an illusion of being quite the only pebble, the only boulder on the beach?' – and, returning to a point he made in 'The Manila Manifesto', he suggests that this urge to stand out derives from the uniqueness of childhood, a time when 'everything we did was hailed as superb', when 'we learnt about rhythm and we learnt new ways of making a noise, and every noise we made was praised.' But then 'primal erasure' causes us to forget this happy phase and, as 'The Manila Manifesto' puts it, 'The remainder of our lives is spent in recapturing that initial sense of discovery. This is the second poetry'.

Relaxed in style and approach, the lectures cover a deal of ground and engage with a multiplicity of themes – betrayal, war, cowardice, homosexuality, women and poetry, envy, secrecy. Nationhood, and what the diminished 'post-imperial *patria*' might turn out to be, constitutes another interesting strand of Fenton's thinking. What links many of the lectures is a thought-provoking consideration of what enables, or disables, poetry for the vulnerable individual. Thus Keats had to wrestle with Wordsworth's vanity; Wilfred Owen had to find a way on from the rhetorical poeticisms of his juvenilia, a process much more complex and uncertain, Fenton thinks, than the neat teleology of 'an Owen shocked into the twentieth century by war'; Larkin had to come to terms with his rejection by the army and by Bletchley, his failure to fulfil his Romantic aspirations, his sense of Britain being in decline; Plath, in discovering the persona of Lady Lazarus, 'subscribed to a fatal vocation'.

Many of Fenton's themes converge in the final three lectures, all of them about Auden. In 'Auden on Shakespeare's Sonnets', Fenton defends Auden convincingly against those who have accused him of hypocrisy and cowardice in not being frank about Shakespeare's sexuality, out of a desire to conceal his own. Again, the focus is on relationships – Shakespeare's with the young man, Auden's with Gerhart Meyer. In 'Blake Auden and James Auden', Fenton suggests that 'in Auden's work prose and poetry interpenetrate to a far greater extent than in the work of any other English-language poet of this century': and while 'Blake sat at Auden's left when he wrote, urging concision, definite views, plain language', at his right sat Henry James, 'suggesting fascinating syntaxes and ways of prolonging a sentence'. Going on to discuss the impact of these twin influences on Auden, 'a rhetorician of the highest powers', Fenton again comes to the poet's defence, this time against the onslaught unleashed by Orwell following the publication of the poem 'Spain' (though Nancy Cunard's letter of 1937 surely did not request contributions for a book called *Authors Take Sides on Vietnam*). The final lecture, 'Auden in the End', returns to the subject of Shakespeare's sonnets, and repeats Auden's comment to Spender (already quoted in the preceding lecture) that 'Art is born of humiliation'. Fenton links this with Auden's own experiences in love, distinguishing between poems of transparency and those written in a kind of code, while suggesting that 'a poem may be at the same time transparent and undisclosing'. In the end, though, Fenton sees Auden as not only the most gifted poet of his time, but alienated in many respects and homeless. This contrasts strongly with Marianne Moore, of whom Fenton writes in the sixth lecture, 'I have said that she did not always lead a sheltered life, but she certainly never (after Bryn Mawr) left home, and the home she never left was a force field of astonishing strength and durability.'

When it comes down to it, what Fenton's lectures convey is that only self-knowledge, self-belief and the deployment of the given talent may offer the poet shelter from his or her accusers, or a way on from hurtful experience, or, after the lost childhood, a sense of home short of the long home. Perhaps the strength of poetry is that, for all the imbalance with which it is associated, it can somehow go on celebrating memorably the complex character of a species trapped, in Pascal's words, between nothingness and infinity, 'un milieu entre rien et tout': and in doing so, maintain the imagination's bulwark against oblivion.

# The King's Head

In book XIX of *The Odyssey* Homer relates how Odysseus, still guarding the secret of his true identity, arrives home on Ithaca and gives Penelope a fictitious account of his adventures, complete with a story about his encounters with her husband and his conviction that he will return within a month. Then he goes to bathe, attended by his old nurse Euryclea. She fetches water and chats about her absent master who, she comments, must be about the same age as the stranger and indeed looks uncommonly like him. Any suspicion she might have is confirmed when she feels the scar on his knee, a wound sustained while hunting a wild boar on Parnassus. The dramatic moment of recognition is engagingly rendered in Pope's 1725 translation:

> Deep o'er his knee inseam'd remained the scar:
> Which noted token of the woodland war
> When Euryclea found, the ablution ceased:
> Down dropp'd the leg, from her slack hand released;
> The mingled fluids from the base redound;
> The vase reclining floats the floor around!
> Smiles dew'd with tears the pleasing strife express'd
> Of grief and joy, alternate in her breast.
> Her fluttering words in melting murmurs died;
> At length abrupt – "My son! – My king!" she cried.

A less operatic but equally telling instant of royal recognition is related by Henry Moore's biographer Roger Berthoud, in connection with one of Moore's most famous bronzes, *King and Queen*. The piece dates from 1952, the year of King George VI's death and the present queen's accession, but Berthoud suggests that if these events did enter into Moore's thinking, they did so unconsciously. He gives a fascinating account, though, of the sculpture's coming into being: 'One day he [Moore] was playing with a piece of mod-elling wax when it began to resemble a horned, bearded, Pan-like head. It grew a crown, and he recognized it as the head of a king, so he gave it a body, using the strength of the wax when it hardens to repeat the slender, aristocratic refinement he had found in the head.'

It's that notion of recognition, as distinct from discovery, which is so intriguing: that moment not quite within the gift of reason when the artist knows what has come alive. When the poem falls into focus. One aspect of it is the business of attending to the material – or, in terms of writing, to the initial image or first idea. What does it want to become? And, sooner or later, *how* is it to become? A whole lineage of creative thought has nurtured the theme of receptivity, the writer as much worked upon as working, from a prophetic or shamanistic possession to Keats's 'negative capability' to the artist as conduit, the instrument upon which creation in some form or other plays its tunes. But quite apart from the taboos of one kind or another which prevent us from recognising the consciously forgotten or the suppressed, let alone what we misremember or have a complete blind spot for, is an entirely objective attentiveness, ego-free, really possible? Auden, in his essay 'Pride and Prayer', seemed to think so: 'To pray is to pay attention to, or shall we say, to "listen" to someone or something other than oneself. Whenever a man so concen-trates his attention – be it on a landscape or a poem or a geomet-rical problem or an idol or the True God – that he completely forgets his own ego and desires in listening to what the other has to say to him, he is praying.' What poets of many times and tem-peraments agree on is the impossibility of willing a poem into being – and that something altogether more mysterious is going on, part of a process which they describe in various ways. Shelley, for instance, memorably: '. . . the mind in creation is like a fading coal, which some invisible influence, like an inconstant wind, awakens to transitory brightness; this power arises from within, like the colour of a flower which fades and develops as it is devel-oped, and the conscious portions of our natures are unprophetic either of its approach or its departure.' Or Yeats, asserting in *Essays and Introductions* that 'a poet writes always of his personal life, in his finest work out of its tragedy, whatever it be, remorse, lost love, or mere loneliness; he never speaks directly as to

someone at the breakfast table, there is always a phantasmago-
ria', while also maintaining that the poet 'is never the bundle of
accident and incoherence that sits down to breakfast; he has been
reborn as an idea, something intended, complete.' And quite
apart from breakfast, which seems to be a considerable measuring point, Yeats contends that 'all that is personal soon rots; it
must be packed in ice or salt.'

Auden wrote, with his characteristic sweep, that for the poet
'every poem he writes involves his whole past'. Robert Frost
burrows into this question instructively in 'The Figure a Poem
Makes', suggesting that 'the initial delight is in the surprise of
remembering something I didn't know I knew . . . there is a glad
recognition of the long lost and the rest follows.' But there is more
to this than might seem at first: 'It must be a revelation, or a series
of revelations, as much for the poet as for the reader. For it to be
that there must have been the greatest freedom of the material to
move about in it and to establish relations in it regardless of time
and space, previous relation, and everything but affinity.' He
goes on to define this freedom as 'the condition of body and mind
now and then to summons aptly from the vast chaos of all I have
lived through.' The chaos includes a view of the way in which
poets acquire knowledge: 'They stick to nothing deliberately, but
let what will stick to them like burrs where they walk in the
fields.' In a letter to John T. Bartlett, Frost also reminds us that
'recognition' is a concept not limited to the writer and his or her
past: 'A word about recognition: In literature it is our business to
give people the thing that will make them say, "Oh yes I know
what you mean." It is never to tell them something they don't
know, but something they know and hadn't thought of saying. It
must be something they recognize.' But, to return to 'The Figure
a Poem Makes', in the act of creation 'the artist must value
himself as he snatches a thing from some previous order in time
and space into a new order with not so much as a a ligature clinging to it of the old place where it was organic.'

So something almost alchemical happens, if Shelley and Yeats
and Frost are right, to transmute the past – to recognise it in a new
way. One of the clearest considerations of what such a process
might involve is to be found in Mary Warnock's *Imagination &
Time* (Blackwell, 1994). Briefly, Warnock begins with Hume's
view of the imagination as enabling us to relive the past, but

disagrees with his suggestion that memory is more vivid, concluding that 'memory should be regarded as a sub-class of imagination, not as a wholly separate "faculty"'. Going on to explore elements of the Romantic imagination, she proceeds via Coleridge (considering, from 'Dejection: an Ode', lines including 'My shaping spirit of Imagination') and Kant (who saw the imagination as 'a powerful agent for creating as it were a second nature out of the material supplied to it by the first nature') to Wordsworth, in whose work she sees a crucial interdependence of time and truth:

> For he held that truth could be reached only through remembered perceptions. What happens to a child is retained, and turned, by the adult he becomes, into a truth that has an application beyond himself. There is a kind of alchemy in memory which turns the ephemeral impression into the eternal verity. The child receives immediate and instantaneous impressions which turn out, when he revisits them, to contain what is timeless. Because memory is at the core of this process, it follows that the discovery of truth is personal
> . . .

Thus Warnock sees in, for instance, 'Lines written above Tintern Abbey', a transformation of the established sentimental idiom of a poem of 're-visit' into a truth seen as 'permanent and shared'. Likewise, in the 'Ode: Intimations of Immortality from Recollections of early Childhood', 'the power of the poem . . . lies not merely in its philosophical content but in its emotional swing towards and away from nostalgic melancholy.' And if the conversion of personal experience into something thought of as universal truth seems a process no longer available to the artist, it may still be philosophically the case that, as Warnock suggests later in the book, 'cognitive recognition' (which need not, she thinks, be dependent on language in order to occur) is an essential feature of responding to the past.

Re-reading *The Prelude* (with its alternative title of 'Growth of a Poet's Mind') in the light of *Time & Imagination* emphasised how much there is in it about memory, and about the almost actual changes which Wordsworth sees it as wreaking upon experience. 'Rememberable things', however haphazard or inconsequential they may seem at the time, remain as direct or indirect triggers, 'Until maturer seasons call them forth / To impregnate and to elevate the mind.' (Book I). And the very act of remembering plays its part in transmuting 'those fleeting moods / Of shadowy exultation':

> ... the soul,
> Remembering how she felt, but what she felt
> Remembering not, retains an obscure sense
> Of possible sublimity, whereto
> With growing faculties she doth aspire, ... (Book II)

Book III emphasises the uniqueness of the individual, whose memories are therefore entirely personal: but more and more as the poem goes on it enacts the processes of memory's transformations and the power of language to bring them about, as Wordsworth describes in the closing lines of Book V:

> ... Visionary power
> Attends the motions of the viewless winds
> Embodied in the mystery of words:
> There, darkness makes abode, and all the host
> Of shadowy things work endless changes, – there,
> As in a mansion like their proper home,
> Even forms and substances are circumfused
> By that transparent veil with light divine,
> And, through the turnings intricate of verse,
> Present themselves as objects recognised,
> In flashes, and with glory not their own.

In its examination of 'the curious props / By which the world of memory and thought / Exists and is sustained' (Book VII), and its author's intention of capturing 'the spirit of the Past / For future restoration' (Book XIV), *The Prelude* is both more complex and more interesting than Eliot's dismissal of 'emotion recollected in tranquillity' in 'Tradition and the Individual Talent' might lead us to believe. In fact when Eliot writes that, far from being any such thing, poetry is 'a concentration, and a new thing resulting from the concentration, of a very great number of experiences which to the practical and active person would not seem to be experiences at all; it is a concentration which does not happen consciously or of deliberation', it is hard to see how Wordsworth would have disagreed with him, as it is when Eliot describes the poet's mind as 'a receptacle for seizing and storing up numberless feelings, phrases, images, which remain there until all the particles which can unite to form a new compound are present together.' In his desire to distinguish between 'personal emotions' in poetry and poetry as 'an escape from emotion', Eliot seems to under-estimate the first half of the phrase from the Preface to the second edition of the *Lyrical Ballads*, which sees poetry itself as 'the spontaneous overflow of powerful feelings' and asserts only that it 'takes its origins from emotion recollected in tranquillity'.

A more recent preface, that of David Jones to *The Anathemata*, brings epic perspectives to the notion of recollection. The poet states his belief that poetry involves anamnesis, and that 'there is, in the principle that informs the poetic art, a something which cannot be disengaged from the mythus, deposits, *matière*, ethos, whole *res* of which the poet is himself a product'. He sees engagement with these 'deposits' as indispensable in seeking a definition of poetry. Explaining the title of his work, which he traces from an English plural meaning 'devoted things', Jones relates it to 'the blessed things that have taken on what is cursed and the profane things that somehow are redeemed . . . the donated and votive things, the things dedicated after whatever fashion, the things in some sense made separate, being "laid up from other things", or some aspect of them, that partake of the extra-utile and of the gratuitous. . .'. In a crucial footnote, he offers a gloss on the idea of anamnesis, quoting from Dom Gregory Dix's *The Shape of the Liturgy*:

> The dictionary defines its general meaning as 'the recalling of things past'. But what is the nature of this particular recalling? I append the following quotation as being clear and to the point: "It (anamnesis) is not quite easy to represent accurately in English, words like 'remembrance' or 'memorial' having for us a connotation of something *absent* which is only mentally recollected. But in the Scriptures of both the Old and New Testaments *anamnesis* and the cognate verb have a sense of "recalling" or "representing" before God an

event in the past so that it becomes *here and now operative by its effects."*

That making present, or re-presentation, of the past, is strongly reminiscent of *Remembrance of Things Past* in which, as Mary Warnock writes, 'the existence of the past . . . is assured by its encapsulation in a present experience. Proust's narrator then determines to capture this reality, to cause it to live longer than the moment in which the two sensations, present and past, coexist, one overlaid on the top of the other before evaporating.' The 'self-haunting spirit' of *The Prelude* would have understood exactly what Proust meant by the joy that was to be experienced in the process – a manifest creative affirmation no less faithful in its way than David Jones's *The Anathemata*, which John Heath-Stubbs describes in *The Literary Essays* (Carcanet, 1998) as 'his *Odyssey,* a voyaging home through the seas of memory'.

# 2003

# Acquainted with Grief

Over the last year the word associated by Isaiah with 'a man of sorrows' has been widely used in contexts of public mourning as well as private loss. 'Grief': clenched, terse, almost gruff, the sound of the word half stifles what it expresses. It carries the sense of hurt and damage, the weight of its Latin origin. Like its German equivalent 'Gram', it retains a rough edge, in contrast with the mellifluous French, Italian and Spanish – douleur, dolore, dolor – whose vowels seem as near to balm as to pain. In any language, grief can outflank the social and ritual mechanisms designed to both articulate and dissolve it. Raw, without compromise, unleavened, it is stasis, with the abyss opened: perhaps that is something of what Dr Johnson meant when he remarked to Mrs Thrale in April 1781 that 'grief is a species of idleness'. Only rarely does grief induce the heightened awareness of the protagonist in Robert Graves's 'Lost Love': 'His eyes are quickened so with grief, / He can watch a grass or leaf / Every instant grow.' More often the best that can be hoped is an empathetic understanding, of the kind present in the opening lines of Blake's 'On Another's Sorrow':

> Can I see another's woe,
> And not be in sorrow too?
> Can I see another's grief,
> And not seek for kind relief?

By the end of the poem, that capacity for fellow-suffering has been explicitly transferred to the sorrowing Christ evoked by Isaiah ('He becomes a man of woe; / He doth feel the sorrow too' – and, in the words of the closing lines, 'Till our grief is fled and gone / He doth sit by us and moan').

In its public manifestations, grief partakes of something else –

a sense of drama and occasion, historical heightening of a kind which can characterise not only mourning but celebration. This is the spirit common to the crowds hacking at the Berlin Wall in 1989, the spectators at Princess Diana's funeral and participants at events commemorating the first anniversary of the attack on the World Trade Centre. And public grief has an element of solidarity, even of sociability, which is absent from its private equivalent. Yet it, too, speaks powerfully to the individual, as Rowan Williams highlights in his thought-provoking meditation on the events of 11 September 2001, *Writing in the Dust* (Hodder & Stoughton, 2002). Granting that we need 'time and opportunity to grieve', he also seeks 'to ask whether anything can *grow* through this terrible moment'. Himself close to Ground Zero at the time of the attack, he spots, even in the eerie choking aftermath of dust and what seemed to him quietness, the possibility of a breathing space. For him, the breathing space of grief can lead to the rediscovery of hope. But, towards the end of his meditation, he emphasises the importance of learning 'to grieve properly':

> Of course, we just grieve anyway, 'properly' or not; but where does our grief take us? And what do we mourn for? If, as St Augustine says in his *Confessions*, we can fail to 'love humanly', then surely we can also fail to grieve humanly, to grieve without the consolation of drama, martyrdom, resentment and projection. Are there words for grief that can make us more human, so that we mourn, not just for ourselves but for those whose experience we have come to share, even for those whose moral poverty is responsible for murder and terror?

Williams's questions present writers and artists with a particular challenge. It was restated specifically by Peter Conrad a year on from 11 September 2001, in an *Observer* article headlined 'The Presumption of Art'. Conrad writes of the dangers inherent in art's 'double function', its truth-telling by fiction, while acknowledging that 'the temptation to see that day in artistic terms . . . is understandable, because it pacifies the raw, enraged pain: the aesthetic is the anaesthetic.' He goes on to note the 'inadvertent, possibly shameful wonderment' which characterised literary

descriptions of the attack and asks: 'How can we forgive ourselves for feeling, along with our terror, so fiercely elated?' Art
may empathise, it may enable the recovery of humour, it may
even assist 'what the gurus on talk shows call "the healing
process"', but finally it should not presume to be able to achieve
more than a limited amount. For Conrad, it is musicians rather
than writers or playwrights who have best understood what he
sees as the prime human need in such a situation, the need not to
be alone. Yet he also suggests that, among all the acts of remembrance one year on, 'the most apt tribute will be the most
minimal: an inventory of almost 3,000 names, to be read out
during the hour and a half that separated the first plane's colli-
sion and the crumbling of the second tower.' In the event, the
reading aloud of the names of the victims was indeed powerful,
even at television's anodyne remove, representing a stark conjunction of the public and the personal, as well as a reminder of
the essentially private nature of grief. And as if unwittingly illus-
trating the mismatch between grief and the everyday, the reading
of the names took much longer than anticipated.

Such sorrowful naming, when it involves the committal of the
personal to the public realm of print, is a zone well explored by
poets, whether as exorcism, celebration or elegiac convention.
And many of the best explorations of grief have to do with time,
the tyranny which sorrow seems strong enough to arrest or dis-
locate ('And time remembered is grief forgotten', wrote
Swinburne of the arrival of spring, in 'Atalanta in Calydon').
Whether time can ever really heal is the question confronted by
Emily Dickinson in one of her longer poems, 'I measure every
grief I meet': considering the various causes of grief ('There's
Grief of Want – and Grief of Cold – / A sort they call "Despair"
– / There's Banishment from native Eyes – / In sight of Native
Air –'), she characterises each as one form of the suffering borne
by Christ and finds herself at the end of the poem 'Still fasci-
nated to presume / That Some – are like My Own –'. Another,
shorter, poem, also probably written in 1862, Dickinson's superabundant year, begins ''Tis good – the looking back on Grief –',
and provides an answer to the first poem's question about grief
and time. In time, it is suggested here, grief can become transparent, seen in the perspective of a past which Dickinson
conveys in a beautiful image:

To recollect how Busy Grass
Did meddle – one by one –
Till all the Grief with Summer – waved
And none could see the stone.

To look back on grief is also to take courage when confronted
with present trouble:

And though the Woe you have Today
Be larger – As the Sea
Exceeds its Unremembered Drop –
They're Water – equally –

It could be argued that grief resides centrally in the inarticulate
nature of its immediacy: as Benedick puts it in Act III of *Much Ado
About Nothing*, 'Well, everyone can master a grief but he that has
it.' In this perspective any poem of lament is already a retrospect,
and the act of artistic making an achievement of distance from the
rawness of the emotion itself, even if also a recalling of it: often it
is as much invocation as evocation. Many elegiac poems have
also been part of a long convention of memorial verse. Thus
George Herbert, for instance, in the first of his sequence of nine-
teen Greek and Latin poems in memory of his mother, begins by
asking 'Ah Mater, quo te deplorem fonte? Dolores / Quæ guttæ
poterunt enumerare meos' ('Ah, mother, with what fountain may
I weep for you? / What drops could enumerate my sorrows?')
and concludes '. . . et ista Dolor nunc tibi Metra parit' ('. . . and it
is for you that my grief now gives birth to these poems'). One of
the best known of English memorial poems is Henry King's 'An
Exequy To his matchless never to be forgotten Freind', written in
honour of his wife, Anne, who was buried in London on 5
January 1624. The affection of the title is wonderfully sustained
through the poem's 120 lines, with never a trace of self-pity or
sentimentality even though, as the survivor, King knows 'How
lazily Time creepes about / To one that mournes'. The poem's
argument, the way in which it meditates upon the interplay of
grief and time, braces it. To remember his dead wife is in fact to
make time go backwards. Were this condition of grief the case
only for a limited time, it might be tolerable: 'But woe is mee! the
longest date / To narrowe is to calculate / These empty hopes.'

Only the end of the world will bring an end, by reuniting them at the last judgement. Till then, the poet commends his wife to the care of death:

> Be kind to Hir: and prethee look
> Thou write into thy doomsday book
> Each parcell of this Rarity
> Which in thy Caskett shrin'd doth ly . . .

Envisaging his own death, King measures time future as the distance between him and his wife ('Each minute is a short Degree, / And ev'ry Howre a stepp towards Thee'). His wife may have been in the van, 'But hark! My Pulse like a soft Drum / Beates my Approach; Tells Thee I come'. Miraculously, in the midst of lament, the muffled funeral drum becomes a lover's signal. By defining all measures of time in terms of his love for his wife, King accurately conveys the static, ubiquitous nature of grief. At the very end of the poem, he asks his wife's pardon for his own sense of consolation, his ability to go on living. This, too, enacts the parabola of grief, the survivor's sense of guilt and need to be forgiven.

Two hundred and fifty years after the death of King's wife, Peter Porter followed exactly the same form – 120 tetrameters in rhyming couplets – in 'An Exequy' (published in *The Cost of Seriousness*, Oxford 1978), likewise written following the death of his wife. Like King, he registers the arresting effects of grief on our perception of time – 'The channels of our lives are blocked, / The hand is stopped upon the clock'. If these lines are reminiscent of Auden when writing in the same vein (as in the final section of 'Autumn Song' – 'Stop all the clocks, cut off the telephone'), elsewhere Porter echoes the model for his poem. For example, King's 'So close the ground, and 'bout hir shade / Black Curtaines draw, my Bride is lay'd' is subtly ghosted here:

> *O scala enigmatica,*
> I'll climb up to that attic where
> The curtain of your life was drawn
> Some time between despair and dawn

Porter's fine poem, which also recalls time spent with his wife in Italy, ends with the thought that she might return to lead him out, helping him to overcome fear. His is an exequy apt for his time, more personal and with no convention of consolation, so that he seems an altogether lonelier survivor.

Among the most memorable of contemporary poems of memory and celebration are those in Douglas Dunn's collection *Elegies* (Faber, 1985), written in memory of his first wife. In one of the very best, a sonnet entitled 'The Kaleidoscope', the poet finds himself unable to fight free:

> I climb these stairs a dozen times a day
> And, by that open door, wait, looking in
> At where you died. My hands become a tray
> Offering me: my flesh, my soul, my skin.
> Grief wrongs us so. I stand, and wait, and cry
> For the absurd forgiveness, not knowing why.

But it is the death of children, with its unnatural distortion of human time, which has called forth some of the most poignant responses by poets, from Ben Jonson, whose son (also called Benjamin) died of the plague in 1603 ('Rest in soft pease, and, ask'd, say here doth lie / BEN. JONSON his best piece of *poetrie*') to Jon Silkin's affecting and perhaps best known poem, 'Death of a Son'. From Eichendorff to Enright, Victor Hugo to Dylan Thomas, Elizabeth Barrett Browning to A. S. Byatt, the theme is a recurrent one, testing the borderland between grief and its articulation, the outrage of loss and something approaching acceptance. It is also the subject of *Representations of Childhood Death* (Macmillan, 2000), an absorbing collection of essays edited by Gillian Avery and Kimberley Reynolds. From a wide variety of historical sources – folklore, ballads, church memorials, the evan-gelical tradition, Victorian and Edwardian writings including Dickens, Kingsley and Barrie, as well as adolescent horror fiction and childhood death as depicted in films – the contributors build up a picture as fascinating as it is challenging in its contemporary implications: not least, as the editors note in their introduction, since 'the violent death of children has again become sadly topical'. Part of the book's interest lies in the details it includes: for instance, the Devon belief that the ghosts of unbaptised infants appeared as butterflies or moths. In Brittany, they were said to turn into birds and to be heard 'twittering faintly at dusk'. The illustrations include two remarkable photographs of seventeenth-century monuments: the cradle tomb of Princess Sophia Stuart and, no less striking, a stoneware portrait of Lydia Dwight on her deathbed, done by her father John. Chubby, cocooned in coverings and bedclothes, her eyes relaxedly closed, the broad-faced child clasps with both hands a lively posy of flowers.

The book points to interesting historical differences and emphases. In the seventeenth century, there was the notion that death in childhood curtailed the life of a potential sinner: in the nineteenth, comfort books risked reviving the Puritan attitude towards early death as worthy of celebration, by implying that it offered early access to heaven. Here and elsewhere the book touches on the dark taboo, present in legends and fairy tales, of the death of children seen as something desirable. Elizabeth Clarke, considering the deaths of children as recorded in seventeenth-century women's manuscript journals, notes differences in the possibilities of response as between men and women: 'Fathers make didactic spiritual texts from their responses to the deaths of children, and often publish them. Mothers' responses are written in manuscript, into spiritual journals, in discourses which can themselves constitute an act of silencing.' Reading this, I was reminded of Hugo, whose daughter Léopoldine drowned in a boating accident soon after her marriage. Hugo, who wrote in a letter that his love for his child was beyond his power to express in words, nonetheless returned to the subject again and again (most notably in *A Villequier*, a noble lament which veers between bafflement and acceptance): for several years he wrote a memorial poem each September. Léopoldine's mother Adèle, as André Maurois relates in *Olympio*, his biography of Hugo, had only the threadbare consolation of keepsakes: 'All day long the mother sat holding a strand of the drowned girl's hair in her fingers. . . . On the walls and tables were portraits of the vanished pair, and on an embroidered bag the words: "The dress my daughter was wearing when she died: a sacred relic."'

One of the essays, by Eda Sagarra, focuses on Friedrich Rückert's *Kindertotenlieder*. This cycle of more than 100 poems was written, astonishingly, in less than six months 'between late December 1833 and May 1834, following the illness and death from typhoid fever of his two-year-old daughter Luise on New Year's Eve 1833, followed by that of the five-year-old Ernst in mid-January 1834, who died after protracted and intense suffering from an accompanying brain haemorrhage. Three other children got the fever and for nearly three months hovered between life and death, but they survived. A year earlier, another son had died in infancy.' Sagarra comments that 'an important motif [of the cycle] is the consolation of poetry in times of great human suffering', and that 'a substantial part of the *Kindertotenlieder* charts the long process of grief, the poems operating collectively as a kind of bereavement self-counselling.' And the poet himself 'suggests at one point that it is much harder for the mother of the dead children to come to terms with the tragedy than the father, presumably because she cannot articulate it in poetry. But then he makes her speak in her own voice, telling the reader of the special place of the youngest children in a mother's life . . .'.

Rückert (1788–1866) is characterised as a skilful writer immensely popular in his own lifetime and for some time after, but whose work is now largely forgotten, except in the case of poems set by composers such as Schubert (for instance, 'Du bist die Ruh', or 'Lachen und Weinen') and so rescued from oblivion. Surprisingly, no mention is made of Mahler's well-known settings of five of the *Kindertotenlieder*. Begun in 1901, a year before the composer's marriage, they were completed in 1904, by which time he was father to two little girls. Intense, plangent, richly textured and making the most of the poems' interplay of light and darkness, his settings are among the most touching artistic expressions of grief. From the composer's point of view, they involved the empathetic use of the imagination. Yet only three years after the completion of the *Kindertotenlieder* settings, Maria, the elder of his daughters, was to die. Mahler wrote: 'I put myself in the place of a man who had lost his child. Later, when I actually lost a daughter, I would not have been capable of writing these songs.'

# The Double Echo

In 'Poésie et pensée abstraite', one of the pieces collected under the title *Théorie poétique et esthétique*, Valéry distinguishes between prose and poetry by characterising the former as walking and the latter as dancing. While walking is undertaken with a specific goal in mind, dancing is an end in itself and aims at the pleasures of movement and rhythm. All that the two modes have in common is language, and they deploy it very differently. Above all, suggests Valéry, poetry is language built to last. He illustrates his point by asking the reader to imagine a pendulum swinging symmetrically between two points. One of these points represents form, sound, accent, timbre – the voice in action: the other, images, sense, ideas, feelings – our capacity for understanding. Whereas in prose the balance between these two points is unequal, in poetry the pendulum moves equally from one to the other and back again: 'entre la Voix et la Pensée, entre la Pensée et la Voix, entre la Présence et l'Absence, oscille le pendule poétique' ('Between Voice and Thought, between Thought and Voice, between Presence and Absence, swings the poetic pendulum'). He concludes that the value of a poem resides in the indissolubility of sound and sense: though they are discrete elements, the poet's task is 'de nous donner la sensation de l'union intime entre la parole et l'esprit' ('to give us the feeling of the intimate connection between the spoken word and the mind'). Elsewhere, Valéry urges the poet to make the most of everything that separates verse from prose.

Not everyone would have agreed with him. Théophile Gautier, for instance, wrote that the desire to separate poetry from prose was a modern folly which would prove catastrophic. More strikingly, well before Valéry wrote there were the examples of Bertrand's *Gaspard de la Nuit*, Baudelaire's *Le Spleen de Paris* and Rimbaud's *Les Illuminations*, all exploring and exploiting the

295

possibilities of the prose poem. But what exactly is a prose poem? Mention of it tends to provoke uneasiness or, in teaching situations, an intense desire to look away. It seems to be a difficult beast to corral. Is it an expanded haiku, aimed at the qualities of a single moment or experience? Does it have any narrative constituent and, if so, is that hidden or occluded in some way? Can it to any good effect be quoted from, or is it, like Valéry's definition of poetry, indissoluble? Does it need the company of other prose poems in order to be fully appreciated? Underlying such questions is that of our expectations of poetry and prose, and the extent to which the prose poem depends on them. Baudelaire raised the issue in his well-known letter of 26 August 1862 to Arsène Houssaye:

> Which of us has never imagined, in his more ambitious moments, the miracle of a poetic prose, musical though rhythmless and rhymeless, flexible yet strong enough to identify with the lyrical impulses of the soul, the ebbs and flows of revery, the pangs of conscience?

The extent to which he succeeded in meeting this challenge may be judged by his own prose poems, available to readers of English in the bilingual edition with translations by Francis Scarfe (Anvil, 1989) from which the above comes. If a case is to be made for the prose poem as a distinct form, clearly it has to be something more than a passage of purple prose, and other than an attenuated version of free verse. Scarfe concedes in his introduction that it is 'a particular, highly debatable form' and defines the appeal of Baudelaire's work as lying 'in its wide range of subjects, its variations of tone and mood, its great variety of presentation and above all its psychological subtleties.' Certainly the scope is impressive, from anecdotes and memorable vignettes (did Kafka, I wonder, know 'Le vieux saltimbanque'? The old acrobat could easily be related to his 'hunger artist') to litanies, celebrations and philosophical asides: whatever his subject, Baudelaire always writes with a relish that almost defeats his disillusionment. And it is particularly interesting to look at those prose poems such as 'Un hémisphère dans une chevelure', 'L'invitation au voyage', 'Le crépuscule du soir' and 'L'horloge' in the light of the poems which Baudelaire also wrote on the same themes, often with the same title (these are by no means the only ones: among others are 'Les veuves', 'Déjà' and 'A une heure du matin').

The poems and prose poems seem closest to one another, in tone as well as expression, in those which hypnotically evoke exotic fragrances and distant idyllic locations, the sumptuous and near-stifling world of Baudelairean 'correspondances'. Here Baudelaire seems to fulfil his injunction (in *Journaux intimes*) to 'always be a poet, even in prose': and it is noticeable that these prose poems often make use of such poetic elements as refrain and repetition in conveying a mood of drowsy intoxication. Where there are striking differences between the poems and the prose poems, it is often one of tone and emphasis, and a number of the prose poems have more distant perspectives, philosophical and almost essayistic. On the other hand, it is surprising to find that the poems have a much stronger sense of moral engagement, whether the empathetic sense of injustice informing 'Les petites vieilles', the note of self-disgust in 'L'examen de minuit' or the grim sense of the ineluctable in 'L'horloge' (the prose poem of the same title is, by comparison, a light *jeu d'esprit*). But none of this quite establishes a clear definition of the prose poem as a form. It is easier to say what it is not, just as it is tempting to conclude that the poems are more memorable, their closed worlds more powerfully able to encapsulate Baudelaire's characteristic sense of time, remorse and regret, as well as the potent sensuality of the worlds summoned by his experience and imagination.

Perhaps the most convincing case for the prose poem is represented by Rimbaud's *Les Illuminations*: here is language seized and rattled, wild with allusiveness, brilliant with dislocations, a restless theatre in which the scenes are always changing, a circus of mad parading figures, hallucinatory views of crazy cities, a world in which Scarborough and fairyland, magical flowers and remembered or half-hidden childhood, energy and enigma all play a part. A terrific dynamism fuses the combined effects of hallucination, the flux of mental processes and associations, a riddling element and astonishing linguistic verve. Here everything is caught up together, so that although the reader notices the occasional use of end-rhyme or refrain, on the one hand, and the movement (though not the direction) of prose on the other, more important is the challenging relationship of the prose poems to one another, and the recurrences of vocabulary, theme and structure which bind them together. Above all, *Les Illuminations* has a stubborn irreducibility which defies ready classification: but 'prose poem' comes near to it. It is, as Martin Sorrell puts it in the introduction to his fine bilingual edition of Rimbaud's *Collected Poems* (Oxford, 2001), 'writing which dances on a tight-rope strung between coherence and chaos'.

If Rimbaud had a successor it was surely the poet and painter Henri Michaux, 'a surprising inheritor of the Baudelairean urge to be "anywhere out of the world"', as Peter Broome describes him in his introduction to *Spaced, Displaced* (Bloodaxe, 1992), a bilingual edition translated by David and Helen Constantine. The French title, *Déplacements Dégagements*, calls to mind Rimbaud's 'dérèglement de tous les sens': and for Michaux, as for Rimbaud, there is the poet's sense of being alive at a time of decisive, revolutionary change, together with what Broome calls 'a dislocation and reorientation of perception', in Michaux's case partly fuelled by experimentation with mescalin, whose effects he describes in one piece as 'toujours ces sortes de *gifles dans le mental*' ('these continual *slaps in the mind*, if I can call them that'). Another link with Rimbaud is Michaux's sense of theatre, his ability to conjure vivid moments and scenes which risk arbitrariness but achieve their own authority, such as the cityscape described in 'Voyage qui tient à distance', seen as a 'mise en scène pour une pièce inconnue, prête à être jouée' ('the set for an unknown play about to be staged').

There have been many other writers of prose poems, among them Mallarmé, with his dense *Poëmes en Prose* and *Un Coup de Dés*, whose disjointed typographical layout is another way of challenging the reader's expectations; Hugo von Hofmannsthal; Claudel (*Connaissance de l'Est*); Max Jacob. Then there are Léon-Paul Fargue's evocations of Paris; Francis Ponge's meditations on minutely observed objects; and, as a recent English instance, Geoffrey Hill's *Mercian Hymns*, with their very particular blending of history and autobiography. A less familiar aspect of the prose poem's development is its adoption in Japan, amply demonstrated in *The Modern Japanese Prose Poem* (Princeton 1980), compiled and translated by Dennis Keene. Including the work of six poets, the oldest born in 1898 and the youngest in 1931, the anthology bears witness to the continuing range and vitality of the prose poem, or *sanbunshi*, which Keene sees as the supreme example of 'the whole modernist attempt in Japanese poetry'. In his thorough introduction he gives the context of the French tradition, and traces the development of the prose poem in Japan from the 1920s, a time of dissatisfaction with traditional forms. Alluding to Kitagawa Fuyuhiko's article (in a 1929 issue of *Poetry and Poetics*) which put forward the prose poem as written in opposition both to naturalist description and to lyricism, Keene suggests that poets were now 'technicians who selected from innumerable words those which could be built into one single and perfected construction. The words and phrases were to be fitted together like bricks . . ., the perfect construct being an expression of the arbitrary nature of the material arranged.' He points to the relative rarity of this image of the poet in the English literary tradition, and goes on to consider the French antecedents. In doing so he has interesting things to say about the prose poem as a form – which he sees as basically a paradoxical one:

> . . . it aims at formal freedom and yet is obliged to realize that, as a poem, its existence depends upon its language being structured. When poets begin to feel that the principal aim of their art is a restructuring of personal experience and thus of reality itself (as Rimbaud believed), then the prose poem is the poem *par excellence*, a true image of that striving toward new structure which the poetic act, indeed the poetic apprehension of the world, becomes.

The prose poem may also imply a reaction against the autonomy of the traditional poem in its apartness from the world, as well as a desire to reflect the restlessness of the modern world by exploring modes other than those of sequential prose, while retaining its characteristic rhythmic movement. Considering the prose poems of Mallarmé, in which the traditional flow of prose is broken up by 'a greater use of abstract nouns and a cutting away of verbs', Keene concludes that the task for the reader is then to 'set his concentration upon the existence of each phrase as it exists mysteriously by itself. . .'. However, as he points out, a whole series of such intense insights might become intolerable, given the concentration demanded by each one: 'The problem the prose poem must raise is that of whether poetic insight can truly be contained in prose contexts or not.'

Solutions of a kind are proposed by Robert Bly, in 'The Prose Poem as an Evolving Form', the postscript to his 1994 collection of prose poems somewhat egregiously titled *What have I ever lost by dying?* (Weatherlight Press). Here he distinguishes three kinds of prose poem: the fable; the story dominated by 'image and fiery language' (presumably *Les Illuminations* would come under this heading); and 'the object poem', his own kind, for which he sees Jiménez and Ponge as forerunners. (I wonder, though, whether the traditional fable can really feature as a prose poem, given the necessary sequential relation between the text and its conclusion. Perhaps Bly has in mind the simply fabulous). As to the difference between 'the metered poem' and 'the thing poem', the former 'has two subjects: the thought of the poet and the meter itself. One is personal, the other impersonal. The thing poem written in prose has two subjects but quite different ones: the movement of the writer's mind and the thing itself. One is personal,the other impersonal. While the poem concentrates on the object, the movement of his mind cannot be hidden.' Furthermore, the basic unit of the prose poem is that of prose, the sentence rather than the line, while 'the nearest relative of the thing poem is not the essay or short story but the haiku . . . The good haiku is evidence that the poet has overcome . . . the category-making mentality that sees everything in polarities.' Bly detects a Buddhist element in the attitude adopted by the writer of prose poems, and so in the prose poem itself:

> Its mood is calm, more like a quiet lake than a sea. When our language becomes abstract, then the prose poem helps to balance that abstraction, and encourages the speaker to stay close to the body, to touch, hearing, color, texture, moisture, dryness, smell. Its strength lies in intimacy. One could also say that in the object poem in prose, the conscious mind gives up, at least to a degree, the adversary position it usually adopts toward the unconscious, and a certain harmony between the two takes place.

Certainly this viewpoint is apposite for Bly's own prose poems, the best of which combine close observation with an affable mild detachment.

In some respects to read what has been written about the prose poem as a form, as well as many actual examples, is to be reminded of another medium altogether, that of film. The breaking of sequential narrative, the swift cutting between one image and another, the reliance upon the imagination's ability to inhabit the literal and quickly to move beyond it by associative cues often subtly introduced, the ability to move between close-up and panoramic views – these seem real affinities. In the realm of the word, perhaps there can never be an entirely definitive description. Essentially the prose poem builds upon two absences, or near-absences, and the reader's familiarity with them: that of prose with its emphasis on narrative and plot (though character hardly gets a look in); and that of poetry's challenging, musical language conveyed in stress or metre. Every now and then, as in the case of Rimbaud or Michaux, it seems to flare into life as a dislocated, highly individual presence. More often, as the name given to the form suggests, it retains and ultimately depends on a double echo: of the onwardness of prose, the inwardness of poetry.

# List of subscribers

Dannie Abse
Peter J. Adcock
Susan Andrew
Cary Archard
Mrs M. E. Badman
Beryl Bainbridge
Jill Balcon
Glencairn Balfour-Paul
Holly & Henry Ball
Dr Iain Bamforth
George & Helen Berry
George & Margaret Bird
Michael & Simone Bird
Ben Bradshaw
Laurie & Fiona Bristow
Sandy Brownjohn
Catherine Byron
Alison Cairns
Felicity Calderari
Jean & Per Campbell
Margie & Jim Campbell
Martin Campbell-White
Caroline Carver
Colin Caverhill
Valerie Cherry
Sir Robin Chichester-Clark
Austin & Hilary Clegg
John Cole
Kate Collins
Caroline Cornish
Justin & Xanthe Cross

Gillian Crossley-Holland
Kevin & Linda Crossley-
    Holland
James Crowden
Simon Curtis
Graham Davies
Richard Debenham
Helen Den Dulk
Carol DeVaughn
Diana Devlin
R. G. Dickens
Belinda Dodd
Peter Doenhoff
Simon & Caroline Drew
Patrick Drysdale
Helen Dunmore
Jane Duran
Tom Eason
Michael & Mary Easty
Nick & Helen Elam
Richard Eyre
Professor German Filippovsky
Duncan Forbes
Catriona & David Games
Christopher Gardner-Thorpe
Damian Gardner-Thorpe
James Gardner-Thorpe
Elizabeth Garrett
Fiona Gimson
Andrew Gimson
Nick Grant

Rosemary Gray
Peter & Henrietta Greig
John Griffith-Jones
Paul Groom
Patricia Haitink
Ella Halkes
Maurice Hardman
Simon A. Hawkins
John, Susan & Libby Henton
Andrew Hoellering
Jeremy Holmes
Lorna Howe
Richard Ings
Fran Jenkin
Nick & Linda Keen
Emily Keyte
Ulrich Kleiner
Thilo Kloss
Kathleen Kummer
Mustapha Laljee
Alastair Langlands
Sue Larkin
Paula & Jeremy Lawford
Andrew & Briony Lawson
Vaughan & Frances Lewis
Penelope Lively
Jill Lloyd
James Long
Mr & Mrs Iain MacCallum
Avril Maddrell
Madingley Hall Library
Bill Mander
Jules Mann
Hermione Mathieson
Michael Mayne
Fokkina McDonnell
Richard McLaughlin
Beverley Meeke
Alison & Henry Meyric
    Hughes

Rosalie Michaelson-Yeates
Margaret Miles
Adrian & Julia Miller
Peter Mills
John Moat
Yvonne Moisey
John Mole
Hubert Moore
The Hon. Mrs Elizabeth
    Morris
Jenny Morris
Felicity Murdin
Beverley Naidoo
Dennis O'Driscoll
Andrew & Lucy Oliver
Micheal O'Siadhail
Laurence Overend
Elizabeth & Richard
    Parkinson
David Payne
David Pease
Martin Pierce
Katherine Pierpoint
Neil Powell
Simon Powell
John Press
Roger Press
Teresa Probert
Simon Rae
Tim Raine
Elizabeth Rapp
Jim & Ann Reed
Carol Rees
Ann & David Revill
D. W. Rice
Edward Richards
Cheryl Ronaldson
Richard Rycroft
Zoë Ryle
Erica Sail

Carole Satyamurti
Clive Scott
Jan & Peter Selby
Norman & Bridget Shiel
Michael J. Sidebottom
Matt Simpson
Stephen Sims
Graham & Dorothea
  Smallbone
Jonathan Smith
Brigid Somerset
Martin & Claire Sorrell
Christopher Southgate
Mary Spencer

Angus Stephenson
Nicholas Swarbrick
Peter Symes
Ann & Anthony Thwaite
Ian Tugwell
Daniel Weissbort
Sir John Weston
Simon Wilkinson
Aran Williams
Patrick Williamson
Peter & Greta Williamson
Derek Wilson
Mary Wortley
Barbara, Gar, Tom & Paul Yates